THE KNITTING ANSWER BOOK

The
Knitting
Answer Book

BY MARGARET RADCLIFFE

Storey Publishing

*The mission of Storey Publishing is to serve our customers
by publishing practical information that encourages personal
independence in harmony with the environment.*

Edited by Gwen Steege and Sarah Guare
Cover and text design by Kent Lew
Text production by Jessica Armstrong
Illustrations by © Alison Kolesar
Indexed by Christine R. Lindemer, Boston Road Communications

Storey books are available for special premium and promotional uses and for
customized editions. For further information, please call 1-800-793-9396.

Printed in China by R.R. Donnelley
10 9 8 7 6 5 4 3 2

Library of Congress Cataloging-in-Publication Data

Radcliffe, Margaret.
    The knitting answer book / by Margaret Radcliffe.
       p. cm.
    Includes index.
    ISBN-13: 978-1-58017-599-9; ISBN-10: 1-58017-599-6 (pbk. : alk. paper)
    1. Knitting—Miscellanea. I. Title.

TT820.R24 2005
746.43'2—dc22

                2005016466

Contents

Introduction 9

Chapter 1: Casting On 11
Basic Cast Ons • All about Casting On •
Special Cast Ons • Provisional Cast Ons •
Solving Problems

Chapter 2: The Basics 45
The Knit Stitch • The Purl Stitch • Hows and
Whys of Knits and Purls • Stitches, Rows, and
Counting • Tips for Lefties • Discovering Your
Personal Knitting Style • Twists and Turns •
Solving Problems with Knitting and Purling •
Fixing Mistakes • The Slipped Stitch • Edge
Stitches • The Yarn Over • Personal Factors •
The Big Picture

Chapter 3: Binding Off 87
Standard Bind Offs • All about Binding Off •
Solving Problems • Special Situations

Chapter 4: Tools 105
Knitting Needles • There's More to Knitting
than Needles

Chapter 5: Yarn 125

Yarn Labels • All about Yarn • Working
with Yarn • Solving Problems

Chapter 6: Reading Patterns 159

Sizing • Gauge • Measurements and
Schematics • Materials and Tools •
Abbreviations and Charts • Knitting
Instructions • Solving Problems with
Knitting Patterns

Chapter 7: Pattern Stitches 189

Basic Pattern Stitches • Special Stitch
Manipulations • Working with Pattern
Stitches • Solving Problems • Cables • Lace

Chapter 8: Circular Knitting 209

Getting Started with Circular Knitting •
Gauge • Working Circularly • Changing
Colors in Circular Knitting • Pattern Stitches
in Circular Knitting • Binding Off •
Converting Flat Knitting to Circular

Chapter 9: Color 235

Stripes • Stranded Knitting • Mosaic
Knitting • Intarsia • Variegated Yarns

Chapter 10: Shaping 255

Increases • Decreases • Special Situations

Chapter 11: Fitting 279

Before You Begin • While You Work • After
You're Done • Solving Other Problems with Fit
• Short-Row Shaping

Chapter 12: Finishing 305

Blocking • Sewing Up • Solving Problems •
Kitchener Stitch • Borders • At Loose Ends •
Solving Problems during Finishing • Wash
and Wear

Chapter 13: Embellishments 347

Beads • Bobbles • Cords • Pompoms,
Tassels, and Fringe • Duplicate Stitch

Resources 363

Acknowledgments 387

Index 388

What's *Your* Question?

I frequently teach a class for all levels of knitters called "Knitting Tips and Techniques." At the first class, I always ask my students what they want to learn. Some come armed with a detailed list of techniques that they want to try or they don't understand. But most say, "I know how to knit, but I want to knit better." This book is dedicated to all of them.

The best way to get answers to your questions about knitting is to ask an experienced knitter. In the past someone from an older generation was usually handy to help the novice knitter. Lucky is the knitter today who has access to such a mentor at the moment she (or he) is needed. This book is meant to fill the place of that experienced knitter, so you can get answers to your questions quickly and get back to more important things — like your knitting!

I wrote this book with all levels of knitters in mind. Some of the questions posed here are those only a more experienced knitter would think to ask. Others are questions I frequently get from beginning knitters. Although much of this book focuses on questions from those who are already knitting, I've included detailed instructions of every step from beginning to end. Get yourself some worsted weight wool yarn and some needles, cast on (chapter 1), then learn the basics of knit and purl (chapter 2). Next, learn to bind off (chapter 3). Find out about tools and yarns before you purchase more of each (chapters 4 and 5). Spend some time learning to follow a pattern (chapter 6), work new stitches (chapter 7), knit circularly (chapter 8), use color (chapter 9), and shape your knitting (chapter 10). Discover how to get the best fit (chapter 11), and after you finish knitting, find out how to sew up (chapter 12) and embellish (chapter 13) your work.

When you talk to knitters and seek advice from other books, you'll soon discover that there is no one "right" way to do anything in knitting, from casting on to the final finishing touches. In *The Knitting Answer Book* I suggest several of the most effective ways to accomplish what you want to do, then explain how to choose among them. You'll be able to try them all, and you'll soon discover your own "right" way to knit.

⋁⋁⋁⋁⋁⋁⋁⋁⋁⋁⋁⋁⋁⋁⋁⋁⋁⋁⋁⋁⋁⋁

CHAPTER 1

Casting On

⋁⋁⋁⋁⋁⋁⋁⋁⋁⋁⋁⋁⋁⋁⋁⋁⋁⋁⋁⋁⋁⋁

The foundation of your knitting is the cast on. Finding the right cast on for a particular project is essential. Firm cast ons support shawls and necklines. Hats and socks fit comfortably thanks to stretchy ones. Decorative cast ons add a special edge to dressy garments. Many knitters remain loyal to just one cast on, which will be perfect for some projects, but may be too loose, too tight, or just won't look right on others.

Basic Cast Ons

Q I know how to do only one cast on, but I know there are others. Should I learn them?

A You'll find it very helpful to know several of the basic cast ons (oftentimes abbreviated "CO" in knitting instructions) so you can choose among them, depending on the situation. You should probably be familiar with the Loop and Backward Loop Cast Ons, the Knitted Cast On, the Cable Cast On, and the Long-Tail Cast On.

LOOP CAST ON

Many knitters start out using the Loop Cast On as beginners and continue to use it for the rest of their lives. It is not the best cast on, but it is the easiest to learn, can be tightened or loosened later, and is thin and unobtrusive. On the other hand, it can be loose or uneven, is difficult to work into on the first row, and has a tendency to spiral around the needle (only a problem for circular knitting); in addition, the loose single strand at the edge of the fabric does not wear well.

WHEN TO USE IT: Good all-around cast on for sweaters, hats, socks, scarves, shawls, or anything where you want the edge to stretch.

GET READY: Use one needle and a single strand of yarn. Hold the cut end of the yarn in the left hand with the needle, and the working yarn (attached to the ball) in your right hand.

HOW TO DO IT:

1. Point your thumb toward yourself, under the yarn. Turn your thumb away from you.

2. Slip the needle up into the loop on your thumb.

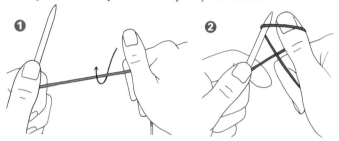

3. Slip your thumb out. Repeat steps 1 through 3 until there are enough stitches on your needle. (A stitch is one loop around the needle.)

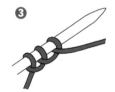

VARIATIONS:

▶ **Use your index finger** instead of your thumb.

▶ **The Backward Loop Cast On** twists the loops in the opposite direction. Hold the needle and cut tail of yarn in your left hand exactly as described for the Loop Cast On. In step 1, point your thumb away from you, then turn it toward you in step 2. When you knit the first row, it will further twist the cast-on stitches, tightening them and making the edge more elastic.

▶ **Switch hands.** Hold the needle and cut tail of yarn in your right hand. If you follow the directions for the Loop Cast On, you'll make a Backward Loop Cast On. To duplicate the Loop Cast On exactly, point your thumb away from you in step 1, then turn it toward you in step 2.

Plan Ahead

If there will be a seam beginning at the cast-on edge, leave a long tail and use it to sew the seam. When you finish, there will be fewer ends to weave in.

KNITTED CAST ON

Because the cast-on stitches are made just like regular knit stitches, this is an excellent cast on for beginners. It is easier to work into on the first row, its twisted bottom edge is more resilient, and it wears better than the Loop Cast On. It can look a little holey if worked too loosely, however, and can be difficult for beginners to tension evenly.

WHEN TO USE IT: Good all-around cast on for sweaters, hats, socks, scarves, shawls, or anything where you want the edge to stretch.

GET READY: Use two needles and a single strand of yarn. Make a slip knot as shown on page 17, leaving a short tail, and place it on your left needle.

HOW TO DO IT:

1. Knit a stitch, leaving the original stitch on the needle. Hint: Work the new stitch a little more loosely than usual.

2. Insert the left needle up into the new stitch from the front.

3. Pull on the yarn to tighten the stitch.

Repeat these three steps until you have enough stitches. The original slip knot counts as the first stitch.

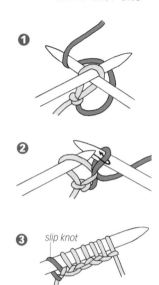

slip knot

CABLE CAST ON

A version of the Knitted Cast On, this method creates an even, cablelike edge that wears well. It is not stretchy, however, and produces a pronounced, horizontal edge that some knitters dislike. On the other hand, the ribbed variation is excellent for garments that begin with K1P1 (knit 1 purl 2) ribbing (see Variation, page 16).

WHEN TO USE IT: Perfect for edges that need to be firm. It can be used for sweaters, but take care to work loosely. Consider the ribbed variation when a great deal of stretch is required (for example, the bottom of a hat or the top of a sock).

GET READY: Use two needles and a single strand of yarn. Begin with a slip knot, then cast on one more stitch, using the Knitted Cast On. Hint: Work the second stitch a little more loosely than usual.

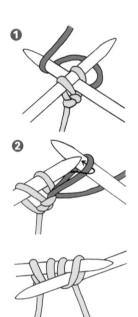

HOW TO DO IT:

1. Insert the right needle between the two stitches.

2. Knit up a stitch, leaving the two original stitches on the left needle.

3. Insert the left needle up into the new stitch from the front and slip it off the right needle.

Repeat these three steps, always knitting the new stitch up between the last two stitches on the needle, until you have enough stitches.

ribbed cable cast on

VARIATION: The **Ribbed Cable Cast On** stretches more and is a good general-purpose cast on, especially for K1P1 ribbing. Make it by alternately knitting and purling between the last two stitches. To purl, insert the needle between the two stitches from the back.

SEE ALSO: *Page 192 for Knit 1 Purl 1 Ribbing*

Tying a Slip Knot

1. Hold the end of the yarn in your hand.

2. Wrap the yarn one and a half times around two fingers to end at the back. Poke a loop of the yarn through between your fingers.

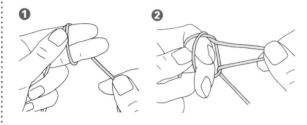

3. Slip your fingers out and tighten by pulling on the cut end and the loop.

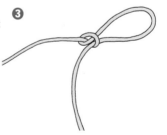

LONG-TAIL CAST ON

This cast on is known by many other names: Y, Sling Shot, Continental, and Two Strand are just a few. This is probably the best of the basic cast ons. Once learned, it can be executed very quickly. It is stretchy but not loose and creates a neat, even edge that's not too thick. Its two sides are noticeably different; you can decide which you prefer for the outside of your garment.

WHEN TO USE IT: The Long-Tail Cast On can be used for almost anything that requires a medium amount of stretch.

GET READY:

1. Use one needle and a single strand of yarn. Pull out a length of yarn for the "long tail." Make a slip knot at this point and place it on the needle. Hold the needle in your right hand with your index finger on top of the slip knot to keep it from sliding. The long tail should hang from the front of the stitch, and the working yarn from the back.

2. Pinch your thumb and index finger together and insert them between the two strands of yarn.

3. Spread your thumb and finger apart so that the long tail hangs over your thumb and the working yarn hangs over your index finger.

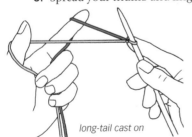

long-tail cast on

4. Catch both strands of yarn against the palm of your hand with your other fingers. *Hint: Don't let these go!*

HOW TO DO IT:

1. Insert the needle up through the loop around your thumb.

2. Bring the needle over and around the strand in front of your index finger.

3. Bring the needle back out through the thumb loop.

4. Let the loop slide off your thumb.

5. Put your thumb behind the long tail and use it to tighten the loop.

Repeat these five steps until there are enough stitches. The slip knot counts as the first stitch.

> **Note:** *As with many knitting techniques, it takes far longer to describe this than to do it. Practice until you can consistently control the tension of both strands by holding them against your palm. Then you'll be able to knit up the stitches very smoothly and rapidly.*

This cast on accomplishes exactly the same thing as if you had used the Loop Cast On and then knit 1 row. Keep this in mind if your instructions say to cast on and then knit 1 row.

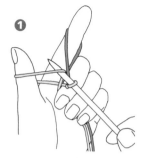

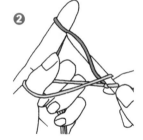

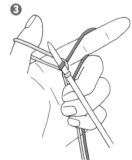

VARIATION: If you find it difficult to hold the yarn in your left hand, then switch. Hold the needle in your left hand and the yarn in your right hand. If you find it difficult to hold both strands of yarn in your left hand, move the working yarn to your right hand. Use a long straight needle and prop it against your leg or hold it under your arm so that you can let it go from time to time. The needle stays still while you do this; only your hands move.

1. Point your thumb up at the ceiling and slip the loop onto the point of the needle.

2. Wrap the yarn around the needle with your right hand. If you like, you can hold the needle with your left thumb and index finger while you do this.

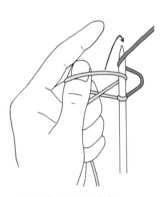

long-tail cast on variation

3. Take the thumb loop back off the needle by bringing your thumb straight over the top of the needle and down the back.

4. Slide your thumb out of the loop and pull the yarn with your left hand to tighten.

5. Point your thumb straight down behind the yarn, then twist it toward you to put the loop back on.

Repeat these five steps until there are enough stitches.

Q The yarn for the tail gets untwisted as I work the Long-Tail Cast On. Why does this happen and what can I do about it?

A Each time you slip the loop off your thumb, you put a half-twist in the yarn. When this twist is in the opposite direction from the twist in the yarn, the yarn gradually untwists as you work. Let go of the yarn occasionally and let it twist back to its original state before continuing. You can roll it between your fingers to help it along. You may not want to use this cast on if your yarn is a bulky one with almost no twist to begin with.

Estimating the Length of the Tail

There are several ways to estimate how long the tail should be before you begin casting on.

▶ Make the tail about three times as long as the width of whatever you are casting on. If it's the bottom of a sweater that is 40" (100 cm), then pull out about 120" (300 cm). This is 3⅓ yards (3 m).

▶ Wrap the yarn around the needle once for each stitch you need to cast on. Unwrap this length of yarn and allow a little extra.

▶ Allow about 1" (2.5 cm) for each stitch. Use less for thin needles, more for fat ones.

All about Casting On

Q What's the easiest cast on?

A Most people consider the Loop Cast On the easiest to learn; however, once you're comfortable with other cast ons, they are just as easy to use.

....

Q What's the fastest cast on?

A The Long-Tail Cast On beats all the rest. Not only can you do it very quickly, but when you're done, you've already knit the first row.

....

Q Is there a way to cast on without measuring out a long tail?

A You can always use one of the methods that doesn't require the tail. If you prefer the Long-Tail Cast On, however, knot the beginning of two balls of yarn together when you make your slip knot. Use one strand for the working yarn and the other for the long tail. Don't include the slip knot in your stitch count. After you finish casting on, cut off the ball you used for the long tail, leaving an end to weave in later. When you get to the end of the first row, unravel the double slip knot.

Q **After casting on, am I now on the right side or the wrong side?**

A It depends! The "right" side is simply the side that you like the best. The "wrong" side is the side you don't like as well. Even if you always use the same cast on, your decision may change depending on what you're making and what pattern stitch you're using. Also keep in mind that the Long-Tail Cast On is the equivalent of casting on using the Loop Cast On and then knitting the first row. If you are working in a pattern where the right-side rows are knit and the wrong-side rows are purled, you will probably want to treat the Long-Tail Cast On as a knitted row, so the following row is the "wrong" side.

Q **The instructions say to cast on stitches at the beginning of the next row. How do I do this?**

A Hold the knitting in your left hand, ready to begin the next row. The working yarn will be hanging ready at the beginning of the row. Use it to work one of the single-strand cast ons — the Loop Cast On or the Knitted Cast On. The Cable Cast On could be used, but it's bulkier and less elastic than the others, which may cause problems when the time comes to sew or pick up stitches along this edge.

Q **What is the best cast on for sweaters?**

A For the bottom edge of sweater bodies and sleeves, use the Long-Tail Cast On because it stretches, keeps its shape, and wears well. The Cable Cast On wears well but is not stretchy. If you like the way it looks, you can use it for sweaters as long as you work loosely or use a larger needle while casting on. If you plan on working in K1P1 ribbing, the stretchier Ribbed Cable Cast On is a good choice.

For cardigans that begin at the neck and are worked down, use the firmer Cable Cast On. It will support the neck edge and prevent stretching. For a neck-down pullover, use the Long-Tail Cast On or the Ribbed Cable Cast On. The upper edge should stretch just enough to go easily over the wearer's head.

....

Q **What is the best cast on for shawls?**

A Shawls vary a great deal in fabric and construction, so there are several answers to this question. If it is a lace shawl, you may want to try the Lace Cast on. If it is a solid shawl, then it will need a flexible cast on, one that drapes nicely and doesn't pull the fabric in. A good choice is the Long-Tail Cast On. If the upper edge of the shawl is cast on and no edging will be worked later along the cast-on edge, then use a firmer cast on to prevent a heavy shawl from stretching out of shape. The Cable Cast On is a good choice.

Q **What is the best cast on for scarves?**

A Any cast on that is flexible and stretchy is good for scarves. Avoid the Cable Cast On, which tends to be too tight.

. . . .

Q **What's the best cast on for K1P1 ribbing?**

A For a firmer edge, use the Ribbed Cable Cast On. For a looser edge, use the Tubular Cast On described on page 27.

. . . .

Q **Is there a more durable cast on I can use for children's clothes?**

A Using extra strands of yarn at the edges of children's clothing can help the garments wear better. If you choose the Loop or Backward Loop Cast On, use two or more strands of yarn while casting on, then switch to one strand. If you use a Long-Tail Cast On, add a second long tail.

DOUBLED LONG-TAIL CAST ON

GET READY: Measure out your long tail using two balls of yarn. Tie both yarns into a slip knot and place it on the needle. Cut the yarn going to the second ball, leaving a tail 6" (15 cm) long.

HOW TO DO IT:
Cast on as described for Long-Tail Cast On (p. 18) with two strands around your thumb, but the usual one strand around your index finger.

VARIATIONS: For more durability or a decorative effect, you can use several strands of yarn for the long tail. To avoid wasting yarn, use a separate ball for each strand and cut them off when the cast on is completed.

> *Note: Don't include the slip knot in your stitch count. When you get to the end of the first row, unravel the slip knot.*

Special Cast Ons

Q **What is the best cast on for socks?**

A The tops of socks have to stretch a long way to be pulled over the heel. Once they are on, they need to stretch enough to be comfortable on the wearer's calf. Of all the cast ons discussed so far, the Long Tail stretches the most while maintaining a neat edge. There are other cast ons that stretch even more. If you plan to work in K1P1 ribbing, try the Tubular Cast On, as shown opposite.

TUBULAR CAST ON

This cast on is very stretchy with no noticeable ridge at the edge, making it excellent for any edge that must be stretched and comfortable against the skin. It's especially suited to K1P1 ribbing. It can be a bit bulky when worked in thick yarn and may be loose when not stretched.

GET READY: Use two needles, contrasting waste yarn, and a single strand of the working yarn.

SEE ALSO: *Page 145 for waste yarn*

HOW TO DO IT:

1. With waste yarn and using the Loop Cast On, cast on half the stitches you need. If you need an odd number of stitches, add an extra stitch. Cut the waste yarn leaving a tail about 6" (15 cm) long. With the working yarn, *K1, yarn over; repeat from * to end of row.

2. Knit the last stitch, but don't work a yarn over at the end of the row. You have now almost doubled the number of stitches.

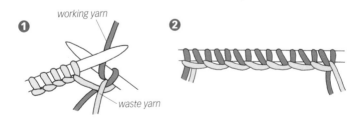

1 working yarn · waste yarn   **2**

3. On the next row, *bring yarn to front (as if you are going to purl), slip 1 stitch purlwise, bring yarn to back, K1; repeat from * to end of row, slipping the last stitch. On the following row, *K1, bring yarn forward, slip 1 purlwise, bring yarn to back; repeat from * to end of row, knitting the last stitch. Repeat these 2 rows once more.

4. Work in K1P1 ribbing. On the first row, knit the knit stitches and purl the slipped stitches.

5. After you've worked a couple of rows of ribbing, pick out the waste yarn.

> *Note: If you need an even number of stitches, adjust for it when the ribbing is completed. To reduce the number of stitches, Knit 2 Together (K2tog) in an unobtrusive spot. If your instructions call for increasing at the top of the ribbing, simply work one less increase so that you end up with the correct number of stitches.*

removing the waste yarn

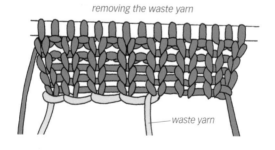

— waste yarn

SEE ALSO: *The Yarn Over, p. 81; The Slipped Stitch, p. 75;* and *p. 264 for Knit 2 Together*

Removing Waste Yarn

1. Cut the waste yarn close to the edge of your knitting.

2. Insert the tip of your knitting needle into the first loose loop of waste yarn at the bottom edge. Gently pull it free.

3. Move to the next loop of waste yarn and pull it free. Continue across.

If you are working across a long edge, cut the waste yarn off frequently to make the job easier.

Q The edge of my Tubular Cast On looks loose and messy. How can I fix this?

A Work the first row with the working yarn using a needle one or two sizes smaller and it will tighten up; however, this will also reduce the amount it can stretch.

. . . .

Q What is the best cast on for lace?

A Lace demands a minimal cast on that will not detract from the lace itself or create a stiff, nonstretchy edge. The optimum choice is the Loop Cast On, which can be adjusted to make the edge looser or tighter. For a more decorative lacy edge, try the Lace Cast On.

LACE CAST ON

This cast on leaves decorative loops across the edge of the knitting. These are also useful for picking up stitches later or for adding fringe.

GET READY: Use two needles and your working yarn. Make a slip knot and place it on the left needle. Hold the slip knot in place with your index finger.

HOW TO DO IT:

1. Wrap the yarn behind the left needle to make a yarn over.

2. Insert the right needle between the slip knot and the yarn over.

3. Wrap the yarn around the right needle and knit a stitch.

4. Slip the new stitch onto the left needle knitwise.

Repeat these four steps, inserting the needle between the yarn over and the previous stitch in step 2.

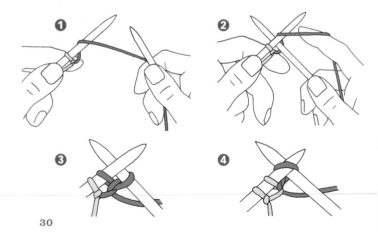

Note: *This cast on always results in an odd number of stitches. If you need an even number of stitches, cast on one more than you need, then unravel the slip knot when you reach the end of the first row.*

. . . .

Q What's the best cast on for fringe?

A The Knitted Cast On and the Lace Cast On leave a loose strand between each stitch that is useful when adding fringe. You may also want to try the Twisted Loop Cast On.

TWISTED LOOP CAST ON

Similar to the Loop Cast On, this one has an extra twist in each loop for an entirely different effect.

GET READY: Use one needle and a single strand of yarn. Hold the tail of yarn against the needle in your left hand.

HOW TO DO IT:

1. Put your index finger under the working yarn, and rotate your finger around twice, twisting the yarn.

2. Slip the loop onto the needle.

3. Pull the yarn to tighten.

Repeat these 3 steps until there are enough stitches.

Provisional Cast Ons

Q What is a provisional cast on and when would I use it?

A Provisional cast ons, also known as open cast ons, will be removed either while the knitting is in progress or as part of a finishing step. To make removal easier, use a contrasting color for the waste yarn. The Loop Cast On is used as a provisional cast on in the Tubular Cast On (p. 27). Here are three others.

....

CROCHETED CAST ON

GET READY: Use one knitting needle, one crochet hook (about the same size as your needle), a ball of contrasting waste yarn, and the yarn for your project. With the waste yarn, make a slip knot and place it on the crochet hook. Hold the needle in your left hand, with the crochet hook in front of it in your right hand. Make sure the yarn is behind the needle. You can

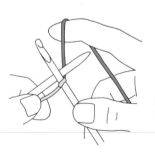

hold the yarn in either hand — whichever is most comfortable for you. To secure the tail, hold it against the needle.

preparing for the crocheted cast on

HOW TO DO IT:

1. Put the waste yarn behind the needle and hook it with the crochet hook.

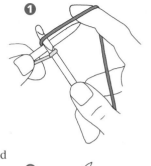

2. Use the hook to pull a new loop through the loop already on the hook.

Repeat these two steps until there are enough stitches on the needle. (Remember to keep the yarn behind the needle and the crochet hook in front of it.) Enlarge the last loop on the crochet hook until it's about 4" (10 cm) tall, then cut the yarn at the top of the loop and pull out the yarn attached to the ball. Avoid pulling on the remaining tail; keep it loose so it will be easier to remove later.

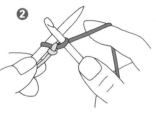

Using your working yarn, knit across leaving a tail 6" (15 cm) long, then begin working your project. When you are ready to remove the cast on, start at the corner where there are two tails: one of the waste yarn and one of the project yarn. Insert a knitting needle into the stitch where the tail of waste yarn emerges and loosen it up, then pull the tail out. Pull on the tail to unravel the crocheted chain. If any fibers are tangled and prevent it from unraveling, use a small pair of sharp scissors to snip the offending fibers. Slip a knitting needle into the loose stitches. If you are a careful sort of person, you may wish to do this every few stitches so they can't unravel before you get them on the needle.

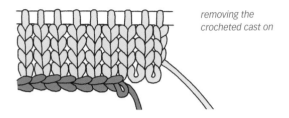

removing the crocheted cast on

INVISIBLE CAST ON

GET READY: Use one needle, a strand of waste yarn, and a ball of your working yarn. Tie the waste yarn around the end of the working yarn. Arrange the yarn with the waste yarn around your thumb, the working yarn over your index finger, both strands held taut against your palm, and the point of the needle under the knot. Keep the knot from sliding off the needle with your index finger.

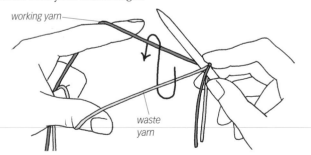

working yarn

waste yarn

HOW TO DO IT:

1. Point your thumb up and insert the needle under the waste yarn from front to back to scoop up a strand of the working yarn.

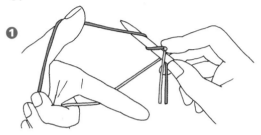

2. Draw the working yarn back under the waste yarn. (Be sure to go behind the working yarn, then under it.)
3. Point your thumb down and use the needle to scoop up a strand of the working yarn. (Again, go behind it, then under it.)

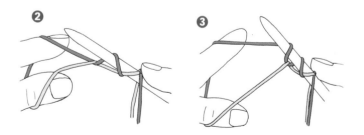

Repeat these three steps until there are enough stitches.

Cut the waste yarn leaving a tail and continue with the working yarn.

invisible cast on

Note: Space the stitches out along the needle to keep them loose. If they are too close together, it will be hard to pick up the stitches when the waste yarn is removed. Try to keep the waste yarn taut so that it runs along the bottom of the needle.

When the time comes to remove the waste yarn, untie the knot. (If this is difficult, simply slide the working yarn out of the knot.) Cut the waste yarn close to the edge of the knitting. Holding its other end, pull the waste yarn straight to the side to remove it. Slip a needle into the stitches.

Go Easy on Yourself

Choose your waste yarn with care. Using a firmly twisted, smooth, or slippery waste yarn (for example, smooth cotton, rayon, or silk) minimizes tangles and helps the waste yarn to slide right out of the knitting when the time comes. Avoid fuzzy yarns, such as mohair, because they leave noticeable bits of fluff on your project when removed. Choose a strong yarn; weak yarns tend to break as they are pulled out.

RAVEL CORD

Ravel cord is a very strong, slippery nylon cord used by machine knitters. Good substitutes are dental floss or fine, soft nylon cord from your hardware or craft supply store. Smooth, slippery, unbreakable knitting yarns, such as a multi-ply silk, may also work, if strong enough.

GET READY: Use two needles, waste yarn, working yarn, and ravel cord.

HOW TO DO IT:

1. With waste yarn, cast on as many stitches as you need, any way you like.

2. Knit 1 row. Cut the waste yarn.

3. With ravel cord, knit 1 row. Cut the ravel cord.

4. With working yarn, knit 1 row, then begin working the project.

> *Note: Ravel cord can be very slippery, so leave long tails, or tie it loosely to the other yarns at both ends. If it doesn't bother you, don't cut the ravel cord. Just leave it dangling and it can be reused many times.*

When the time comes to remove the ravel cord, remove any tangles or knots. Pull the ravel cord firmly, straight out to the side. When all the slack is pulled tight, the ravel cord will slide out of the fabric. Slip the stitches onto a needle.

Q Is there some way to make my cast on match my bind off?

A Yes, work the Crocheted Cast On using the working yarn, rather than the waste yarn. When you have one fewer stitch than you need, slip the loop off the crochet hook and onto the needle. Don't cut the yarn; just start knitting. This makes a chain stitch along the cast-on edge that matches the chain of the Basic Bind Off.

SEE ALSO: *Crocheted Cast On, p. 32; and Basic Bind Off, p. 88*

Q Can I make a hem when I cast on?

A Yes. Use a provisional cast on, then work in Stockinette Stitch for the length of the hem. Decide what kind of edge you want. For a rolled edge, simply continue in Stockinette. For a straight, flat edge, work one or two rows in Reverse Stockinette (two rows will make a squarer edge). For a picot edge, repeat yarn over, K2tog across the row. Work in Stockinette again until the length above the fold equals the length below the fold. To join the two layers, remove the provisional cast on and place those stitches on an extra needle. Fold the hem to the inside and use a third needle to knit the stitches

picot edge

on the two layers together to join them. Continue with the body of your garment.

· ·

Q How can I avoid bulky hems?

A Work the inner layer of hems with thinner yarn. If none is available, use fewer stitches on the inside section of the hem or work this section on smaller needles.

Solving Problems

Q My cast on is too tight. How can I fix it?

A There are several solutions to this problem.

▶ **Use a needle one or two sizes larger** for casting on, then switch to the correct size needle on the first row. If you end up with a too-loose edge or stitches that are too tall, try the next solution.

▶ **Space your stitches farther apart** on the needle as you cast on. Stitches that are compressed as tightly as possible have a little less yarn in them than stitches that are spaced about ¼" (.5 cm) apart on the needle. If your needle is too short, use a longer needle.

▶ **Change to a different cast on.** If you are using the Cable Cast On, which is characteristically tight and inelastic, learn the Long-Tail Cast On.

....

Q My cast on is too loose. How can I fix it?

A Try one of these solutions to the problem.

▶ **Use a needle one or two sizes smaller** for casting on, then switch to the correct size needle on the first row. Sometimes this results in an edge that is too tight and stitches too tight to knit easily on the first row. If you have these problems, try the following method.

▶ **Space your stitches a little more closely** on the needle as you cast on. Stitches that are compressed tightly have a little less yarn in them than stitches that are spaced farther apart.

▶ **Change to a different cast on.** If you are using the Loop Cast On or the Knitted Cast On, both of which tend to be loose, learn the Long-Tail Cast On or the Cable Cast On.

Q **Why are my cast-on stitches so tall?**

A This usually happens with the Long-Tail Cast On when you switch to a larger needle to prevent the edge from being too tight. The larger needle makes the stitches larger, but when you knit the first row at normal tension, the stitches are squeezed together and thus become narrower and taller. To fix this problem, switch back to the normal size needle and space your stitches slightly farther apart as you cast on.

· ·

Q **One of my cast-on stitches fell off and unraveled. What do I do?**

A The answer depends on which cast on you used.

▶ **Loop or Backward Loop Cast On.** Insert the right needle under the loose strand of yarn (from the back as shown for the Loop Cast On, from the front for the Backward Loop Cast On). Slip it back to the left needle, twisting it to match the stitches on either side (insert the left needle into the front as shown for the Loop Cast On, from the back as shown for the Backward Loop Cast On).

picking up a dropped loop cast on

▶ **Long-Tail Cast On.**

1. Pick up the loose strand at the very bottom, as described in the previous solution.

2. When it is on the left needle correctly, insert the right needle into it as if you are going to purl.

3. Take the tip of the needle under the loose strand. Pull it through to the back.

4. Slip the stitch off the left needle. Finally, slip the stitch purlwise back to the left needle.

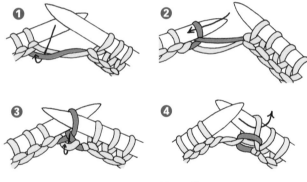

picking up a dropped long-tail cast on

SEE ALSO: *The Slipped Stitch, p. 75*

▶ **Knitted Cast On.** The dropped cast-on stitch is the strand that now lies in front of the next stitch on the needle.

1. Insert the right needle under the front of this strand.
2. Insert the left needle into the front of it and slip it off.

picking up a dropped knitted cast on

▶ **Cable Cast On.** It is nearly impossible to put this cast on back together if it unravels. The good news is that if one of the stitches slips off the needle, it is held tightly in the twisted strands at the bottom edge and rarely unravels completely. Just slip the left needle back into the stitch.

· ·

Q **The slip knot leaves a bump at the corner of the knitting. Is there a way to get rid of it?**

A The slip knot is usually hidden in a seam or by a border, but if it's in a position where it bothers you, simply untie it. Insert the tip of your knitting needle into the knot and loosen it. Finally, pull the end out of the knot and gently tighten the stitch by pulling on the tail.

This won't work for the Long-Tail Cast On, where the slip knot isn't at the beginning of the yarn. To get rid of the slip knot, begin the Long-Tail Cast On by measuring out the tail and position your yarn in your hand as shown. Remember that the long tail goes over the thumb.

1. Put the tip of the needle under the yarn. Lift the needle a little and twist it in a full circle.

2. When you get to the end of the first row, if your loop seems a bit loose, work into the back of the stitch to tighten it up.

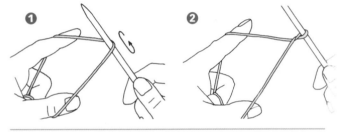

SEE ALSO: *Page 194 for knitting or purling into the back loop*

Q When I make cables, my cast on flares out below them and the bottom edge ripples. How can I prevent this?

A Cast on one or two fewer stitches below each cable. Then, on the row before you cross the cables for the first time, increase in each cable section to get the correct number of stitches. If you place the increases at the center, where the cable crosses, they won't be noticeable.

SEE ALSO: *Increases, p.256*

CHAPTER 2

VVVVVVVVVVVVVVVVVVVVVVVVVVVV

The Basics

VVVVVVVVVVVVVVVVVVVVVVVVVVVV

Knitting is made of just two stitches, knits and purls, which are combined to create unlimited patterns. "The Basics" details two of the most common knitting techniques used in North America and Europe, but around the world people use a multiplicity of methods to form the two basic stitches. Suggestions in this chapter will help you become a more comfortable and efficient knitter, so that you can discover your own "right" way to knit.

The Knit Stitch

Q What is a knit stitch and how do I make one?

A The knit stitch (K) is the basic building block of knitted fabrics.

WHEN TO USE IT: Constantly. It's difficult to imagine a project without any knit stitches.

HOW TO DO IT: There are two prevalent methods of making a knit stitch. They both accomplish the same thing, but the yarn is held differently and the needles manipulated differently.

ENGLISH METHOD

This is also known as the American or right-handed method.

1. Hold the needle with stitches on it in your left hand. Hold the yarn and the empty needle in your right hand. Insert the

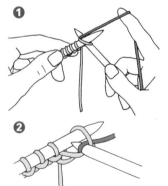

right-hand needle into the front of the stitch. Make sure the working yarn (the yarn connected to your ball) is behind the needles. Wrap the yarn around the needle counterclockwise.

2. Pull the yarn through the stitch with the tip of the right needle.

3. Slip the original stitch off the left needle.

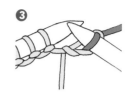

After you become used to this, you will be able to work faster, and it will become a smooth in-around-and-out motion, rather than three separate steps.

CONTINENTAL METHOD

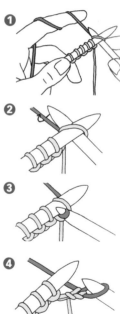

This is also known as the German or left-handed method.

1. Hold the needle with stitches on it in your left hand and the empty needle in your right hand. Hold the yarn in your left hand, pulled taut behind the needle. Insert the right needle into the stitch and behind the yarn.

2. Hook the yarn with the tip of the right needle.

3. Pull the yarn back through the stitch with a twist of the right needle.

4. Slip the original stitch off the left needle.

After you've practiced this for a while, the four separate steps will merge into a smooth in-hook-and-out motion.

The Purl Stitch

Q **What is a purl stitch and how do I make one?**

A A purl stitch (P) is simply a knit stitch in reverse. Knit stitches make a smooth V shape on the fabric facing you as you knit. Purled stitches make a small horizontal bump or bead on the side facing you. If you look at the back of a knit stitch, you'll see the telltale bump of a purl. If you look at the back of a purl, you'll find the V of a knit.

WHEN TO USE IT: Use the purl stitch in combination with the knit stitch to create everything from the ubiquitous Stockinette Stitch to ribbing to complicated textured brocades.

SEE ALSO: *Pattern Stitches, chapter 7*

ENGLISH METHOD

1. Hold the needle with stitches on it in your left hand. Hold the yarn and the empty needle in your right hand, in front of the needles. Insert the right-hand needle into the stitch from right to left.
2. Wrap the yarn around the needle counterclockwise.

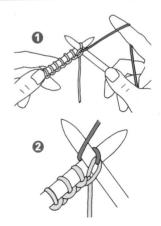

3. Pull the yarn through the stitch with the tip of the needle.

4. Slip the original stitch off the left needle.

CONTINENTAL METHOD

1. Hold the needle with stitches on it in your left hand and the empty needle in your right hand. Hold the yarn in your left hand, pulled taut in front of the left needle. Insert the right-hand needle into the stitch from right to left. (Make sure the tip of it is behind the yarn stretching up to your index finger.)

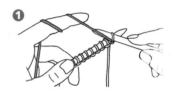

2. Move your left index finger down and to the front so that the yarn is taut over the tip of the right needle.

3. Hook the yarn back through the stitch with the right needle.

4. Slip the original stitch off the left needle.

Hows and Whys of Knits and Purls

Q I have trouble holding the yarn — it's always too tight or too loose. Is there a better way to hold it?

A The simplest method is to pass the yarn over the index finger and then across the palm, providing tension by holding it gently with the last two or three fingers of your hand against your palm or against the needle. If you feel the tension on the working yarn is too loose, wrap it around your index finger once more, or wrap it around the base of your little finger so you don't have to worry about holding on to it. You can also weave it in and out between your fingers.

....

Q I understand how to make a knit stitch, but how do I string them together?

A Regardless of whether you use the English or the Continental method, knit stitch by stitch across the needle until all the stitches are on the right needle (one row), then turn the needle, put it in your left hand, and knit another row. If you repeat the knit stitch in this manner, row after row, you are doing what is known as Garter Stitch.

SEE ALSO: *Page 192 for Garter Stitch*

Q Why would I use a purl stitch?

A Whether you use the English or Continental method, if you alternate knit rows with purl rows, you get Stockinette Stitch.

....

Q When I'm beginning a row in Stockinette Stitch, how do I know whether I should knit across or purl across?

A Look carefully at both sides of the fabric. The knit side is made up of smooth, V-shaped stitches. The purl side is made up of lots of horizontal bumps. Hold the needle with the stitches in your left hand with the knitting hanging down from it. If the purl bumps are facing you, then purl. If the knit Vs are facing you, then knit.

....

Q I've heard that Continental knitting is better than English. Is this true? Should I change the way I knit?

A Many people insist that the way they knit is the only proper way, better than any other method. The fact is that no one method is better than any other. Some Continental knitters insist that their method is most efficient, because less movement of the right hand is involved. But they have to hold the yarn under tension with the left index finger all the time and use the right hand to manipulate the needle, creating stitches. While this is less work than the English method when there isn't much knitting on the needle, it's a different story if the whole back of a sweater is hanging from the right needle. In that case, Continental knitters must lift the full weight of the piece every time they make a new stitch, whereas English knitters simply move a strand of yarn around the needle. On the other hand, English knitters are at a disadvantage doing K1P1 ribbing or Seed Stitch, because they must pass the yarn from front to back between the needles for every stitch by moving the whole right hand. Continental knitters can move the yarn into the correct position with a slight adjustment of the index finger.

If you're knitting comfortably and are happy with the fabric you're making, then there's absolutely no need to change the way you knit. Keep in mind that the styles of knitting detailed in this book are only two of many used around the world. There are advantages to learning to hold your yarn several different ways and being able to knit in either the Continental or the English manner.

▶ Holding one strand of yarn in each hand when working with two colors allows you to knit color patterns more efficiently.

▶ If you have problems with pain or fatigue caused by knitting, you can switch hands to alleviate the problem.

▶ If you're working with a slippery yarn, you may want to be able to hold it under more tension. (For more ways to knit, check Brown-Reinsel's "Beyond the Basics: Different Ways to Knit"; see Resources, p. 363.)

SEE ALSO: *Page 192 for Knit 1 Purl 1 Ribbing; and p. 190 for Seed Stitch*

Stitches, Rows, and Counting

Q **What are stitches and rows?**

A Knit stitches are made up of two legs that form a small V. Purl stitches make tiny horizontal bumps in your knitting. Rows are made up of stitches. All the stitches across your needle make one row, as does each horizontal line of stitches below the needle.

. . . .

Q **How do I count stitches?**

A To count stitches on your needle, spread them out and count each loop on the needle as one stitch. To count stitches farther down in the knit fabric, work horizontally across a row, counting the Vs or bumps. To count rows, work vertically up or down a column of stitches. There are eight stitches in the horizontal box and eight rows in the vertical box in the illustration. In Garter Stitch, every two rows makes a noticeable ridge, so it's easier to count each ridge as two rows. If you look closely at Garter Stitch you'll see that the ridges are made up of curved interlocking strands that look like smiles and frowns. To count stitches in Garter Stitch, hold your knitting right-side up (that is, with the needle at the top and the fabric hanging down), and count all the frowns across the top of one ridge. Each frown is a stitch.

SEE ALSO: *Page 192 for Garter Stitch; and p. 192 for Stockinette Stitch*

Q **Do I need to count my stitches after every row?**

A When you are learning to knit, this is a very good idea. Unless you intentionally work increases or decreases in the course of a row, or cast on or bind off stitches, you should always have the same number of stitches at the end of the row

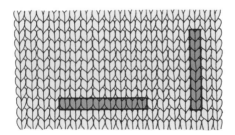

8 stitches and 8 rows

as you did when you started. If the number changes, then look back across the row for inconsistencies. This is how you'll begin to recognize mistakes. When your knitting becomes more consistent, you need to count only if you think there's a problem or if you just want to make sure everything is correct.

SEE ALSO: *Casting On, chapter 1; Binding Off, chapter 3; Increases, p. 256; and Decreases, p. 264*

Tips for Lefties

Q **I'm left-handed and I've been told I need to learn to knit backward, sitting opposite someone who knits and doing a mirror image of what that person does. Is this really true?**

A Most emphatically, no! Knitters knit with both hands and there are many ways to hold and manipulate the needles and yarn. There isn't a left-handed versus a right-handed way of knitting. If you learn to knit backward you'll be working in the opposite direction from most of the knitting world. Whenever you follow written instructions, you'll have to reverse references for "right" and "left." If you are already knitting this way, there's no need to change. But if you are just beginning, all the books, patterns, and technical information will make more sense if you work in the same direction as the vast majority of the world's knitters.

Q Is either the Continental or the English method better suited to left-handed knitters?

A Not really. Many people who are left-handed hold the yarn in the right hand and many people who are right-handed hold the yarn in the left hand. Some people who know how to crochet feel more comfortable holding the yarn in the left hand as they do when crocheting. For some, it's just the reverse. Just keep in mind that there are many correct ways to knit, and it's up to you to find one that's comfortable.

Discovering Your Personal Knitting Style

Q I find it difficult to insert the right needle into the stitch. Do you have any tips?

A Prop the right needle against your leg or tuck it under your arm to stabilize it. Instead of moving the right needle, move the left needle, pushing the stitch onto the right needle. Wrap the yarn, then move the left needle up and over the tip of the right needle to pull the new stitch through.

Q I find it difficult to get the right tension. What's the secret?

A If you generally knit English style, try learning Continental style and hold the yarn in your left hand. However, if you find it difficult to tension the yarn with your left hand, switch to knitting English style with the yarn in your right hand.

. . . .

Q I want to learn Continental style, but I find it difficult to pick up the yarn with the right needle point and pull it through to make a new stitch. Is there a way to make this easier?

A You may find it easier to move your left hand or index finger to wrap the yarn around the needle, rather than move the needle tip around to catch the yarn.

. . . .

Q Is there an easy way to pull the new stitch through the old one? It keeps slipping off my needle.

A Use a fingertip to push the point of the needle back through the old stitch.

Twists and Turns

Q **I've been told that my stitches are on the needle the wrong way. How can I tell?**

A The so-called right way is with the right leg of the stitch in front of the needle. The so-called wrong way is with the right leg of the stitch behind the needle. It would probably be better to call these orientations standard and nonstandard. More than a few knitters place some or all of their stitches on the needle in the nonstandard orientation. Continental knitters often have standard knit stitches and nonstandard purl stitches, because it's easier to purl this way.

standard

nonstandard

Some English knitters wrap their purl stitches in the opposite direction from their knit stitches. Most of these knitters automatically compensate for their nonstandard approach by knitting these stitches through the back loop, thus ensuring that they are not twisted. (In this book, unless it states otherwise, the assumption is that your stitches are on the needle in the standard direction.)

Does it matter that my stitches are on the needle the wrong way?

It matters only if you are twisting your stitches inadvertently. It's important to recognize the non-standard position and compensate for it to avoid twisted stitches. If you have standard knit stitches and nonstandard purl stitches, work into the back of the loop of the purl stitches when working on the knit side and into the front of the loop when working on the purl side.

· ·

Is there any difference in the way stitches are positioned on the needle when you're knitting circularly, as opposed to flat knitting on straight needles?

If you work standard knits and nonstandard purls, you'll need to work into the front of the purl stitches in circular knitting to prevent them from twisting. This is because each stitch begins life as a knit stitch (which is standard), not a purl stitch (nonstandard).

Q I'm one of those knitters who knits into the back of my knit stitches and purls into the front of my purl stitches. What should I do if my pattern instructions say to "knit into the back loop?"

A You can substitute knitting into the front of the stitch to twist it intentionally. Although this will twist it in the opposite direction, the change of direction may not matter. On the other hand, if the twist is part of a pattern, you may end up with stitches that don't all slant in the same direction.

Q I've been told that I twist my stitches. How can I tell if they're twisted?

A Twisted stitches cross at the bottom. Untwisted stitches have a little space between their two legs. Twisted stitches are sometimes used intentionally to tighten the knit fabric, especially in ribbings, or for decorative purposes.

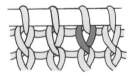

twisted stitches

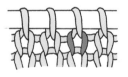

untwisted stitches

Q Why are my stitches twisted and how do I prevent it from happening?

A Here are a couple of suggestions that may help.

▶ **Try the front.** Knitting or purling into the back of the stitch can cause it to twist. Look at the stitch waiting on your left needle to be worked. Is it already twisted?

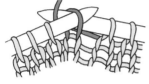 

knitting into the back of a stitch   *purling into the back of a stitch*

If it isn't, then you are working into the back of the stitch, causing it to twist as you form the new stitch on the next row. Work into the front of the stitch instead.

working into front of stitch on a knit row

working into front of stitch on a purl row

▶ **Orient yourself.** The standard is to wrap the yarn counterclockwise around the needle on both knits and purls. If you knit with the yarn in your left hand, you may be bringing the right needle up under the yarn (instead of over it) to form a knit stitch or bringing the needle over the yarn (instead of under it) to form a purl stitch. Knit a stitch. Look carefully at the new stitch on your right needle. The working yarn attached to that stitch should be hanging from the back of the needle. Try the same thing with a purl stitch. If the yarn exits a stitch in front of the needle, it's not in the standard position. Correct this by working into the back of these stitches on the next row to untwist them or by forming your stitches in the standard way, described earlier in this chapter.

SEE ALSO: *The Knit Stitch, p. 46; and The Purl Stitch, p. 48*

Q How do I fix a twisted stitch if I come across one while knitting?

A Simply work into the back of it to untwist it, then check the results. If it was twisted more than halfway or was twisted in the opposite direction, knitting or purling into the back may not solve the problem. In that case, take the stitch off the needle and pull on the working yarn to unravel the new stitch you just made, then untwist the original stitch and put it back on the left needle in the standard orientation.

Q For knitters like me who take the nonstandard approach, decreases can be very confusing. How do I handle a K2tog if I knit into the back of my knit stitches?

A If the stitches are nonstandard, working K2tog results in a left-slanting decrease, the opposite of the result with standard stitches. In order to work a right-slanting decrease, the stitches must be rearranged before the K2tog is worked. (For more on other knitting orientations, check Zilboorg's *Knitting for Anarchists* and Modesitt's *Confessions of a Knitting Heretic*; see Resources, p. 363.)

SEE ALSO: *Decreases, p. 264*

Solving Problems with Knitting and Purling

Q I set my knitting down in the middle of a row. How can I tell in which direction I was going?

A The working yarn (that's the yarn connected to your ball) will be hanging from the last stitch you worked. Make sure this is dangling from the right-hand needle when you begin again.

Q My knitting looks fine, but my stitches are so tight I can hardly move them across the needles. How can I make them looser?

A Here are a few hints.

▶ **Don't stop short.** You may be forming new stitches on the tapered tips of your needles. Make sure that you're sliding the stitches all the way onto the wider, straight part of the right needle each time you make a new stitch.

▶ **Change your tension.** If you are wrapping your yarn around any of your fingers, stop doing this and just hold it gently against the palm of your hand.

▶ **Ease up.** You may have gotten into the habit of tightening each stitch after you work it by tugging on the yarn. Stop doing this! Instead, after you make a new stitch, lift up gently on the right needle to make the stitch just a little bigger. Make sure you are holding the yarn loosely while you do this.

▶ **Let it slide.** If you are using wood needles, switch to metal, which allows the yarn to slide more easily.

Q My knitting looks messy. How can I knit more evenly?

A If some stitches are loose and some are tight, it's because you're not tensioning your yarn consistently. If you're a new knitter, your technique will improve with practice. Try different ways of holding your yarn until you find one you can use comfortably and consistently. Remember that no one's knitting is completely even. If there are just a couple of rebellious stitches that are looser or tighter than their neighbors, take the tip of a knitting needle and coax the yarn across the row on either side to even out the tension. Washing and blocking your work will also improve its appearance.

SEE ALSO: *Blocking, p. 306*

Fixing Mistakes

Q I worked all the way across the row and now I'm ready to start the next one, but the yarn's attached to the second stitch, not the first one. How do I fix this?

A When you worked the last stitch of the row, the yarn you wrapped around the needle somehow slipped off, so it never got pulled through to make a new stitch. Turn your knitting around so that the problem stitch is on the left end of the needle. Take your empty needle and slip the stitch onto it. Now knit (or purl) it as usual.

....

Q How do I pick up a dropped knit stitch?

A Pinch the fabric just below the dropped stitch so that it won't unravel and insert the left needle into the stitch from the front. If it has already unraveled, there will be a loose strand above the stitch. You must knit up the loose strand before putting the stitch back on the needle. You can do this with the tip of your knitting needle, but it's easier to use a crochet hook. Lay your knitting down on a flat surface, being careful not to stretch it (which may cause further unraveling). Insert the crochet hook through the stitch from the front, hook it under the loose strand, pull the strand through to the front, and put it on your left needle.

SEE ALSO: *Solving Problems, p. 318*

Q How do I pick up a dropped purl stitch?

A Like a dropped knit stitch, pinch the fabric below the stitch and insert the left needle into it from the front. If the stitch has unraveled, turn the fabric over so the knit side is facing you and use a crochet hook to pull the loose strand back into the stitch (as described for knit stitches, opposite). Then turn your knitting back to face you properly. If the renegade stitch is on the right needle, slip it to the left so you're positioned to begin purling again.

....

Q How can I fix a mistake several rows below? Do I have to rip it all out back to that point?

A If the mistake involves just one stitch, work to the point in the row where the stitch directly above the mistake is at the tip of a needle and slip it off the needle. Unravel just this one stitch down to the mistake. Now you must work the stitch back up in pattern.

▶ **Stockinette Stitch.** Turn your knitting so that the knit side is facing you. Insert a crochet hook into the stitch from the front and hook the lowest unraveled strand through to the front. Don't remove the crochet hook. Instead, continue to work your way up from the lowest strand to the highest, hooking each one out to the front to reknit another stitch. At the top, put the stitch back on the needle.

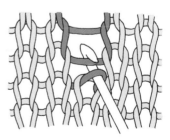

▶ **Ribbing.** Turn your knitting so that the knit side of

picking up dropped stitch on knit side

the stitches to be corrected is facing you and hook the strands back up just as described for Stockinette Stitch.

▶ **Garter Stitch or other pattern stitches.** Where there is a combination of knits and purls facing you, you will need to hook up the knit stitches from the front and the purled stitches from the back. If you find it difficult to insert the crochet hook from the back, simply turn your knitting over and hook up the stitch from the other side, then return to the front to capture the next knit stitch. Take care to pick up the strands in the correct order from bottom to top.

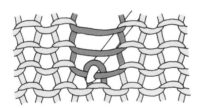

picking up dropped stitch on purl side

Q Is there any way I can work back a few stitches to fix a mistake without taking the knitting off the needles?

A Yes. Insert the left needle tip into the stitch directly below the one on the right needle. Slip the right needle out of this stitch and pull on the yarn. The newest stitch will unravel, and the stitch from the row below will be secure on the left needle. Continue doing this across your knitting until you reach the mistake. Unknitting stitch by stitch like this has come to be called tinking in knitting parlance, because "tink" is "knit" backward.

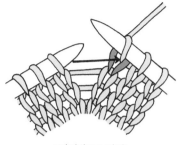

unknitting a stitch

Q **My needle accidentally came out of my knitting. What should I do?**

A Gather the knitting up into a bunch to prevent stretching, which may unravel your stitches. If you are right-handed, work from right to left with the needle in your right hand and insert the tip into the stitches from the back, one at a time. Gradually ease them farther up the needle as you work. If you are left-handed, work from left to right, inserting the tip of the needle into the front of the stitches. Careful attention to inserting the needle into each stitch from the correct direction may still not result in all the stitches being placed consistently on the needle. Some may have unraveled; some may be twisted. You can correct the problems as you work across the next row, or you can slip each stitch to another needle and make corrections as you replace them on the working needle.

Easy Does It

Here are a couple of tips that make replacing stitches on your needles easier.

▶ A needle several sizes smaller is easy to slip into the stitches. Either slip the stitches back to the correct-size needle after you pick them all up, or just work across using the correct-size needle.

▶ If you use a circular needle you won't have to worry about ending up with the working yarn hanging from the wrong end of the needle.

Q If I need to rip out a sizable chunk of my knitting, how do I do it?

A Slide your needle out of the knitting and pull on the yarn to unravel it. If you are a bold, brave knitter, unravel as far as you like and then slip your needle back into the stitches as described on page 69. If you are not quite so fearless, especially if you are working with slippery yarn, or fine yarn and tiny needles, stop unraveling one row above the desired point. Take the needle in one hand and the knitting in the other and insert the needle into each stitch as you unravel the final row.

Q What is frogging?

A In current knitting slang, action described in the answer above is called frogging, because you "rip it, rip it, rip it."

....

Q I keep ending up with extra stitches. Why is this happening?

A This is a common problem, with a variety of causes. Take a good look at your knitting, checking for sloppy stitches, a steadily increasing width, or holes in the fabric. These issues are addressed in the next three questions. You may have just one of these problems, or you may be making several different mistakes.

....

Q I have some sloppy stitches on my needle that cross other stitches. What is happening?

A Any of the following problems could cause this.

▶ **Incomplete stitch.** You inserted your needle into the stitch and wrapped the yarn around the needle, but you slipped the old stitch off the left needle without pulling the new stitch through it. Both the old stitch and the

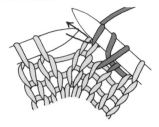

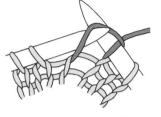

tinking to the mistake

fixing an incomplete stitch

new one are now on your right needle. To fix this, slip the intervening stitches back to the left needle or unknit the intervening stitches and put them on the left needle. Then, simply lift the old stitch from the row below over the incomplete stitch on the current row.

▶ **Inserting incorrectly.** You inserted the needle into the stitch a little lower than you should have, catching the stitch on the row below. When you pulled the new stitch through, you exited in the correct place, leaving the stitch from the row below on your needle along with

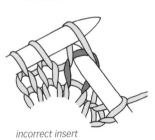

incorrect insert

the new stitch. To fix this, work across your needle to the mistake. Slip the double stitch off and unravel the stitch. You'll need to hook two rows back up with a crochet hook and put it back on the needle.

▶ **Exiting incorrectly.** You began the stitch correctly, but when you pulled the new stitch through the old one, you accidentally went too low and picked up the stitch from the row below. Now the new stitch and the one from the row below are both on your right needle. Fix this in the same way you fix incorrectly inserted stitches.

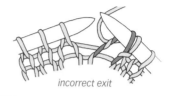

incorrect exit

Q **Why does my knitting get wider at the edges when I'm just trying to knit straight?**

A You are probably adding a stitch each time you begin a row. This can be caused in two ways.

▶ **Pulling too hard.** Many knitters feel that the first stitch of the row is too loose, so they pull on the yarn to tighten it before they begin. They pull so hard that the stitch one row below is pulled up over the needle. If you look closely at a knit (or purl) stitch, you'll see that it has two legs. Pulling that first stitch causes both legs of the stitch below to slide up over the needle, making two stitches where there was only one.

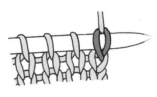

pulling up stitch from row below

▶ **Starting off wrong.** The yarn may be in the wrong position when you begin the row. Make sure that the yarn is behind both needles when you begin to knit and in front of both needles when you begin to purl. Making this mistake consistently at the beginning of every row adds one new stitch per row and makes a diagonal edge rather than a straight one. To fix a piece of knitting with this problem, unravel back to the point where your knitting started getting wider. When you desire a diagonal edge, you can intentionally position the yarn incorrectly at the beginning of the row to make a yarn over. This is one way that triangular shawls and other diagonal edges are shaped.

SEE ALSO: *The Yarn Over, p. 81*

Q **Why does my knitting have holes in it?**

A Holes are caused by accidentally wrapping the yarn around the right needle between stitches. This can happen if the yarn is in the wrong position before working a stitch. When this is done intentionally, it's called a yarn over and is used to create lace or eyelets. To avoid unwanted holes, make sure the yarn is in back before knitting and in front before purling. To fix the hole, unravel the whole column of stitches down to the hole. Don't worry; it can't go any farther than this. Use the tip of a needle to coax the slack in the yarn into the stitches on either side. If your knitting is too loose or there are too many holes, you may need to unravel back to the point where the hole was formed.

SEE ALSO: *Solving Problems during Finishing, p. 342*

The Slipped Stitch

Q **What is a slipped stitch?**

A A slipped stitch (Sl) is one that is simply moved from the left needle to the right needle without wrapping the yarn to create a new stitch above it.

WHEN TO USE IT: Use slipped stitches to create decorative patterns or to make a denser, more substantial fabric, on the heels of socks, for example.

HOW TO DO IT: Insert the right needle into the stitch on the left needle, then slide it off the left needle.

Q **When I slip a stitch, should I insert the needle as if I'm knitting or as if I'm purling?**

A If your pattern doesn't specify, then slip as if you are purling (also called purlwise). If you slip knitwise, you change the orientation of the stitch. Working into the front of it on the next row causes it to twist, changing the appearance of the stitch and making the fabric even tighter. Of course, you can decide for yourself which look you prefer.

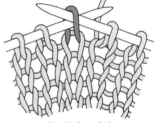

slip stitch purlwise

If your stitches are on the needle in the nonstandard direction, check your slipped stitches carefully after slipping to make sure they are on the needle the same way as all the other stitches. Turn them around if necessary.

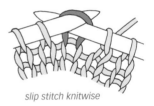

slip stitch knitwise

Q **Where should the yarn be when I'm slipping, in front or in back?**

A If your pattern doesn't specify, then leave the yarn wherever it already is. This is in back if you are knitting and in front if you are purling. Take a look at the effect. The yarn makes a longer horizontal strand across whichever side it's on when you slip the stitch. If it doesn't look right, then hold it in the other position. In general, if the horizontal strand in front of the slipped stitch is not part of a decorative effect on the right side of the fabric, then slip the stitch with the yarn held on the wrong side of the fabric.

. . . .

Q **If I forget to slip a stitch, how do I fix it?**

A If you discover the mistake within a few stitches, "tink" back to it, then slip it properly and continue to work across the row. If you discover it on the next row, simply unravel that one stitch and put it on your left needle ready to be worked. Make sure the loose strand of yarn you unraveled is in the proper position (either in front of the fabric or in back). Use the tip of your knitting needle to work the slack from this strand into the stitches on either side. They will be a little loose but should even out once the item is finished. If the stitches are too loose (for example, if you unraveled several slipped stitches in the same area), you'll need to take out the whole row and do it again. Or, you can pull out all the slack into a loop on the wrong side, cut the loop, and weave in the ends to secure them.

SEE ALSO: *At Loose Ends, p. 340*

Q I've been working a slipped stitch pattern, but the rows are so tight I can hardly go on. Why?

A Instead of slipping purlwise, you're probably slipping knitwise (twisting the stitches), which makes the fabric much tighter when the stitches are twisted on the next row. If this isn't the problem, then it's simply that slipped stitch patterns characteristically make a tighter fabric. Try consciously to make your stitches a little looser as you work, or stop and spread them apart on the right needle periodically. You may need to use a larger needle.

Edge Stitches

Q What are edge stitches?

A Edge stitches are the stitches at either end of the row of knitting. These are characteristically uneven, alternating long and short, tight and loose up both sides. Some knitting patterns call these selvages and give instructions for special treatment. (For more check "The Edges of Knitting" in *Hand-knitting Techniques: From Threads Magazine*; see Resources, p. 363.)

Q **Should I knit the first stitch of every row?**

A Probably not. If you knit the first stitch of every row, then that edge stitch will be in Garter Stitch, rather than in Stockinette or whatever pattern stitch you are working. It will also leave a little bump in every other row. My preference is to work the first and last stitch of every row in Stockinette Stitch because it forms a neat edge and makes picking up stitches and seaming easy.

On the other hand, if this is the finished edge of your knitting and you like the look, then by all means knit the first stitch of every row. The little bumps are also very convenient if you later want to pick up one stitch every other row for a border or to add another section of knitting. You can easily sew a seam between two pieces of knitting by simply zigzagging back and forth between the bumps on the edges of the two pieces to be joined. This makes a very flat seam, but it is not substantial enough to stand up to a lot of wear.

. . . .

Q **Should I slip the first stitch of every row?**

A I find that plain Stockinette Stitch is the best choice for edges that will be seamed or where a border will be added. When you're making the heel flap of a sock, however, always slip the first stitch of the row because it contributes to the shape of the flap. I also like to slip the first stitch and purl the last stitch of each row when working in Garter Stitch, because it creates a very pleasing chain effect along the edge. Many knitters prefer a slipped-stitch edge on all their knitting, and if you like the results of slipping the first stitch, then you may want to proceed that way.

Q The edges of my knitting are uneven and loose. How can I fix this?

A All knit edges are uneven, with alternating loose and tight stitches up the edge. If some of your edge stitches are way too loose, however, try this. Knit the first stitch of the row, then place your index finger on top of the stitch to hold the yarn in place and lift up on the right needle, gently pulling the slack out of the stitch below. Then pull on the working yarn to remove the slack. Work normally across the rest of the row. Don't pull on the yarn before making the first stitch of the row, because it may cause you to add an extra stitch.

The Yarn Over

Q What is a yarn over and how do I do it?

A A yarn over (YO) is simply a wrap of the yarn around the right needle between two stitches. A yarn over adds a stitch.

WHEN TO USE IT: Each yarn over makes a hole in the knitting, so it is used individually for buttonholes, spaced across a row for eyelets, or combined with decreases to make knitted lace.

HOW TO DO IT: If the yarn is in your right hand, simply wrap it counterclockwise once around the right needle. If the yarn is in your left hand, either wrap it around the needle with your index finger, or take the right needle over the yarn and around the back.

yarn over

....

Q How do I pick up a dropped yarn over?

A Insert the left needle from the front, under the top strand that stretches between the two needles.

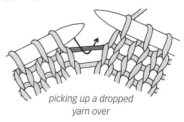

picking up a dropped yarn over

Q I forgot to do a yarn over on the last row. Is there a way to fix this without ripping out?

A Yes. When you come to that point in the row, pick up the top strand as described in the previous answer.

....

Q How do I do a yarn over at the beginning of a row?

A Put your yarn in the "wrong" position before you begin the row. If you plan to knit the first stitch, then put the yarn in front of the right needle. If you plan to purl the first stitch, put the yarn in back. Either way, when you work the first stitch, the yarn will make an extra loop over the needle; that's your yarn over. If you are about to purl, the yarn over will be on the needle in the nonstandard position. When you come to it at the end of the next row, just work into the back of it to untwist it.

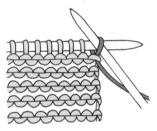

yarn over at beginning of purl row

SEE ALSO: *Twists and Turns, p. 58*

Q How do I do a yarn over at the end of a row?

A You can't. Turn your work and make the yarn over at the beginning of the next row.

....

Q How do I make a double yarn over?

A Just the same as a regular yarn over, but wrap the yarn around the needle a second time. This makes a bigger hole. On the next row, the instructions may say to work into the yarn over, letting the extra loop fall off the needle. In this case, knit or purl into it as usual, then slip the extra loop off when you slip the stitch off the needle.

....

Q My instructions say to K1, P1 into the yarn over from the previous row. How do I do this?

A Knit into the yarn over as usual, but don't slip it off the left needle. Instead, bring the yarn between the needles to the front, insert the right needle again as if to purl, purl a stitch, and then finally slip the yarn over off the needle. If this was originally a double yarn over, let the first loop slip off the needle before making the purl stitch. If the instructions say to P1, K1 into the yarn over, simply work the purl stitch first, then take the yarn to the back before making the knit stitch.

Personal Factors

Q **My shoulders, hands, and elbows hurt. Is there something I'm doing wrong?**

A Avid knitters often fall prey to repetitive stress injuries by overdoing it. Carpal tunnel syndrome and tennis elbow are among the most persistent and debilitating, but a host of other aches and pains can plague knitters. The good news is, you can prevent such injuries. Follow these guidelines.

▶ **Good posture.** Sit up straight!

▶ **Moderation.** Don't knit for hours in one position.

▶ **Stay in shape.** Exercise to build up strength in your arms and shoulders; put down your knitting and stretch frequently.

▶ **Vary your knitting.** Move between several projects using different size needles, with different levels of difficulty.

▶ **Check your glasses.** If your near-distance prescription needs to be adjusted, you may be holding your work in an awkward position in order to see it better.

▶ **Avoid pain.** If it hurts, stop! If pain persists, see your doctor.

Step Away from the Knitting

Take the time to stop what you're doing and check your work.

▶ **Are there mistakes?** Hold up your knitting periodically and glance at the fabric. Dropped stitches, holes, and cables twisted the wrong way will all pop out at you. You'll be amazed you didn't notice them before. If you're working with dark yarn that's hard to see, take it outside into natural light occasionally so you can get a good look at it. The more often you step back and check your work, the sooner you'll find errors and the easier they'll be to correct. There's nothing more disheartening than finishing a sweater, sewing it up, adding the borders, weaving in all those ends, putting it on, and only then catching sight of an obvious error the first time you walk past a mirror.

▶ **Is it the right size?** If you're making something that is supposed to fit a certain way, stop and measure it or hold it up against yourself to see if it's shaping up properly. You may be reassured that it's perfect, or you may discover you've chosen the wrong size or misinterpreted the instructions and it can't possibly fit. If it looks like it won't fit, you can take action to fix it right away.

The Big Picture

Q **I've been working on a sweater and I'm not sure I like the feel of it. Do you have any suggestions?**

A Back off and take the larger view. Squeeze your fabric, stretch it, fondle it. Each project needs the optimum fabric to be a success: soft and stretchy for a hat, soft and caressing for a sweater, light and stretchy for a shawl, thick and substantial for a pot holder or purse. If you're knitting from a pattern, then the designer has decided on the fabric for you, but it's still up to you to create it. Check to see if your stitch and row gauges match the ones specified in the pattern. If you're knitting from your own design, you've assumed full responsibility! So take the time to notice whether or not you like the fabric as you knit. If you're still in doubt about the project, try these suggestions.

▶ **Change needle size.** Larger needles create a softer fabric, and smaller ones tighten it up.

▶ **Change yarn.** Maybe a different yarn or a different color is what you really need.

▶ **Change patterns.** Perhaps it's the design itself that's the problem.

SEE ALSO: *Gauge, p. 162*

^^^^^^^^^^^^^^^^^^^^^^^^^^^^^^

CHAPTER 3

Binding Off

^^^^^^^^^^^^^^^^^^^^^^^^^^^^^^

Binding off serves two purposes: It removes your stitches from the needles, and secures them so they can't unravel. Binding off is one of those seemingly simple finishing touches that can make or break a garment. You'll find times when the bind off should be tight, others when it should be loose. For instance, at the top of a garment the bind off needs to be tight to support the neckline, but if it's too tight, the sweater won't go over your head. Across the top edge of a shawl you need a loose bind off, or the drape of the fabric will be distorted.

Q What's the difference between casting off and binding off?

A They are just two different terms for the same thing.

Standard Bind Offs

BASIC BIND OFF

The Basic Bind Off (BO) is easy to learn and makes a neat, firm edge. It creates a chain along the edge that attracts attention.

WHEN TO USE IT: Most of the time. If you have a special situation where it just doesn't look right or behave properly, try one of the other methods described in this chapter.

GET READY: Knit the first two stitches.

HOW TO DO IT:

1. Insert the left needle into the right-hand stitch on the right needle and lift the stitch up.

2. Pull the other stitch through it with the right needle.

3. Drop the stitch off the left needle.

4. Knit the next stitch.

basic bind off, step 2

Repeat these four steps until all the stitches on the left needle are bound off. A stitch will remain on the right needle.

Enlarge this stitch so that it's about 6" (15 cm) tall, then cut the yarn at the top of the stitch. Pull out the yarn still connected to the ball.

Hint: Use a crochet hook the same size as your needle instead of the right needle to make binding off easier.

Knitting without End(s)

If there'll be a seam at the end of the bind off, leave a long tail and use it to sew the seam. You'll have fewer ends to weave in when you're done.

KNIT 2 TOGETHER BIND OFF

This method may be useful if you find it difficult to lift one stitch up and pull the other through it.

GET READY: Knit one stitch.

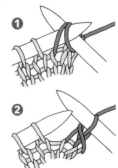

HOW TO DO IT:

1. Slip one stitch knitwise. Insert the left needle into the two stitches on the right needle.

2. Knit these two stitches together.

Repeat these two steps until all the stitches are bound off.

SEE ALSO: *The Slipped Stitch, p. 75*

All about Binding Off

Q When a pattern says to bind off a certain number of stitches, I find it very confusing to know how many I've actually bound off. Is it the number of stitches I've knit, or the number I've passed over them?

A It's the number of stitches you've passed over, because these are the ones that have actually been bound off. The question logically arises because you always have to work one additional stitch in order to pass the previous one over it. This stitch remains on your needle, however, and will be worked on subsequent rows, so it's not included in the count of bound-off stitches.

· ·

Q My pattern says to bind off in knitting on the wrong side. What does this mean?

A Work across a right-side row as usual. At the end of the row, turn your knitting so that the wrong side is facing you. Now, work the bind off as usual, knitting each stitch and passing the previous stitch over it and off the needle. To bind off in purl, purl all the stitches as you work the bind off; this makes the characteristic chain along the edge form on the side away from you.

Q My pattern says to bind off in ribbing. How do I do this?

A As you bind off, follow the rib pattern you've established on the item, knitting the knit stitches and purling the purl stitches. For example, in K1P1 ribbing, knit the first stitch, purl the next stitch, then pass the knit stitch off over the purled stitch. The next stitch on the left needle is a knit stitch, so knit it, then pass the purled stitch over it. Continue across, alternately knitting and purling stitches as you go. Working the bind off in ribbing makes the chain of bound-off stitches sit along the edge of the fabric rather than lie prominently along the knit side.

SEE ALSO: *Page 192 for Knit 1 Purl 1 Ribbing*

Q I don't like the chain that forms across the edge when I bind off. Is there a way to get rid of it?

A The Basic Bind Off always forms a chain, but it doesn't need to be on the right side. You can bind off in purl (or from the other side of the fabric), and the chain will form on the back. Or you can bind off in ribbing, and the chain will form along the edge instead of across the front. You can also use one of the other techniques, such as the Sewn Bind Off or the Tubular Bind Off.

SEE ALSO: *Sewn Bind Off, p.99; and Tubular Bind Off, p. 97*

Q Should I bind off on the knit side or the purl side?

A That depends on how you want the bound-off edge
to look. If you knit each stitch while you bind off, the
chain of bound-off stitches will appear on the side facing you.
If you prefer that this chain be on the knit side, then bind off
with the knit side facing you. If you prefer that the chain be
on the purl side, then bind off with the purl side facing you.
Keep in mind that if the edge will be sewn into a seam or is
the base for a border, it will be hidden and the appearance
of the bind off won't matter.

. . . .

Q After binding off, what do I do with the yarn that I cut off?

A If you will be sewing a seam there, leave a long tail and
use it to sew the seam. Otherwise, when you are done,
weave the end in on the wrong side.

SEE ALSO: *At Loose Ends, p. 340*

Q Is there a way to take out the bind off?

A Yes. Tease the cut end out through the last stitch with
the tip of your needle. Pull on the tail and the bound-off
edge will unravel. If the yarn is a little felted (matted or meshed

together) and does not pull freely, use a sharp, pointed pair of scissors to carefully snip just the tangled fibers.

Solving Problems

Q When I bind off, the edge is always too tight. What should I do?

A This happens because the stitches need to lie sideways across the edge of the knitting, but knit stitches are wider than they are tall, so the bound-off stitches naturally pull in a little compared to the stitches below them. Here are some tips that may help.

▶ **Use a larger needle** (or crochet hook) while binding off. It automatically makes the stitches a tiny bit bigger, allowing them to stretch a bit more across the edge. Be sure to form each stitch on the straight part of the needle, instead of on the needle tip.

▶ **Loosen up.** Each time you bind off a stitch, lift the right needle up a bit, pulling the stitch looser, before you knit the next stitch. If you are a firm knitter, stifle the urge to tighten each stitch as you go.

▶ **Try a different bind off.** The Yarn Over Bind Off, Sewn Bind Off, and Tubular Bind Off are all looser and stretch more than the Basic Bind Off.

YARN OVER BIND OFF

This bind off produces a very stretchy edge that's not too bulky. It can look a little ruffled when it's relaxed, and it does not support the edge.

WHEN TO USE IT: Perfect for any edge that needs to be very loose. For example, for lace (especially shawls), around the outer edge of a curve, at the edge of a ruffle, or the top of a sock.

GET READY: Knit the first stitch.

HOW TO DO IT:

1. Yarn over.
2. Lift the knitted stitch up over the yarn over and off the needle.
3. Knit the next stitch.
4. Lift the yarn over up over the knit stitch and off the needle.

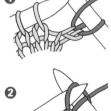

Repeat these four steps until all the stitches from the left needle are gone. Enlarge the last stitch and fasten off as for the Basic Bind Off.

VARIATIONS: You can fine-tune the width of this bind off by making a yarn over after every two or three stitches, instead of after every stitch.

SEE ALSO: *The Yarn Over, p. 81*

Special Situations

Q Is there a way to add cording as I bind off?

A Yes, you can bind off and add I-Cord at the same time.

SEE ALSO: *Page 354 for information on I-Cord*

I-CORD BIND OFF

GET READY: Cast on 3 stitches at the beginning of the row, using the Knitted Cast On or the Loop Cast On.

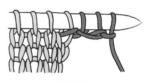

cast on 3

HOW TO DO IT:

1. Knit two stitches.
2. Slip the next stitch knitwise.
3. Knit one more stitch.
4. Pass the slipped stitch over the knitted stitch and off the needle.
5. Slip three stitches back to the left needle purlwise. Do not turn. Pull the yarn firmly across the back of the three I-Cord stitches.

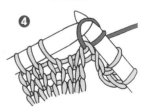

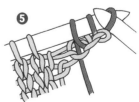

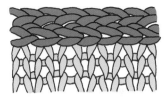

*completed I-Cord
bind off*

Repeat these five steps until all stitches across the row have been bound off. Cut your yarn and pull the end through the three I-Cord stitches.

VARIATIONS:

▶ Cast on two stitches for a very narrow edging, or more stitches for a wider cord. This bind off is usually most successful with three to five stitches.

▶ For a quicker version, substitute K2togtbl (knit 2 together through the back loop) for steps 2 through 4.

SEE ALSO: *Page 266 for Knit 2 Together Through the Back Loop*

Q Is there a bind off I can use that doesn't leave a noticeable ridge?

A Yes, you can use the Tubular Bind Off. This is most successful used with K1P1 ribbing.

TUBULAR BIND OFF

GET READY: Cut the yarn, leaving a tail about three times the width of the knitting and thread it through a yarn needle.

HOW TO DO IT:

1. Insert the tip of the threaded yarn needle knitwise into the first stitch and slip it off the needle.

2. Insert the yarn needle purl-wise into the third stitch and pull the yarn through.

3. Insert the yarn needle purl-wise into the second stitch and slip it off the needle.

4. Bring the needle and yarn around to the back of the knitting, and insert the yarn needle knitwise into the fourth stitch. Pull the yarn through.

Notice that you've dropped two stitches off the needle and already worked into the first two stitches that remain. These will be the first and second stitches as you work through the instructions again.

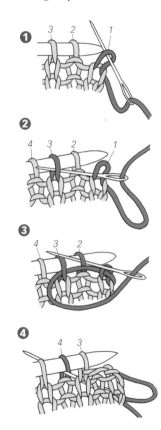

Repeat these four steps until all stitches have been secured. As you become familiar with the process, you'll be able to merge these steps into two simple movements, working steps 1 and 2 together and steps 3 and 4 together.

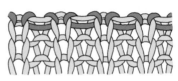

completed tubular bind off

VARIATIONS:

▶ Divide the stitches alternately, with the knit stitches on the front needle and the purl stitches on the back needle if you are binding off K1P1 rib fabric. You can do this most easily by slipping the needle out of the stitches completely. The knit stitches naturally spring out to the front and the purl stitches to the back. Slip one needle back into the knit stitches and a second needle into the purl stitches. Make sure both needles point the same way, with the yarn hanging at the point of one needle. Follow instructions for Kitchener Stitch.

▶ If you have been working in K1P1 ribbing, before cutting the yarn and starting the Tubular Bind Off, work four rows, knitting the knit stitches and slipping the purl stitches (purlwise) with the yarn in front.

SEE ALSO: *The Slipped Stitch, p. 75; and Kitchener Stitch, p. 321*

Q What's the best bind off for lace?

A For a plain but very loose bind off, use the Yarn Over Bind Off. If you crochet, you can crochet an edging, working one stitch at a time or working groups of stitches and decorative loops. (For more on crocheting, check Eckman's *The Crochet Answer Book*; see Resources, p. 363.)

....

Q Which bind off is the most stretchy?

A The Tubular Bind Off is, if you are careful to work it loosely, although it tends to stretch out of shape. The Yarn Over Bind Off is stretchy and retains its shape better.

....

Q Can I make my bind off match my cast on?

A The Sewn Bind Off is a good match for most cast ons, and you can control the tension to make it looser or tighter.

SEWN BIND OFF

GET READY: Cut the yarn about twice as long as the width of your knitting. Thread it through a yarn needle and use it to sew through the stitches. Hold the knitting in your left hand and sew with your right.

HOW TO DO IT:

1. Sew through two stitches from right to left.

2. Sew back through the first stitch from left to right.

3. Slip that stitch off the needle.

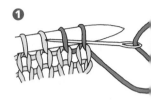

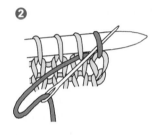

Repeat these three steps until you have only one stitch left on the needle. Sew once more through this last stitch and slip it off the knitting needle. You'll need to decide which side of this bind off you prefer. If you are left-handed, you may reverse the directions. Sew with your left hand, from left to right. In step 1 sew through two stitches from left to right, and in step 2 sew through one stitch from right to left.

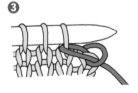

. . . .

Q I've heard of a way to join two pieces of knitting when you bind off. How do you do this?

A This is known as the Three-Needle Bind Off. It's an excellent way to join the top of two pieces of knitting, such as the shoulder seams of a sweater. It supports the fabric with just a slight stretch and makes a very neat join. Binding off with the right sides of the knitting held together hides the seam on the wrong side. Or, you can hold the wrong sides of the knitting together so that the seam forms a decorative ridge on the outside of the knitting.

THREE-NEEDLE BIND OFF

GET READY: Hold the two pieces to be joined, with either right sides or wrong sides together. The two needles should be next to each other, pointing in the same direction, with the working yarn hanging from one point.

HOW TO DO IT:

1. Using a third needle (or a crochet hook), knit together one stitch from the front needle and one from the back needle.

2. Repeat for the next stitch on both needles.

3. Pass the first stitch on the right needle over the second to bind it off.

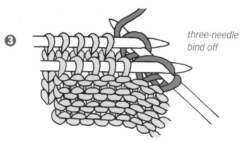

three-needle bind off

Repeat steps 2 and 3 until all stitches are bound off. Cut the yarn and pull it through the last stitch.

Q I've been working in a pattern stitch with cables. How do I bind it off so that the edge doesn't ripple and flare?

A Cables pull the fabric in substantially. To prevent the bound-off edge from fanning out, work one or two decreases at the top of each cable, either as you bind off or on the row before. You can experiment with decreasing when you bind off your swatch.

....

Q Can I make a hem when I bind off?

A Yes. Work in Stockinette to the edge of the garment. For a gently rolled fold line, simply continue in Stockinette. For a straight, flat fold line, work one or two rows in Reverse Stockinette (two rows will make a squarer edge). For a picot edge, repeat yarn over, K2tog across the row at the fold line. Work in Stockinette again until the length above the fold equals the length below the fold. Cut the yarn, leaving as long a length as is comfortable to sew with. To join the two layers, fold the hem to the inside of the garment and use a yarn needle to sew through each stitch on the needle, then through one stitch on the garment. You may bind off very loosely and then sew the hem, but the result will be bulkier.

For a Slimmer Hem

For less bulk, work the inside layer of the hem with thinner yarn, use fewer stitches, or switch to smaller needles.

Q I've been working in a pattern stitch that has increases and decreases. How do I bind it off so it looks good?

A You need to bind off "in pattern." As you work across the row, instead of knitting each stitch, work the stitches to correspond to a normal pattern row. For example, if you are working a ribbed pattern, continue knitting and purling in pattern across the row while you bind off. You may want to continue to make some or all of the increases or decreases as you bind off.

Let's use the example of a chevron pattern. On the wrong side, you purl across. On the right side, your pattern calls for you to work yarn overs and decreases. Each time you have two stitches on your right needle, pass the right stitch over the left stitch, even when the left stitch is a yarn over. When it is time to work a decrease, such as K2tog, work the decrease, then pass the right stitch off the needle over it. Although the difference between binding off in pattern and binding off normally may be subtle, your stitches are less likely to become distorted if you bind off in pattern.

Q How do I get rid of "stair steps" when I bind off over several rows?

A When shaping armholes, shoulders, and necklines, you frequently need to work several groups of bound-off stitches, resulting in "stair steps" going up the sloped edge of your knitting. If you create a smooth diagonal edge, on the other hand, it will be easier to seam or to pick up stitches.

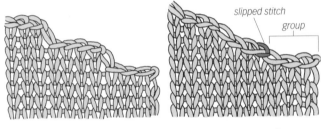

stair-step bind off

slipped stitch

group

smooth bind off

You can smooth the edge by slipping the first stitch of each group before you bind it off. To do this, bind off the first group as you normally would. When it is time to bind off the next group, slip the first stitch knitwise. Knit the next stitch. Pass the slipped stitch over the knitted stitch and off the needle. Continue binding off the rest of the stitches as usual.

CHAPTER 4

Tools

All you really need to get started with knitting is some yarn and a couple of pointed sticks. I've been known, in an emergency knitting situation, to knit with two pencils. When you walk into a yarn shop, look at a catalog, or shop on the Internet, however, you find seemingly thousands of kinds of knitting needles and hundreds of small accessories with uses you can't even imagine. So, what do you really need?

Knitting Needles

 What types of needles are available, and when would I use them?

 Knitting needles seem to be sold with more options than there are knitters on earth. Choosing the right needle can be daunting when you're presented with such a wide array of possibilities. Things to consider are needle type (straight, double-pointed, or circular), size, length, material, and shape. All of the information you need is in the chart on the next page.

. . . .

 How do I know what needle size to choose?

 Needle size is given either as an arbitrary number in the U.S. system (smaller numbers are for thinner needles) or as a millimeter measurement in the international system. Size refers to the thickness (diameter) of the needles. Thinner needles generally are used with finer yarn, fatter needles with thicker yarn. Like all knitting rules, however, this one is meant to be broken. You may want to knit lace with a larger needle and very fine yarn, so that it appears even more open. Or, if you wanted to create a thicker, less stretchy fabric for a bag or a pair of bulky socks, choose thinner needles.

Knitting Needle Know-How

TYPE	USES	NOTES
Straight needles have a point at one end and a knob of some sort at the other.	Flat knitting, where you knit across one row, then turn and knit back across the next.	Sold in pairs. If knitting instructions don't specify double-pointed or circular needles, then this is the kind they mean. Also called single-pointed.
Double-pointed needles are also straight but have points at both ends.	Socks, mittens and sweater sleeves; anything that involves knitting a small tube circularly.	Sold in sets of 4 or 5 needles. Also used for some special purposes such as knitting cords. Convenient for knitting narrower flat pieces because they are shorter than straight needles.
Circular needles have 2 pointed ends with a long flexible cable between.	Circular knitting of larger tubes, such as hats and bodies of sweaters.	Useful for flat knitting as well, especially wide projects like blankets and shawls. May be used 2 at a time for smaller projects, such as socks, or for very large projects.

Pattern instructions include a recommended needle size and a gauge for each project. The right needle size is the one that gives you the correct gauge. This may be different from the size recommended. If you're not working from a pattern, then refer to the yarn label for a recommendation on needle size. Work a sample on that size needle, and see if you like the fabric. If the fabric is too loose, use a smaller needle. If it's too tight or stiff, use a bigger needle. If the ball band gives you no hints, then use a needle gauge to determine needle size. Double the yarn, and hold it across the holes in the gauge. Try using the needle size of the hole that the doubled yarn just covers.

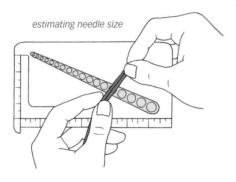

estimating needle size

SEE ALSO: *Gauge, p. 162; Yarn Labels, p. 126; and p. 120 for rulers and gauges*

Knitting Needle Sizes

	DIAMETER (MM)	US SIZE NUM	SUGGESTED YARN WEIGHTS
Limited Availability	.5	0000000	Extremely fine yarn and thread
	.75	000000	(lace weight)
	1	00000	
	1.25	0000	
	1.5	000	
	1.75	00	
Wide Availability	2	0	Superfine (sock, fingering, baby)
	2.25	1	
	2.75	2	
	3.25	3	Superfine to fine (sock, fingering, baby, and sport)
	3.5	4	Fine (baby, sport)
	3.75	5	Fine and light (baby, sport, DK, light worsted)
	4	6	Light and medium (DK, light worsted, worsted)
	4.5	7	
	5	8	
	5.5	9	Medium and bulky (worsted, heavy worsted, chunky)
	6	10	Bulky (chunky)
	6.5	10½	
Limited Availability	8	11	Super bulky and multiple strands or unspun roving
	9	13	
	10	15	
	12.75	17	
	15	19	
	19	35	
	25	50	

Q **My local stores carry metal, plastic, and wood needles. Which kind is best?**

A Knitting needles are available in all sorts of materials, but you may find only a limited selection in smaller knitting shops and large craft chains.

▶ **Metal** choices include stainless steel, aluminum, and nickel-plated brass, both coated and polished.

▶ **Wood** needles are made from walnut, birch, rosewood, ebony, and mahogany. Bamboo needles are included in this classification.

▶ **Synthetic** materials and composites include plastic, nylon, casein, and cellulose acetate.

Choosing the material you like best is simply a matter of personal preference. You may find that different kinds of yarn knit up more easily on a particular type of needle. The comments in the chart on pages 112–113 come from my own experience, as well as that of other knitters.

Q **Aren't all knitting needles shaped the same: long and pointy?**

A No. The tips of the needles are shaped differently. For some knitters, the shape of the points is the most important detail. Some are round and blunt, some long and

best for knitting firmly or working pattern stitches

best for knitting loosely or plain knitting

tapered, and others concave. A few are so pointy they may prick your fingertips. If you knit firmly or work pattern stitches like cables or lace that involve a lot of stitch manipulation, you probably prefer longer, tapered points. If you knit more loosely or stick to plain knitting, you may prefer blunter tips. If you tend to help the needles along by pushing the points through stitches with your fingertips, avoid sharp-tipped needles.

Circular needles have the added complication of cables, which differ widely in style. Some are metal, others are plastic or nylon. Some are thin monofilament, while others are thicker plastic tubes like tiny hoses. The older braided metal cables sometimes come loose at the join between needle and cable, one wire at a time, snagging each stitch as it passes over the join. Nylon and plastic cables become brittle after many years of service and can crack. If you knit firmly, it can be difficult to slide your stitches along the thicker plastic tubes. In some brands, the cable connects to the needle points with a little bump, particularly on bamboo or wood needles with nylon cables. Although the bump looks innocuous, trying to slide the stitches over it can be very annoying. Look for circular needles with very smooth joins.

Knitting Needle Materials

	METAL	WOOD
PROS	Good if you knit tightly or for yarns that tend to stick to the needles, because stitches slide easily. Very durable. Not usually chewed by puppies or kittens.	Especially good for lace, circular knitting on double-pointed needles, and slippery yarns. Provides more friction than metal, so stitches don't slip off, and needles don't fall out of the knitting. Recommended for beginners and for working complicated patterns. Feel warm, lightweight, quiet. Somewhat flexible, so good for people with arthritis or other hand problems. Dark woods make it easy to see when knitting light yarns.
CONS	Too slippery if you knit loosely or for slippery yarns. Click while knitting; clang when dropped on a hard surface. Feel cold, can be heavy, and are not flexible, unpleasant features if you have arthritis or other hand problems. Some are very shiny, making it difficult to see if your vision is poor or if glare bothers you.	Tend to break more easily that metal needles, especially in very thin sizes; bamboo is more resilient than wood. Can develop splinters (easily fixed with a little sandpaper). May become slightly curved with use (usability is not affected). Dark wood may make it difficult to see when knitting dark yarns. Easily destroyed by puppies and kittens, which like to chew them.

PLASTIC & NYLON	CASEIN	CELLULOSE ACETATE
Flexible.	Smoother than wood but not as slippery as metal, so a good compromise.	Slightly flexible.
Not easily broken.		Not easily broken.
Quiet and lightweight.		Quiet.
Come in a range of colors.	Feel warm, light-weight, quiet.	Come in a range of colors.
	Come in a range of colors.	
May be hard to use with cotton yarns, which sometimes stick to them.	Not as widely available as metal, wood, and plastic (availability increasing).	Larger sizes are hollow with a reinforcing wire inside, which may jangle annoyingly when in use.
May become curved over time with use (usability is not affected).	May become curved over time (usability is not affected).	
	Some people report a strong chemical smell if the needles get wet. Very attractive to some pets because they're made from milk protein.	

Q Can I switch needles in the middle of a project?

A Yes, you can. In fact, in some projects you'll have to change needles. For example, you start a hat at the bottom on a 16"-long (40 cm) circular needle, but when you decrease for the crown you have fewer stitches and must switch to double-pointed needles to finish the hat. Be aware, though, that you will not necessarily get the same gauge on two different needles of the same size. You may find that you knit more tightly on slippery metal needles, so the stitches are smaller than when knitting the same yarn on wood needles of the same size. Also keep in mind that needles from different manufacturers may vary in diameter, even if the packaging says they are identical. Be particularly suspicious of old needles inherited from other knitters. In the past, needles were not always produced in standard sizes, and other countries used different sizing schemes. Your grandmother's size 8 may not be the same as a current size 8. Use a needle gauge to check your needles for consistency.

SEE ALSO: *Page 120 for rulers and gauges*

Q **I'm using a circular needle and the cable curls so much — it's really annoying. How can I straighten out the cable?**

A Once the needle is full of stitches and you've knit a couple of inches, the weight of the knitting usually brings a kinky cable under control. You can also relax the cable by dipping it briefly in a pan of boiling water. You can purchase a hanging storage case for your circular needles, which allows them to dangle freely, without being coiled up. Some knitters store their circular needles on skirt hangers, securing the cables with the two clips and leaving the points hanging. Both methods of storage keep the cables relaxed and kink free.

Q **If I lose a needle, what can I do?**

A Some needle manufacturers and distributors will replace a single needle, especially if it's one of a set, either for free or for very low cost. You can find corporate contact information on the packaging that the needles came in, in advertisements in knitting magazines, and on the Internet. If these resources don't turn up a street address, phone number, or e-mail address, have a retailer who sells the product put you in contact with the company or its sales representative.

Q **If my metal needles get rough, can I fix them?**

A You can use a fine metal file to smooth the rough places, but the finish of the needle in that spot may continue to annoy you afterward. To polish the metal, try rubbing it with a piece of wax paper.

. . . .

Q **If my needles feel sticky, can I correct this?**

A First, clean them. Wash plastic, nylon, or metal needles with a little soap and water and dry them thoroughly. Expose wood needles to as little water as possible; just wipe them off with a damp cloth and dry them immediately. If they still don't feel clean, go over them lightly with fine sandpaper or fine steel wool. An old set of steel needles that are a little rusty may benefit from fine steel wool. Avoid buffing any area that doesn't need it, because it will roughen the finish. If the needles don't seem as smooth as in the past, rub them with a piece of wax paper.

. . . .

Q **Can I fix wood needles that get rough or splinter?**

A Yes. Use fine sandpaper or an emery board to smooth the problem spot, then polish it with wax paper.

Q I'm tired of never having exactly the right needle, so I'm thinking of buying an interchangeable needle set. Which kind is the best?

A There are currently three types of interchangeable needle sets on the market: one with metal needles, one with plastic needles, and a couple with bamboo needles. The cables connect to the needle points in a variety of ways. Some require a separate tool to lock them in place. Others screw in or simply twist and lock. Anything that screws in can come unscrewed as you work, so look for long-threaded screws rather than short ones. Cables for most sets are made of nylon, but cables for the plastic set are made of tiny plastic tubes that resemble little hoses. If you are a firm knitter, you may find it annoying to slide your stitches along these cables. Frequently, extra cables and ends are included that can be used as stitch holders.

Each of these sets allows you to build needles in a variety of sizes and lengths. Sets vary most in the number of different size needles included. Some have a wide range of sizes, 2 through 15, while others are limited to sizes 5 through 10. Each set features four or more cables of different lengths, from about 14" to 40" (35 to 100 cm), so that you can assemble whatever size and length needle you want. Some of the sets allow you to connect the cables to each other to make even longer needles. You can also attach a separate cable to each point, with a disk or bead at the other end of the cable, and use them as if they were straight, single-pointed needles.

Needle sets can be very expensive, so it's best to try them out before you buy. Replacement and extra parts for some sets are also available.

There's More to Knitting than Needles

Q **What is a cable needle? Which kind is best?**

A Cable needles are used as temporary holders for some of the cable stitches while the cable is being twisted. They come in several styles: metal gull wings with a curve at the center, metal J-shaped hooks, and straight wood needles with ridges or slightly thicker ends to keep the stitches from falling off. The shape you choose is a matter of personal prefer-

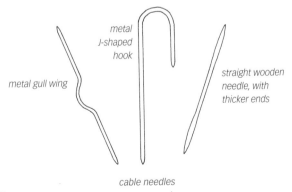

metal J-shaped hook

metal gull wing

straight wooden needle, with thicker ends

cable needles

ence. Cable needles come in several thicknesses. Use one that is the same diameter or smaller than the needles for your project. In a pinch, good substitutes are a short, double-pointed needle, a round toothpick (but you may need to sand it smooth), a straightened paper clip, or anything that's thin enough with a point at both ends.

....

Q Do I need a knitting bag?

A A bag for your knitting keeps your project clean and all your tools, materials, and pattern together. You can get a top-of-the-line knitting bag with all the bells and whistles: pockets, coordinating needle and accessory cases, hooks for your keys, and features you can't even begin to imagine. Or, you can use a 2-gallon ziplock plastic bag. There are, of course, other options in between, like all the promotional tote bags from conferences that grow in a pile on a shelf in your closet. The top-of-the-line bags have the advantage of keeping your knitting supplies organized and making it easy to carry everything you need with you. If you work on only one project at a time, this may be the way to go. If you have multiple projects and tend to work on them at home, ziplock bags may be the low-end solution. They're cheap and can be sealed to protect against moths and marauding cats. Whatever kind of bag you choose, you may want to include a small case, such as an eyeglass case or zippered toiletry bag, to hold tiny accessories that tend to get lost at the bottom of the bag.

Q What should be in my bag?

A Here's what I keep in mine.

▶ **Rulers and gauges.** You'll need a tape measure for measuring your knitting as you go and a knitting gauge for checking needle sizes. Simply slip a needle into the knitting gauge holes; the smallest hole that it goes into indicates its size. If you are the independent sort of knitter who modifies patterns, a bendable ruler is useful. It bends neatly into curves and then holds its position, making it very handy for redesigning armholes and necklines.

SEE ALSO: *Page 108 for illustration.*

▶ **Stitch markers.** Place these rings on your needle to mark specific points in the row. Use small ones on thin needles and larger ones on thick needles. The soft rubber ones are less likely to pop off your needles and fly across the room than the hard plastic ones. Split markers have overlapping ends and can be added to your needle in the middle of the row or hooked into the fabric. Beautiful beaded markers are also now available, and they don't get lost as easily as the garden variety. You can substitute safety pins (ones without coils that catch in the yarn are made just for knitters), paper clips, a small loop of contrasting yarn, or even an earring.

▶ **Stitch and row counters.** These help you keep track of how many stitches you've increased or decreased, and how many rows you've completed. Tiny barrel-shaped row counters slip right onto your needle; advance the counter by hand at the end of each row to keep count. Larger counters that increase each time the top is depressed are also available. Devices with holes and pegs reminiscent of cribbage boards allow for more complicated tracking. Small candies also make good counters: Eat one as you complete each step.

▶ **Scissors, snips, and yarn cutters.** Folding scissors, tiny snips with a cover over the points, or a yarn cutter that can be worn as a pendant around your neck will cut your yarn without poking holes in your knitting bag. If you've progressed to the point of cutting your knitting, a large pair of very sharp sewing scissors is also a necessity.

▶ **Stitch holders.** Several tools are available to keep stitches on hold until they are needed again later in your project. Metal holders like giant safety pins are widely available, as are rods resembling short knitting needles with a spring closure. In a pinch you can place your stitches on large safety pins (or coilless safety pins), on a strand of yarn, or on an extra circular needle (particularly good for large numbers of stitches).

▶ **Yarn needles** are used for sewing knit pieces together and weaving in loose ends. They are big sewing needles with large eyes and blunt points, and can be made of metal or plastic and are straight or have a bent tip. Choose whichever style you like. The only requirement is that the eye be large enough to accommodate your yarn. For finer yarns, you can use tapestry needles. Darning needles with large eyes and sharp points may make it easier to sew up some projects.

▶ **Crochet hooks.** Some knitting instructions may call for crocheted edgings, but crochet hooks are also very handy for hooking up dropped stitches and for crocheting pieces of knitting together. As with knitting needles, crochet hooks come in a range of sizes and in metal, wood, and plastic. If you use them only to correct mistakes, you don't need a full range of sizes. One small and one medium hook should be sufficient.

▶ **Extras.** These aren't required, but you may find them handy to have around.

• *Point protectors,* to cover the points of your needles so that stitches don't fall off and so that needles don't poke holes in your bag. You can also use them to convert double-pointed needles to straight needles for small projects.

• *Calculator,* for calculating how many stitches you should have.

- *Hand lotion,* to smooth rough hands that are getting in the way of knitting.

- *Wax paper,* for polishing needles.

- *Sandpaper or emery board,* for emergency needle repairs.

- *Pencil and notepad,* for taking notes. Small pads of graph paper are great for charting patterns.

- *Sticky notes,* for keeping track of your place in lengthy pattern instructions.

Q **Are there other knitting tools I should know about?**

A Here are suggestions for other tools that are helpful, although you may not want to carry them in your knitting bag.

▶ **Knitting needle cases.** If you own more than a few needles, you'll want a way to organize them. Most needle cases are made of cloth, with pockets to organize your needles. The top folds over to keep the needles from falling out, and then the case is rolled or folded and tied. Cases for circular needles come in several designs. Small booklets with see-through pockets for each size are particularly handy to carry around with you. Hanging cases allow you to store cable needles without coiling them. (Kinky cables can be very annoying to knit with).

▶ **Yarn bras** are little mesh bags each designed to hold a ball of yarn. They are invaluable for keeping slippery yarns from becoming tangled. A knee-high stocking makes a good substitute. You can also seal your yarn in a ziplock sandwich bag, with one corner snipped open to pull the yarn through.

▶ **Document stand and magnetic placeholder** can hold your pattern while you work. Some stands come with a magnifying placeholder.

▶ **Ball winders and nostepinnes** are used for winding balls of yarn. Ball winders clamp to a tabletop and wind yarn very quickly when cranked. Nostepinnes, which are easily carried in a knitting bag, form a base for a ball wound by hand.

SEE ALSO: *Illustrations of ball winders and nostepinnes on page 133*

▶ **Swifts** hold skeins of yarn while they're being wound into balls. Wooden swifts tend to be larger and can handle bigger skeins. The metal and plastic ones are smaller, lighter, and more portable. Some models are freestanding, while others clamp to a table. All rotate to feed the yarn to your ball winder and are adjustable to hold skeins of various sizes. You can also put your skein around the top of two straight chairs set back-to-back, over an upturned laundry basket, or on a friend's hands. Swifts are also useful for winding yarn into skeins if you want to wash the yarn before knitting.

CHAPTER 5

Yarn

Yarn is probably the single biggest factor affecting what you knit. After all, it's the material your sweaters, mittens, hats, bags, and so on are made from. Happily, you'll discover a very wide variety, from plain worsted wool to glamorous novelty yarns. There are even yarns made from bamboo, stainless steel, and soy by-products.

Yarn Labels

Q **When I buy yarn, how do I know what I'm getting?**

A The simple answer is to look at the label. Unfortunately the label can be very confusing. There is a movement in the United States to standardize yarn labels, but because yarn comes from around the world and the standards are voluntary, you can still expect some variations in the information on a yarn label.

. . . .

Q **How can I tell how much yarn is in a ball?**

A Yarn amounts are measured by weight and length. Most balls or skeins are labeled with one or both of these measurements. Weight is given in ounces and/or grams. Length is given in yards and/or meters.

Metric Equivalents

WEIGHT	LENGTH
50 grams = 1.75 ounces	1 yard = .915 meters
100 grams = 3.5 ounces	100 yards = 91.5 meters
4 ounces = 114 grams	1 meter = 1.09 yards = 39⅜"
1 pound = 454 grams	100 meters = 109 yards

Q What does "yarn weight" mean?

A Yarn weight describes yarn thickness. The Craft Yarn Council of America has introduced a standard system for yarn weights, but it is by no means universal. The chart below shows how the new system relates to the traditional terms and what the yarn actually looks like.

SEE ALSO: *Page 376 for the Web site containing yarn standards*

Understanding Yarn Weights

NEW WEIGHT STANDARD	TRADITIONAL WEIGHT DESCRIPTION	ACTUAL YARN
1	Superfine, Sock, Fingering, Baby	
2	Fine, Sport, Baby	
3	Light, DK, Light Worsted	
4	Medium, Worsted, Afghan, Aran	
5	Bulky, Heavy Worsted, Chunky, Craft, Rug	
6	Super Bulky, Roving	

Q How can I tell what my yarn is made of?

A Fiber content is given on the yarn label. Yarns are made from wool, mohair, cotton, linen, silk, rayon, acetate, polyester, nylon, and a host of other materials.

. . . .

Q Does it make a difference what the yarn is made of?

A The easiest yarn to knit with and the one that most consistently results in successful garments is wool. This is because wool has a natural crimp or wave in each individual hair that gives the yarn elasticity and resilience. In other words, wool yarn stretches (elasticity) and then returns to its original length (resilience). Other fibers don't have these qualities, so they can be more difficult to work with, and garments knit from them have a tendency to stretch out of shape. These include other animal fibers with no crimp (mohair, angora, alpaca, and even wool from some breeds of sheep), as well as cotton, linen, rayon, and silk. On the other hand, yarns from these fibers often knit up into fabrics with a beautiful drape, making them perfect for creating slinky garments or lace. Synthetic fibers, such as polyester and acrylic, fall somewhere in between these two extremes because they are manufactured to have a bit of stretch. Wool has other benefits: It is less dense than other fibers, because each individual hair contains air pockets. These air bubbles make wool an excellent insulator, even when wet. Because other fibers are heavier, they tend to stretch out of shape more than wool. Some yarns blend fibers to take advantage of their varying properties.

··

Q What does "dye lot" mean?

A Dye lot is a code number that identifies each separate batch of yarn dyed in this color. Be careful to choose balls from the same dye lot for a project because yarns from different dye lots may vary in color. Some yarns are labeled "no dye lot." These are synthetic fibers, for which the color is produced as part of the chemical process of creating the yarn rather than by dyeing afterward. The color should be identical in every batch.

··

Q There are round and square symbols on the label with no explanation. What do they mean?

A These are cleaning instructions, most often for washing and drying, but they occasionally stand for dry cleaning. Symbols also exist for bleaching and ironing, but they don't always appear on yarn labels. Examples of common symbols are shown below. European symbols are similar. Go to

Resources, p. 363, for links to Web sites that offer complete information on United States and European laundry symbols.

hand wash

do not iron

dry flat

dry clean

· ·

Q **I don't understand the symbols for needle size. Can you explain them?**

A Needle size symbols have not been standardized. The symbol shown below is just one example. It indicates that a size 8 US, 5 mm, or size 6 Canadian needle should be used to create a knitted fabric with 18 stitches and 24 rows in a 4" x 4" (10 cm x 10 cm) square. This is only a recommendation, intended for the average knitter making an average garment like a sweater. In reality, a range of needle sizes can be used successfully with any yarn. If you knit tightly or loosely, or want to make a fabric that is tighter or looser, you should choose your needle size accordingly.

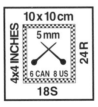
yarn symbol

Q Can you tell what gauge a yarn will produce before knitting it?

A Yarn labels frequently include a recommended gauge, usually given as stitches per inch or stitches per 4" (10 cm) and sometimes for rows as well.

SEE ALSO: *Gauge, p. 162*

All about Yarn

Q Is there any difference between skeins and balls of yarn?

A They are just different ways of packaging yarn. Balls are rounded and usually must be unwound from the outside. Pull skeins are longer and cylindrical; the yarn can be either pulled from the center or unwound from the outside. Hanging skeins or hanks of yarn are simply giant loops of yarn, which are tied in several places to keep them from becoming tangled. Sometimes they are twisted to further discourage tangling. They must be wound into balls before knitting. Yarn may also come on a cone or a spool; you can knit directly from either.

Q How do I wind a ball of yarn?

A The main thing to remember when winding yarn for knitting is not to stretch it. The ball should be soft and a little loose when you're through winding. If you knit with yarn that's stretched to its limit, the garment will return to its natural state the first time you wash it, meaning that it will shrink!

You need something to hold your skein while winding it. Hanging skeins can be held most efficiently on a rotating swift, but a friend's hands, two chair backs, or an upturned laundry basket are all good substitutes. You can wind a ball using your hands, a simple tool called a nostepinne, or a ball winder.

SEE ALSO: *Page 124 for swifts, nostepinnes, and ball winders*

▶ **Hands.** Begin by wrapping about 10 loops around your fingers. Then place this bundle of yarn against your fingers lengthwise, and wrap about 10 more loops around

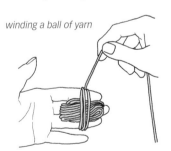

winding a ball of yarn

your fingers and the yarn. Continue to remove the yarn from your fingers and to wrap around the yarn and your fingers, gradually increasing to 15 or 20 wraps as the ball grows, varying the position of the yarn each time. Including your fingers in the wrap ensures that the finished ball is loosely wound and the yarn isn't stretched.

▶ **Nostepinne.** The nostepinne serves as the base for your ball. Make a slip knot to attach the end of the yarn to the top, where there is a notch to keep it from slipping off. Wrap diagonally around the shaft, turning it a tiny bit each time you wrap. Slip the ball off over the end, then disconnect the yarn from the tip of the tool. This makes a neat center pull ball. Nostepinnes are tapered to make it easy to remove the ball, but you can use any smooth round object in its place, such as a piece of dowel, a child's block, or a wooden spoon handle. Winding around a core ensures that the ball is wound loosely when the core is removed.

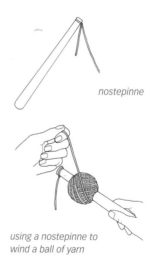

nostepinne

using a nostepinne to wind a ball of yarn

▶ **Ball winders.** This is the fastest way to wind a ball of yarn, but you need to have something to hold the skein, such as a swift. The advantage of swifts is that they rotate around a center shaft, feeding the yarn freely without tangling. If there's too much tension on the yarn, the ball winder can't work properly. Ball winders have a cone at the center that is removed after the ball has been wound. Follow the instructions that come with the ball winder.

· ·

Q What difference does the yarn structure make?

A Structure affects both the way the yarn looks and the way it behaves. Yarn is made from plies. Yarns with only one ply (one twisted strand of fiber) are sometimes called singles. Yarns can also have multiple plies; 2-ply, 3-ply, and 4-ply yarns are common. In these yarns, each single is first spun in one direction, and then groups of them are plied by twisting the singles together in the opposite direction. A 4-ply yarn is

4-ply bulky yarn

single-ply bulky yarn

not necessarily fatter than a single-ply yarn; it all depends on how thick the individual singles are to begin with.

The way in which some yarns, such as the following, are plied gives them a unique appearance.

▶ **Marled yarns.** Plies of different colors are twisted together for a barber-pole effect. The yarn has a tweedy look when knit.

▶ **Cabled yarns.** Singles are spun in one direction, then paired and plied in the opposite direction, and finally two pairs are plied with each other, twisting in the original direction. Because cabled yarns provide excellent stitch definition when knit, they are particularly suited to textured patterns and cables.

▶ **Novelty or designer yarns.** These are made in many different twisted structures, including bouclé, spiral, and chenille. Other structures include knitted and woven tapes and chains. Eyelash yarns have long strands hanging from either a chained or a twisted yarn. Yarns may also have slubs, knots, and garnets. These are just lumps and bumps of fiber, sometimes in contrasting colors, that add texture to the yarn. (For more information on novelty yarns, check McCuin's "Discovering Novelty Yarns"; see Resources, p. 363.)

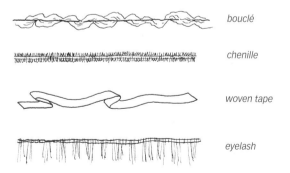

bouclé

chenille

woven tape

eyelash

▶ **Multi-ply yarns** wear better than singles. Pattern stitches and cables are most visible when done in yarns that are round in cross section. If you cut through a single-ply yarn, you'll see that a cross section of this yarn is round. Do the same with a 2-ply yarn and you'll see that it's flat, because the two plies just sit next to each other. If you look at cross sections of multi-ply yarns, you'll see that the more plies, the rounder the yarn is.

For a plain Stockinette or Garter Stitch sweater, any kind of yarn works. For a textured or cabled sweater, a smooth, round yarn shows the stitches best; choose a single or a multi-ply yarn over a 2-ply. If you plan on using more than one color, keep in mind that fuzzy yarns obscure the color changes; for clearer definition, pick a smoother yarn.

....

Q **What does "worsted" mean?**

A This is a confusing term because it is used in two entirely different ways. Most frequently, you'll see references to "worsted weight" yarn or "knitting worsted," the yarn weight most frequently used by knitters. It knits up at about 5 stitches per inch. The other meaning of worsted refers to the way the wool fiber is prepared and spun. Worsted-preparation yarns are very even, smooth-surfaced yarns that wear well. In a knitting context, worsted almost always refers to the thickness of the yarn, whether it is a worsted-preparation or not.

Q **Why do things knit with chenille get little tails all over them?**

A This phenomenon is called worming. Chenille yarns are unique. They are made of a pair of singles, tightly plied to hold short, fine threads in place, forming pile along the whole length of the yarn. Originally, they were made by weaving a fabric where pairs of threads were twined around each other and then the fabric was cut into strips, leaving threads caught in the twisted pairs. Machines now create chenille yarn without the separate steps of weaving and cutting.

Chenille yarns can be both fragile and frustrating for knitters. If they are untwisted or treated roughly, the pile may fall out, leaving only the bare threads at the core. Much chenille is either over- or under-twisted, so that it kinks up on itself. A little loose yarn pulls out from the fabric, the pile prevents it from slipping back in, and the extra twist in the yarn winds it into little tails. Another problem can be biasing, where the fabric develops a distinct slant once it is off the needles.

To prevent these problems, some chenille can be set after knitting by machine washing and drying. Unfortunately, other chenilles fall apart when subjected to this treatment. Knitting chenille more tightly, knitting it together with another yarn, or using a pattern stitch that twists the stitches as you knit may prevent some worming.

Is there any way I can predict how my chenille will behave when knit up?

A Test your chenille to see if worming is a problem. Cut a length of chenille at least a yard long. Discard the first yard at the beginning of the ball or skein, because it may have untwisted (or twisted more) when it was originally cut, and take the second yard for your sample. Immerse this length of yarn in a basin of warm water and wait. As it absorbs water, it will return to its natural state. If it is undertwisted or over-twisted it will begin to writhe and twist back on itself. The more it does this, the bigger the chance that you'll have trouble with worming. If your yarn just lies inert in the water, it should behave itself in the knitted fabric.

SEE ALSO: *Straight Talk, p. 158*

Q **How do I choose the best yarn for my project?**

A If you are working from a pattern, it will tell you what kind of yarn to buy. You don't have to use the yarn specified in the instructions, but pick a similar yarn to ensure success . Consider the yarn's thickness, fiber content, structure, color, and suitability for ultimate use.

▶ **Thickness.** Look for a yarn with about the same number of yards per pound (or per ounce or 50 grams) as the original yarn. If you don't know the yardage per weight of the original yarn, then match the recommended gauge. Purchase the new yarn based on total yardage needed for your project, not on weight or number of balls.

▶ **Fiber content.** Stretchy yarns made from wool or wool blends can be substituted for each other. Wool yarns are more elastic and resilient than other fibers, making them your best bet for bulky sweaters, hats, mittens, and socks. Nonstretchy yarns made with other fibers can also be substituted for each other. Yarns that aren't elastic, especially fine ones, are particularly suited to lace, making them perfect for scarves and shawls.

▶ **Structure.** If you know the structure of the original yarn (for example, single, 4-ply, cabled), look for a similar yarn. If not, then consider whether the yarn will enhance any pattern stitch.

▶ **Color.** If you are planning to use a different color than the original, consider how the finished product will look. If there is a textured pattern and you choose a very dark or a multicolor yarn, then you may not be able to see the pattern when you're done.

▶ **Suitability.** Consider how the finished product will be used. If it is a garment to be worn next to the skin, test the yarn against your own skin to see if it's irritating or scratchy. You can knit a small swatch and tuck it inside your sleeve or waistband. If it's intended for a baby or child, or even for an adult who may not know how to treat natural wool, pick one of the many machine-washable and -dryable yarns available.

••

Q **How much yarn do I need?**

A If your pattern doesn't indicate how many yards are required or if you are designing your own project, ask for help at your yarn store or look for another pattern for a similar garment and use it as a guide. Variations in the amount of yarn needed for pattern stitches, longer or shorter sleeves, and details like collars and pockets make it very difficult to estimate yarn requirements. Simply switching from Stockinette to Garter Stitch increases the amount of yarn significantly. A loose, open fabric uses up much less yarn than a thicker, less stretchy fabric.

A knitted swatch will give you a better idea of how far your yarn will go. Measure your swatch, and multiply length times width to get the area. Then unravel the swatch and measure the amount of yarn used. You can calculate area per yard by dividing the area by the number of yards. Estimate the area of the entire garment by multiplying length times width for each piece and totaling the results, then divide by the area per yard to find the total yards needed for your project. (To find yarn amounts for basic sweaters, check Budd's *The Knitter's Handy Guide to Yarn Requirements*; Gibson-Roberts and Robson's *Knitting in the Old Way*; and Gayle's "Beyond the Basics: How Much Yarn Do I Need?"; see Resources, p. 363.)

....

Q **What are the best yarns for baby clothes?**

A Many people are convinced that wool is too harsh for babies and that babies are allergic to it. Neither belief is true. Although yarn can be contaminated with dust mites, dyes, and chemicals that may irritate skin, true allergies to wool are rare. Natural fibers, such as wool and cotton, are actually more comfortable for a baby because they allow some air to pass through the fabric, preventing the baby from becoming too warm. The softest wool yarns available, made of merino wool, are comfortable against a baby's skin. Smooth yarns are preferable to fuzzy yarns. Fuzz will be caught in the folds of a baby's fingers and hands and inevitably transferred into the mouth. For convenience, choose yarns that can be machine washed and dried.

SEE ALSO: *Page 130 for cleaning symbols*

How do novelty or designer yarns differ from regular kinds of yarns?

The terms "novelty" and "designer" are used interchangeably. They usually refer to yarns with a more complex structure than basic, smooth, plied yarn. These include highly textured yarns like bouclé and chenille, flat tapes and ribbons, and many other structures. Some designer or novelty yarns have a simple structure but are made of a special fiber, such as silk or metal.

....

Can I use two strands of finer yarns instead of the yarn specified in my pattern?

Yes. The two strands must knit up at the correct gauge and make a fabric appropriate for the project (not too thick or thin, too stretchy or stiff).

....

Can I substitute a different yarn for the one given by the pattern?

Yes, but picking a similar one will increase your chance of a successful project.

SEE ALSO: *Page 138 for choosing the best yarn for a project*

Q Can I use a novelty yarn instead of a plain yarn if the gauge is right?

A Sometimes. If a simple pattern stitch or plain Stockinette is used, then you can usually substitute a novelty yarn successfully. Beware of combining a complex, textured yarn with a complex pattern stitch. You may put in a lot of effort and use a very expensive yarn, but end up with a fabric that doesn't show off either the yarn or the pattern stitch to best advantage. If you are making a sweater, be aware that novelty yarns are often neither elastic nor resilient. If you use such a yarn in place of a nicely behaved wool yarn, the sweater will have a tendency to stretch out of shape. You can help to support the sweater by modifying the borders. Knit them on smaller needles, use fewer stitches to tighten them up, and use twisted stitches to make them more resilient. Choose a pattern with seams rather than a pattern knit circularly; the seams will help support the fabric and prevent stretching.

. . . .

Q Can I combine different yarns or colors in a single project?

A Of course! It usually works best if you use yarns that are the same thickness, but you can also intentionally combine very thin and very thick yarns for special effects. When knit with the same size needles, the thin yarns make a loose, see-through fabric while the thick yarns make a tighter and denser fabric. You can also mix various fibers, but you may have to experiment to create a finished product that you like. Ideally, choose yarns that can all be cleaned the same way.

SEE ALSO: *Color, chapter 9; and p. 154 for how to tell if the color will run*

Working with Yarn

Q What does "working yarn" mean?

A The working yarn is the yarn that goes from the current stitch to the ball of yarn you're working with. This term may be used to differentiate between the yarn in use and a contrasting color or different yarn that is not currently in use, between the yarn going to the ball and the cut tail of yarn at the cast on, or between the project yarn and the waste yarn.

Q What does "tail" mean?

A This is the cut end of yarn left at the point where casting on began, after binding off, after changing colors, or after adding a new ball of yarn.

Q What is waste yarn, and why would I use it?

A Waste yarn is used at the beginning of some projects where the cast on will be removed in order to pick up stitches at the bottom edge and work in the opposite direction. It is also sometimes used in the middle of the knitting to hold stitches where something will be added later (a mitten thumb, sock heel, or pocket, for example). You can use any leftover or unwanted yarn, but it's best to choose a smooth, tightly spun yarn the same weight as the real yarn for the project, in a contrasting color. Slippery yarns, such as silk or rayon, have the advantage of being easy to pull out. Avoid fuzzy yarns, such as mohair or angora, which can leave bits of fuzz behind.

· ·

Q How do I start a new ball of yarn?

A You'll find it useful to have several different methods in your repertoire.

▶ **At the edge.** If you're at the beginning of the row or can easily unravel back to the edge, leave at least 6" (15 cm) of yarn from the old ball hanging there. Begin the next row with the new ball, leaving a tail about the same length. Weave the ends into the seam or the inside of the garment later.

SEE ALSO: *Page 68 for unraveling; and At Loose Ends, p. 340*

▶ **In the middle.** If it's not practical to begin the new ball at the edge of the fabric, then you can do it in the middle of a row, leaving ends at least 6" (15 cm) long to be woven in on the back later. If the loose stitches at this point bother you, knot the two ends loosely together (but untie them before you weave them in). You can also overlap the two pieces of yarn for just one stitch to prevent looseness. Don't knit both strands together for more than one stitch, because that spot will be noticeably thicker than the surrounding fabric.

▶ **Splicing.** When it will be difficult to weave the ends in later and you're joining a new ball of the same yarn, you can make an invisible join by splicing. This is useful in lace and on reversible items like scarves or shawls, or if you just hate to weave in ends. Split the ends of the yarn, pulling the plies apart for about 4" (10 cm). Break off half of the plies on each end. Overlap these thin ends and twist or wrap the plies around each other in the same direction that the plies are already twisted. Wet this section of the yarn and rub it a little to help set it. Hold onto the spliced section while you knit the next few stitches.

splicing

Take care not to pull apart the join as you knit. Once it has been knit, it will not come apart. Single-ply yarns may also be spliced. Untwist the ends, gently remove some of the fibers from both ends to reduce the thickness, then overlap and twist.

Splicing is easiest on wool and fuzzy fibers. For smooth, slippery fibers like cotton, linen, and silk you may be able to splice successfully using a longer length, but the join frequently looks different from the rest of the yarn after it is knit.

Q **There's a knot in my yarn. Is it okay to knit it?**

A No! Cut out the knot or problem spot and treat the ends as if you were joining a new ball of yarn.

Q **I dislike weaving in ends when everything else is done. Is there a way to weave in the ends as I knit?**

A Knit two stitches with the new ball of yarn, then begin weaving in the end of the old ball as you go. These instructions assume you are working a knit row in Stockinette Stitch.

▶ **Working yarn in right hand.** Take the tail from the old ball in your left hand and hold it behind your knitting. Simply insert your right needle under it while knitting the next stitch, as shown in the illustration. Alternate knitting normally and knitting under the tail until you've worked about ten stitches.

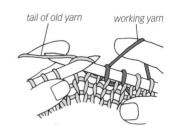

tail of old yarn   *working yarn*

▶ **Working yarn in left hand.** Take the tail from the old ball in your right hand and follow these two steps.

1. Insert the right needle into the next stitch and wrap the tail around the point of it counterclockwise. Wrap the working yarn around the right needle as usual (counterclockwise).

2. Unwrap the tail. Knit the new stitch out through the old one.

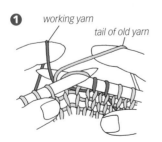

❶ *working yarn*
tail of old yarn

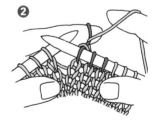

❷

Alternately knit a stitch normally and then knit a stitch catching the tail in (following steps 1–2) until you've worked about ten stitches.

Don't weave in the tail from the new ball this way, because it will pull the yarn in the wrong direction, distorting the first stitch. If you are knitting back and forth, weave in the tail of the new yarn on the purl side on the next row. You must hold the tail in front of your work to do this.

If you are knitting circularly, weave in the new yarn later using a yarn needle. In some pattern stitches it may not be possible to weave in as you go.

SEE ALSO: *At Loose Ends, p. 340*

 Do I need to knit ribbon yarn differently from regular yarn?

A Ribbons can be slippery. Use a yarn bra to keep the ball under control. Ribbon may become slightly twisted as you knit, but it won't be noticeable in the finished fabric. If the ribbon twists into a tight, thick strand, however, untwist it periodically. To avoid this, you can put a knitting needle through the center of the ball, with the ends through holes punched in a cardboard box, so that the ball rotates and feeds the ribbon as you knit.

SEE ALSO: *Page 124 for yarn bras*

Q **Is knitting with hand-spun yarn different from knitting with machine-spun yarn?**

A Hand-spun and machine-spun yarns are interchangeable. Many people think of hand-spun as thick, chunky, uneven yarn, but a good hand spinner can create whatever yarn he or she likes: fine and smooth, thick and thin, or loopy. Look for hand-spun yarns that are plied. Many heavy, loosely twisted hand-spun singles are available, but they don't wear well and they have a tendency to pill or shed. If the yarn is too tightly spun or incorrectly plied, it may kink while you work with it and cause biasing. When you purchase hand-spun yarn, find out if it has been washed. The first time it is washed, the yarn shrinks and becomes loftier. If you can't confirm that the yarn was washed, wash it before using it. If it's not already packaged in hanging skeins, you'll need to skein it first.

SEE ALSO: *Page 158 for preventing biasing; and How to Wash Skeins, p.155*

Q **Can I reuse the yarn from another project?**

A Yes. Unravel the project and you'll notice that the yarn is crimped. To straighten it out, skein it and wash it.

How to Skein Yarn

Wind the yarn around two chairs set back to back; a niddy noddy (a special tool for this purpose available from knitting and spinning suppliers); a swift; an upturned laundry basket; or anything else that will hold the yarn neatly while you wind it into a big loop. Use contrasting yarn (white cotton is best) to tie chokes (short lengths of yarn wrapped around the skein in figure-eight fashion) in at least four points around the skein to prevent the yarn from tangling when washed. Be sure to catch both ends of the skein into chokes so you can find them later.

Q **Is there anything I should know about knitting with coned yarn?**

A You can knit directly from the cone, but sometimes the yarn is stretched tight on the cone and then shrinks the first time the knitting is washed. Some coned yarn may still have spinning oil on it, left from the machine-spinning process. The oil comes off and the yarn fluffs up significantly when first washed. You may find the oil on the yarn unpleasant while knitting. If it bothers you, skein and wash the yarn.

SEE ALSO: *How can I tell if my yarn will shrink?, p. 154*

Q **I have yarn without any label. How can I figure out what it's made of?**

A You can narrow down the fiber content by performing a burn test. It can be quite difficult to determine the fiber content of yarns that are blends of various fibers. If the plies of a yarn appear to be made of different substances, you may want to separate them and twist each type of fiber into little bundles so they can be tested separately. (For more information, check Pizzuto's *Fabric Science*; see Resources, p. 363.)

▶ **Plant fibers** include cotton, flax (from which linen is made), hemp, ramie, and rayon. These fibers burn without melting, leaving a fine gray or white ash. You'll notice a smell of paper or wood as they burn.

▶ **Animal fibers** include wool, cashmere, mohair, angora, alpaca, qiviut, and silk. These fibers also burn without melting, but they give off an odor of hair or feathers. Burning produces a black, pebbly ash that crushes into powder.

▶ **Synthetic fibers** frequently used in knitting yarns include acetate, acrylic, nylon, polyester, and spandex. All of these melt as well as burn, and most leave a hard bead instead of ash. They tend to give off chemical odors while burning, but some have noticeable differences. Acetate smells like paper and vinegar, acrylic like fish, nylon like celery, and polyester somewhat sweet. Burning produces a dark bead in almost all of them; nylon and polyester form a cream-colored bead unless overheated, and spandex has a chemical odor and is identified by dark ash.

Use common sense when doing burn tests.

▶ Work in a well-ventilated area.

▶ Work over a nonflammable surface such as aluminum foil or a baking sheet.

▶ Use a candle to produce a stable flame rather than lighting matches. You may want to use a lighter when evaluating odor, so that the smell of the candle or match doesn't interfere.

▶ Keep your hair out of the flame.

▶ Cut samples of yarn about 4" (10 cm) long and hold them in a pair of tweezers to avoid burning your fingers. Be aware that some synthetic fibers leave a hot melted bead that retains enough heat to burn you for some time after it's removed from the flame. Some yarns are difficult to light, but then flare and burn quickly.

Q How can I tell if the color in my yarn will run?

A Wet a white paper towel, fold it over a strand of the yarn, and rub back and forth. If no color comes off, then the yarn doesn't run. If color does come off, it is best not to combine this yarn with other colors. You can sometimes remove excess dye by skeining the yarn and soaking it in warm water, then changing rinse waters until no more color comes out in the water. Add the surfactant Synthrapol to the wash water to remove excess dye. Retayne is a fixative that helps to set colors in the fabric, preventing them from running. These products, or their equivalents, are available from quilting, dye, and art suppliers. Shout Color Catcher dye-trapping sheets are available with laundry products in grocery stores. Put one or two of these cloths in the wash to absorb excess dye in the water.

Q How can I tell if my yarn will shrink?

A The only way to tell is to test your yarn. Knit a swatch, measure it, wash it, dry it, and then measure it again. If the swatch changes size, you have two options. You can allow for shrinkage by knitting your garment wider and longer, so that it shrinks to the correct size when washed. Or, you can skein the yarn and wash it before beginning your project.

How to Wash Skeins

Fill a basin with warm water. If the yarn is dirty, add soap or detergent but avoid creating a lot of suds. Let the skeins soak, then lift them out of the water and squeeze gently. Run clean water into the basin (never run it onto wool or other animal fibers, because it may cause felting). Press the skeins down into the water and squeeze gently. Repeat until the water is clear, agitating as little as possible. Roll the yarn in a towel to remove excess moisture, stretch it a bit to straighten out the strands, and drape it over a rack or line to dry.

SEE ALSO: *Don't Felt It!, p. 345*

Solving Problems

Q I have two balls of the same yarn, but the colors look different. Why?

A There are several possibilities.

 Dirt. If you think the yarn is dirty, skein and wash it.

 Fading. This can happen if the yarn is stored in direct sunlight. Unwind the top layer of the ball or skein to see if the protected yarn underneath is darker. Discard the faded yarn or save it for another project.

▶ **Dye lot.** Check the labels for different lot numbers. If the yarn was purchased recently, check with the store to see if you can exchange it to get all the same dye lot. If not, the store may be able to get some from its distributor or another store. You could also post a request for the yarn you need on the Internet.

....

Q **What do I do if I can't get more yarn in the same dye lot?**

A Merge the two shades together as you knit. When you come to the end of a ball of one lot, reserve enough yarn for several rows and then alternate one row of the old dye lot with one row of the new. This will blend the two colors together and the change won't be so noticeable. This is easiest to do if you are working circularly. Simply change balls at the beginning of each round. If you are careful not to twist the two yarns around each other, the change will be inconspicuous. When working flat, alternate balls by using a circular needle and working across twice on the right side (once with the old yarn and then once with the new), followed by working across twice on the wrong side. If you find this too confusing or your pattern stitch makes it difficult, work two rows in each yarn. If you have about equal amounts of the two dye lots, you may want to alternate rows throughout the project. There are frequently noticeable variations in hand-dyed yarns even within a single dye lot, making it a good idea to alternate rows from the very beginning so that the yarn looks consistent throughout.

If the colors are very close and you discover the problem late in the project, you can sometimes disguise the difference by working the main part of the garment in one dye lot and just the borders in the other.

. . . .

Q **When I finished knitting, I could see a line where the color changed. I used all the same color yarn. How did this happen? What do I do about it?**

A It could be caused by faded yarn or a variation in dye lots. To catch a problem like this in the future, you can test each new ball of solid-colored yarn before you start knitting. Be sure to do this in good light; daylight is best. Take the end of the old ball and twist it with the beginning of the new ball. If the colors are identical, you will just see a thicker yarn, all the same color. If the shades are slightly different, you'll see striping, like a candy cane.

You can hide the color change with Duplicate Stitch, using yarn from the other dye lot to cover every other stitch going across on both sides of the line. You could also Duplicate Stitch a pattern in a contrasting color, transforming it into an embellishment by adding the same motif in other areas.

SEE ALSO: *Page 129 for dye lots; and Duplicate Stitch, p. 360*

Q I knit a cardigan and it was fine at first, but now it's twisting and the fronts don't hang straight anymore. What do I do?

A Your cardigan has a condition known as biasing. Some pattern stitches cause fabric to bias. The yarn itself can cause this problem if it has too much twist or wasn't plied properly. You can test the yarn by soaking it in water as described for chenille. The larger the garment, the bigger the biasing problem. A little bit of bias in a baby sweater isn't really noticeable. Scale it up to a man's size extra-large, however, and it's hard to miss. If you suspect that biasing may occur, avoid patterns without seams (seams help control the problem). If you work circularly, avoid pronounced vertical patterns, such as cables or ribs, which will spiral around the body. Horizontal motifs, such as purled ridges or stripes, can spiral to their heart's delight without attracting so much attention.

SEE ALSO: *Page 138 for testing chenille*

Straight Talk

Here's how to prevent biasing.

▶ Use a pattern with knits and purls in about equal proportions or use twisted stitches.

▶ Create a fairly tight fabric.

▶ Knit the yarn that tends to bias together with a different yarn.

CHAPTER 6

Reading Patterns

Although the style and presentation vary, all well-written knitting patterns include the same general information: size, gauge, materials, and knitting instructions. Some begin with a description of the item, including fit and construction highlights. A few suggest a level of difficulty, although you won't always agree with it.

Sizing

Q Can you explain how knitting patterns are sized?

A Sizes are shown at the beginning of the pattern. They may be presented as small, medium, or large; as chest measurement or circumference; or as a range of sizes (such as Misses 8–10). For sweaters, you'll usually find a chest measurement, but beware: The measurement given may be either the person's actual size, or the finished size of the garment. If it's not clear, look for a schematic with measurements or a chart of measurements, which almost always indicates the finished size of the garment.

SEE ALSO: *Measurements and Schematics, p. 168*

When there are instructions for multiple sizes, they are usually presented in one of two ways. The smallest size is given first, followed by larger sizes within parentheses or brackets, for example, S (M, L). In the pattern instructions, details for each size are shown the same way. For example, "Cast on 80 (88, 96) stitches," means cast on 80 stitches for small, 88 stitches for medium, or 96 stitches for large. If there are more sizes, they may appear both inside and outside the parentheses, for example, XS, S (M, L, XL, XXL). When only one number is given, it applies to all sizes. It will be easier to work with the pattern if you highlight the instructions for your size all the way through it. If you don't want to mark your original, make a copy to mark up.

Other patterns place instructions in a column on the left side of the page and separate the details for each size in individual columns at the right. It's easier to find the correct size as you work with patterns in this format, but some clarity can be lost when the information for each size is separated from the text.

When complete garment pieces are shown in a chart, lines may define the boundaries of each size.

SEE ALSO: *Abbreviations and Charts, p. 170*

Q **How do I know what size sweater to make?**

A Choose your size based on circumference. In most cases, you cast on the width of a garment and then knit until it's the right length. It's easy to adjust length as you go, but width must be correct from the start. To get a proper fit, first take your chest/bust measurement, wearing whatever you'd normally wear under the garment. (For example, put on a shirt if you plan to wear the sweater over it.) Now add 10–20 percent for normal fit, 20–25 percent for oversize fit. For a fine yarn and a closer fit, use the bottom end of the range given. For a thick yarn and a looser fit, choose the high end. Fit is a matter of personal taste, so a good guideline is to choose a garment of the same thickness, with a fit that you like, and measure it.

These guidelines apply only to sweaters knit conventionally from bottom up or top down. For sweaters knit sideways, the key measurement is length, because the number of cast-on stitches determines the length, but you can made adjustments for width as you knit across.

One Size Does Not Fit All

Some patterns may say "one size fits all" or "one size fits most." This could be true for a poncho or shawl, but probably is not true for a sweater or jacket. Check the measurements carefully to see if you are one of the select few it will actually fit.

SEE ALSO: *Before You Begin, p. 280*

Gauge

Q **What does "gauge" mean?**

A Gauge describes the tightness (or looseness) of your knitting. In U.S. knitting instructions, it refers to the number of stitches and rows per inch in your pattern stitch. Patterns from the United Kingdom (and from New Zealand, Australia, and Canada), use the term "tension." Gauge is usually given in stitches per 4" (10 cm), but may be per 1" (2.5 cm), 2" (5 cm), or any other measurement. In the United States, tension is used more generally when talking about whether knitting is tight, loose, or uneven.

Q Why does gauge matter?

A If you want your garment to fit, it is imperative that your knitting match the gauge specified in your pattern. This is more of a problem with sweaters, socks, and hats that actually need to fit the wearer, than with shawls, scarves, place mats, and bags. A difference of just a half stitch per inch (2.5 cm) can easily make a 4- or 5-inch (10–13 cm) difference in the size of a completed adult garment. For example, a sweater with a pattern gauge of 20 stitches in 4" (10 cm) should have 5 stitches per inch (2.5 cm) and measure 40" (102 cm) around the chest/bust. If you knit more tightly and had 24 stitches in 4" (10 cm), or 6 stitches per inch (2.5 cm), the completed sweater would be only 33 1/3" (85 cm) around. If you knit more loosely, with only 4 stitches, instead of the recommended 5 per inch, your sweater would be too big.

· ·

Q How do I calculate stitch and row gauge?

A The first step is to knit a swatch, about 5" (12.5 cm) square. For example, if your instructions give a gauge of 20 stitches over 4" (10 cm), cast on 24 or 25 stitches, so you'll have room to play with. Work until your swatch is square. Bind off loosely, measure it, wash it, let it dry (blocking it if appropriate), and measure it again to see if it shrank. It's especially important to carry out this procedure, including the washing, if you suspect that the fabric may shrink (a real possibility with cotton or hand-spun yarn that may not already have been washed) and you're beginning a large project like a sweater. If you're working on something smaller, like a hat or a scarf, or with a yarn you know and trust, then you can probably get by without washing.

SEE ALSO: *Page 165 for measuring; Wash and Wear, p. 344; and Blocking, p. 306*

Speed Swatching

I like to measure my stitches per inch when I've worked for only an inch or two of my swatch, to see if I'm at least in the right neighborhood. Then, if the stitches are too loose (too few per inch), I unravel what I have, change to the next smaller needle size, and continue. If they are too tight (too many per inch), I switch to a larger needle. I repeat the process until I seem to have the right gauge, and then continue knitting until I have a square swatch. At this point I bind off.

Q Should I work my swatch in Stockinette?

A If you'll be working your project in Stockinette, work your swatch in Stockinette. With one or more pattern stitches, the instructions usually specify to which pattern-stitch the gauge applies.

Q How do I measure my swatch?

A Lay the swatch on a smooth, hard surface like a table or counter (not a soft one like a chair or pillow). Lay a ruler straight across the center of the swatch and count the number of stitches in 4", avoiding the edge stitches, because they're usually a little narrower than the center stitches. If the swatch curls up, the ruler should hold it flat enough to work with. Don't stretch or compress the swatch while you're measuring. If your swatch isn't wide enough to measure 4", then count your stitches over 3" and calculate how many there would be in the full 4".

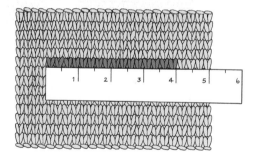

measuring stitches per inch

Measure rows by laying the ruler across the center of the swatch from top to bottom and counting the stitches in a column. Don't unravel your swatch, because it may come in handy for trying out ribbing or borders later. Of course, if you run out of yarn for your project, the yarn in the swatch is still available.

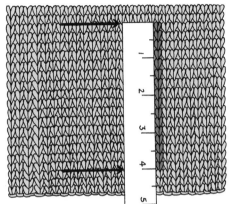

*measuring rows
per inch*

SEE ALSO: *Stitches, Rows, and Counting, p. 53*

Q **What do I do if my stitches match gauge, but my rows don't?**

A If you have the right number of stitches per inch, but fewer rows than you are supposed to, it means that your stitches are too tall. This can happen if your stitches are just a little too loose. Try knitting another swatch on needles that are one size smaller and you may find that you match stitches and rows perfectly. If, instead, you now have too many stitches per inch, you'll need to stick with the original needles. If you can't match both, then matching the correct number of stitches per inch is more important, because you can adjust for a row gauge that's not quite right by simply working the length indicated by the pattern.

....

Q **I can't even see the stitches in this yarn! How can I count stitches and rows?**

A If the yarn is dark, multicolor, or textured, it can be difficult to get an accurate count. You can use a contrasting plain yarn to outline the area you want to measure. Use a pair of double-pointed needles. Work a couple of rows with the project yarn, then knit one row with a plain, light-colored yarn, leaving a long tail of this yarn hanging down at both ends of the row. Slip the knitting back to the other end of the needle and continue the swatch, using the original yarn. As you work the rest of the swatch, use the long tails of the contrasting yarn to mark off the number of stitches at the center called for in the gauge specification by passing the tails from front to back, or from back to front, on each row as you go. This will weave the tails into the fabric and outline the marked stitches. When you've worked the number of rows called for in the gauge, work one row in the contrasting yarn, then bind off your swatch. Now measure the distances between the two contrasting rows and between the woven tails to see if they match the gauge specification.

Measurements and Schematics

Q What is a schematic?

A The actual measurements of the finished garment are usually shown on a diagram of the major garment pieces called a schematic. They may also be shown in chart form. In U.S. patterns, measurements are usually given in inches, followed by centimeters. Patterns produced elsewhere in the world may provide only centimeters.

Q My pattern doesn't list the finished width. Is there a way to figure this out?

A First calculate the number of stitches per inch, then read through the pattern to find the number of stitches for the circumference in your size at the chest/bust. Don't use the number of stitches cast on, because frequently there are increases above the bottom border. Divide the number of stitches by the number of stitches per inch to get the circumference in inches. You can follow exactly the same procedure using stitches per centimeter.

Materials and Tools

Q **How much yarn should I buy?**

A All patterns estimate the amount of yarn needed for the project. For multipart projects (such as a scarf and hat), yarn amounts may be given for the set or for the separate items. If a particular brand of yarn is indicated, the amount may be given in the number of balls or skeins. If the pattern does not call for a specific yarn, the amount is usually given by weight or yardage, or both. Purchase yarn for your project based on yardage, which may vary significantly among different types of yarn, even when packaged in balls of the same weight.

Well-written patterns include information about the thickness and fiber content of the yarn (for example, worsted weight, 100% wool). If a particular yarn is specified, the pattern may also tell you how that yarn is packaged (for example, 100 yards per 50-gram ball). If you want to substitute a different yarn, this information makes it possible for you to find an equivalent yarn.

SEE ALSO: *Yarn Labels, p. 126; and p. 138 for choosing yarn*

Q **How do I know what needles to use?**

A Your pattern recommends the size and type of knitting needles for the project. If circular or double-pointed needles aren't specified, then straight needles are assumed. Frequently, smaller needles are required for borders. Remember that needle size is just a suggestion: You must "test-drive" your needles by knitting a swatch. Some patterns list every possible tool you may need, but most take the commonsense attitude that you'll have basics like scissors, tape measure, yarn needle for sewing up, stitch holders, and markers.

Abbreviations and Charts

Q **What do all the abbreviations mean?**

A Almost every pattern includes some abbreviations. These may be straightforward, for example, *in* for inch and *yds* for yards. Some abbreviations, such as the following, are used so frequently in knitting instructions that you will become familiar with them almost immediately.

ABBREVIATION	DESCRIPTION
BO	bind off
CO	cast on
inc	increase
k or K	knit
K2tog	knit 2 together
p or P	purl
st(s)	stitch(es)

Q Is there a complete list of knitting abbreviations somewhere?

 A You can find lists of the most standard abbreviations in knitting reference books and on the Internet. Not all abbreviations are standard, however. Publishers and editors each have their own preferences, patterns produced in other countries use conventions different from those in the United States, and pattern writers invent new abbreviations so that they can include new or unusual techniques in their designs. These special abbreviations are explained in the individual patterns. In knitting magazines and books, look for abbreviations in a reference section at the front or the back of the volume.

SEE ALSO: *Resources, p. 363*

Q Do pattern instructions usually explain how to do the pattern stitches?

A If a color or textured pattern stitch is used in the project, instructions for it may be included within the knitting instructions or may be placed in a separate section for the sake of clarity. These may be written row by row or charted, or both. While some knitters find it annoying to refer back and forth from the main instructions to the pattern-stitch instructions, independent instructions are actually beneficial when making your gauge swatch and learning the pattern stitch.

SEE ALSO: *Pattern Stitches, chapter 7*

Q What are knitting charts?

A Knitting charts are laid out in a grid, with one square for each stitch. They can represent textured pattern stitches, color pattern stitches, and shaping, all in relation to each other.

Q How do you read a knitting chart?

A Because the first row is at the bottom of a piece of knitting, follow the chart starting at the bottom. When working flat, read the right-side rows from right to left. When you turn your knitting to work back on the wrong side, read the row from left to right. Charts depict what the knitting looks like on the right side of the fabric, so when working on the wrong side, you must mentally substitute knits for purls and purls for knits. When working circularly, you are always on the right side of the fabric and read every row of the chart from right to left.

Look for patterns that provide both charts and row-by-row written instructions; it's useful to be able to check one against the other if you become confused or if there is a mistake in the pattern.

....

Q What do the symbols mean?

A Pattern stitch charts use symbols to represent knits; purls; and stitch manipulations, such as increases, decreases, and cables. Check the chart key in your pattern for an explanation of the symbols. Some pattern stitches are not easily charted. Patterns where the number of stitches changes on every row are difficult to represent in a grid.

SEE ALSO: *Chart Symbols for Knitting, p. 381*

Q Are charts for color knitting different?

A This type of chart may be in color or in black and white with symbols for each color.

SEE ALSO: *Illustration on p. 240*

Q What are the advantages and disadvantages of row-by-row and charted instructions?

A Row-by-row instructions are much longer and can actually be more difficult to follow than charted instructions. For visually minded knitters in particular, charts make it easy to see what the knitting should look like. On the other hand, charts often show just one repeat of a pattern, assuming that you will figure out how to continue the pattern on your own.

Q The chart key in my pattern has a black square labeled "no stitch." What does this mean?

A When the number of stitches decreases from one row to the next, the stitches that disappeared may be

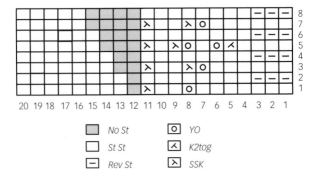

No St · YO
St St · K2tog
Rev St · SSK

represented as black or dark gray squares. You're likely to come across these when shaping takes place in the middle of a piece of knitting. If you're knitting from a chart, just remember that when you come to one of these squares on the chart, there is no matching stitch on your needle. You ignore the square as if it weren't there. In the example, the widening wedge of black squares represents all the stitches that have been decreased.

SEE ALSO: *Decreases, p. 264*

Knitting Instructions

Q **What's included in knitting instructions?**

A The instructions tell you the actual steps necessary to knit your project. Before you begin to knit, be sure to review the entire pattern, including abbreviations, pattern stitches, and charts. Knitting instructions are usually given row-by-row, but they can also be written as general instructions that give you an overview of a section or the entire project, or they may consist completely of charts. The best pattern instructions use a combination of these three.

Q I find patterns for complicated projects like sweaters very confusing. I never seem to know where I am. What can I do to stay oriented? How can I keep track of where I am?

A Take a look at the section headings before you begin, to get an idea of what to expect to do and in what order. In a sweater you'll usually find "Back," "Front," "Sleeves," and "Finishing." Subheadings such as "cuff," "bottom border," "armhole shaping," "neck shaping," and "shoulder shaping" help keep you oriented as you work. Look at the schematic to get an idea of how each piece is shaped. Whenever the instructions say how many stitches there should be on your needle, count them! If you don't have the correct number, then look at the instructions and your knitting to see where you went wrong.

Use sticky notes or a magnetic document holder to mark your place in the pattern as you work. Or, make a copy of the pattern, then use a highlighter to mark each pattern instruction as you complete it. If you plan to make the pattern again, you can use a different color to mark it the second time.

To keep track of your place in your knitting, use markers on your needle to indicate the beginning and end of each section or the location of decreases and increases.

SEE ALSO: *Page 195 for more ways to keep track*

Q I've found some patterns very easy to follow, but others are almost impossible. What should I look for to make sure I'm getting a well-written pattern?

A Avoid patterns where different sizes are made simply by changing needle sizes while using the same yarn: The larger sizes will be very loosely knit and stretch out of shape. Avoid patterns that don't provide gauge, garment measurements, and schematic diagrams, as well as explanations of pattern stitches, special techniques, and abbreviations. Beware of patterns where you can't really see a garment in the photograph. If you can't see details of construction, fit, and shaping, the publisher may be trying to hide problems with the garment.

Q Why don't knitting patterns include information on all the techniques they expect me to use? Where can I find out how to do them?

A Knitting patterns usually assume that you know the basics of knitting. At the very least, these basics include how to cast on and bind off, knit and purl, increase and decrease, and sew pieces together. Most also assume that you already know the basic pattern stitches, such as Stockinette Stitch, Garter Stitch, and ribbing. If the writer had to include all of this information in each pattern, the individual patterns would swell to the size of books. On the other hand, books and magazines usually contain a reference section that may have the answers you're looking for.

SEE ALSO: *Basic Pattern Stitches, p. 190*

Q I want to share a pattern with my friends. Is it okay to make copies?

 Knitting patterns, like all other written materials, are protected by copyright even if there is no copyright notice on the pattern, even if the original is no longer available, and even if you downloaded the pattern from the Internet. If the pattern states clearly that it is "in the public domain" or that you can make multiple copies and distribute them freely, you may make copies for your friends. Otherwise, you may make only personal use copies for yourself. If you found the pattern on the Internet, send the link to your friends and let them download it for themselves. If a pattern is out of print, contact the publisher or author, whoever is listed as the copyright holder, and ask for permission before making copies for friends.

Q The knitting charts in some patterns are so small and complicated that I can't read them. Is there a way to make them bigger and easier to read?

A Enlarge the charts for your own personal use at a copy center or by using your own scanner or copier at home. You can enlarge a chart to fit on several pages, then tape them together. If the chart is for color knitting and you have trouble remembering which symbol represents which color, use a highlighter or color pencils to shade it in on your copy. If you plan to use the chart repeatedly with different colors, make the copy on a transparency and wash off the highlighter before the next use. If the symbols represent pattern stitches that are difficult to distinguish, color-code or label them so you can quickly see what is to be done as you knit.

Q I prefer charts to written instructions, but many patterns don't include them. Is there a way to make my own?

A Yes. Just get a piece of graph paper with large squares, familiarize yourself with the basic charting symbols, and get to work. You may find it helpful to outline the correct number of stitches and rows before you begin. Remember to mark the rows on the chart from bottom to top. If the pattern is written for flat knitting, mark the right-side rows from right to left and the wrong-side rows in the opposite direction. When the number of stitches remains the same on every row, charting is relatively simple, but if there are decreases on one row with corresponding increases on the next row, you will need to black out the stitches that disappear on the decrease row, making a "no stitch" square for each of them. Charting text instructions is also a great way to learn a complicated pattern stitch before you actually start knitting it, as well as being helpful for converting pattern instructions from flat to circular knitting.

Q **I dislike charts, but sometimes patterns don't include written instructions to go with them. How can I cope with this?**

A Sit down with the chart and key and write your own instructions based on it. To avoid mistakes, verify the number of rows on the chart and make sure you write instructions for each row. Ensure that each row of your instructions includes the correct number of stitches. Begin at the bottom of the chart. Remember that for flat knitting, the right-side rows are read from right to left and the wrong-side rows from left to right. In circular knitting, all the rows are on the right side. Work across each row, writing down the instructions for each stitch or group of stitches as you go. After you finish your instructions, try knitting from them to make sure they really work.

Q **I have trouble keeping track of when I'm supposed to do a series of increases or decreases. Do you have any suggestions?**

A Use small safety pins to keep track of your increases or decreases. For example, if the instructions say to decrease one stitch at each edge four times, you'll need eight safety pins. Fasten these together into two chains of four pins each. When you work the decrease at the beginning of the first row, pin one of the chains to the stitch. When you work the decrease at the end of the row, pin the other chain to that stitch. Each time you decrease, remove one safety pin from the bottom of the chain at that edge and pin it to the stitch you just worked. The chains of pins will remind you where you are supposed to decrease, and the individual pins make it easy to count the decreases you've completed. When you've used all the safety pins, you're done decreasing.

· ·

Q **How can I find out the meaning of foreign knitting terms I come across?**

A Unfortunately, the reference book on this topic, *Knitting Languages* by Margaret Heathman (Schoolhouse Press, 1996), is not widely available. If you can't find a copy, an Internet search for "foreign knitting terms" or "knitting translations" will give you several Web sites with crossreferences between languages.

Q My pattern says to change to larger needles after I complete the ribbing. It's hard to slip the stitches onto a larger needle, and when I get done, the working yarn is hanging from the wrong end of the needle. Is there an easier way to do this?

A Instead of slipping the stitches to the larger needle, simply work the next row using the larger needle, then continue with the larger needles from that point forward. Don't forget to exchange the empty needle for a larger one at the end of the first row.

....

Q What do all the parentheses, brackets, and asterisks in knitting instructions mean?

A These are used to indicate instructions that are repeated. For example, K4, P1, K1, P1, K1, P1, K1, P1, K4 can be simplified in several ways:

▶ K4, P1, (K1, P1) three times, K4

▶ K4, P1, [K1, P1] three times, K4

▶ K4, P1, *K1, P1* repeating between * until 4 stitches remain, K4

▶ K4, P1, *K1, P1; repeat from * to last 4 stitches, end K4

Is it okay to make adjustments to patterns?

Yes. There are many things you should not hesitate to do on your own. Here are just a few of them.

▶ **Switch needle size** for ribbing. For example, use a needle one or two sizes smaller to make the ribbing neater and less likely to stretch out of shape.

▶ **Adjust the number of stitches** for ribbing. For example, cast on one extra or one fewer stitch to center the ribbed pattern and make seaming easier.

▶ **Treat the first and last stitch** as edge or selvage stitches, for example, by slipping the first stitch of every row, knitting that stitch, or keeping both the edge stitches in Stockinette. If there is a pattern stitch, you may need to cast on two additional stitches to maintain the integrity of the pattern stitch. In a fine yarn, this will not be a problem, but in a thick yarn it may add as much as an inch to the garment measurement.

▶ **Adjust the body length.** Usually, making the body of a sweater longer or shorter is simply a matter of knitting more or fewer rows between the bottom and the underarm. Remember that a longer sweater requires more yarn.

▶ **Adjust the sleeve length.** If the sleeve is tapered, you may want to space the increases out over a few more rows.

▶ **Change the borders.** For example, substitute K2P2 ribbing for K1P1 ribbing. With care, you may also substitute another noncurling pattern such as Garter or Seed Stitch. Because these tend to be wider and less resilient than ribbing, they may need to be worked on fewer stitches. They can also be tricky around necklines.

▶ **Change the pattern stitch,** as long as the gauge, thickness, and drape of the fabric is the same as the original.

▶ **Change colors.** You should avoid changing a plain-colored pattern to Fair Isle or stranded color work because the gauge will change. However, you can add stripes, work sections in different colors, or add intarsia, as long as the yarn is all the same weight and knits up at the same gauge.

SEE ALSO: *Adjusting Sleeve Length, p. 288; and Color, chapter 9*

Solving Problems with Knitting Patterns

Q I think there's a mistake in the pattern. What should I do?

A Read back through the pattern. Make sure you haven't misinterpreted one of the instructions. Key details to check are whether you interpreted repeated sections in brackets, parentheses, or asterisks correctly; whether the abbreviations mean what you think they mean; and whether you are doing the same type of increase the pattern specifies (some increases make a stitch between two stitches, while others use an existing stitch). If you can't locate the problem, seek help from the shop where you purchased the pattern and materials, members of your knitting guild, or a friend who knits. If you don't have anyone local to turn to, the Internet is a wonderful resource. Check the Web site of the pattern's publisher for corrections to the pattern. If you don't find any, send an e-mail requesting help. Post a request for help to one of the knitting lists or bulletin boards. If you can't get an answer, use common sense to make up your own solution. If your knitting looks okay, is shaped the way you want it, the pieces fit together, and it fits the wearer, then it doesn't matter whether it matches the pattern instructions exactly.

What Does It Mean When a Pattern Says . . . ?

KNITTING JARGON	WHAT IT MEANS
End with a wrong-side row.	Complete the wrong-side row, then follow the next instruction. (The same logic applies for "end with a right-side row.")
End ready to begin a wrong-side row.	Complete the right-side row, then turn your work and follow the next instruction while working a wrong-side row. (The same logic applies for "End ready to begin a right-side row."
In pattern as established.	Work the pattern stitch on future rows so that it continues the pattern already in progress. If there is shaping at the edges, adjust the point where you begin the pattern stitch on each row to stay in pattern.
Maintain pattern.	This is the same as "in pattern as established."
Work even.	Continue on the same number of stitches, without increasing or decreasing.
With right side facing, pick up and knit.	This is used to join a new section of knitting to an existing piece. Use one knitting needle and a ball of yarn to knit up stitches through the edge of the fabric.

KNITTING JARGON	WHAT IT MEANS
Pick up.	This is usually the same as "pick up and knit." If a pattern wants you to place loops from the edge of a piece onto the needle without knitting up stitches from the edge, it will usually say so.
Pick up stitches from holder.	Slip the stitches from the holder onto your knitting needles. Sometimes instructions say to knit the stitches off the holder, rather than slip them.
Work to within last 3 stitches.	Work across the row until 3 stitches remain on your left needle, then go on to the next instruction.
Place marker.	Put a stitch marker on the needle.

SEE ALSO: *Page 276 for working in pattern as established; and Picking Up Stitches, p. 324*

Q I know there's a mistake in the pattern. What do I do about it?

A Let the publisher know. Write a letter or send an e-mail. If the error is in a book, the book may be reprinted with corrections. If you have Internet access, share your solution with other knitters by posting your correction to one of the knitting lists. Tell the people at your local yarn shop, if they sell the pattern, because they are sure to get questions from other knitters. Tell the members of your knitting guild. And don't forget to mark the correction on your copy of the pattern, because you may want to knit it again.

CHAPTER 7

Pattern Stitches

Pattern stitches are made by combining knits, purls, slipped stitches, and yarn overs. An infinite number of patterns can be created by manipulating these basic stitches.

Basic Pattern Stitches

Q Knitting instructions seem to assume that I know what Garter Stitch, Stockinette Stitch, Reverse Stockinette, and ribbing are, but I still find them confusing. What are the differences between them?

A Use the chart on the following pages as a quick reference.

Knit the Knits and Purl the Purls

This instruction can be very confusing, because the reverse side of a knit stitch is a purl, and the reverse side of a purl is a knit. It's what you see while you're working across the row that counts. If you see a knit, knit it; if you see a purl, purl it. If the instructions say to knit the purls and purl the knits, work the opposite of each stitch as you come to it.

Q My pattern calls for me to work a section in Seed Stitch. How do I do it?

A Knit 1, purl 1, and repeat across the row. On subsequent rows, knit the purl stitches and purl the knit stitches.

SEE ALSO: *The Basics, chapter 2*

A New Twist

If you normally work into the back of your stitches to prevent them from twisting, you'll need either to work into the front, twisting the stitch in the opposite direction, or to turn the stitch around on the left needle before working into the back.

Special Stitch Manipulations

Q My pattern says to knit into the stitch one row below, but when I do that the upper stitch unravels into a big loop. What am I doing wrong?

A You are just knitting the single strand of the lower stitch, leaving the upper one to unravel. When you knit into the stitch one row below, you should insert your needle all the way to the back of the fabric, then form the new stitch. This catches both the stitch on the needle and the stitch one row below, and knits them together.

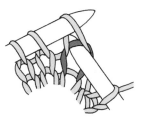

knitting into the stitch below

The Standard Stitches

	PATTERN STITCH	FLAT KNITTING INSTRUCTIONS
	Garter	Knit every row.
	Stockinette	Knit on the right side, purl on the wrong side.
	Reverse Stockinette	Purl on the right side, knit on the wrong side.
	Knit 1 Purl 1 Ribbing (also called K1P1 or 1x1 rib)	Knit 1, then purl 1, alternating across the row. On the next row, knit the knit stitches and purl the purl stitches.
	Knit 2 Purl 2 Ribbing (also called K2P2 or 2x2 rib)	Knit 2, then purl 2, alternating across the row. On the next row, knit the knit stitches and purl the purl stitches.
	Other types of ribbing	Establish your pattern on the first row, then knit the knit stitches and purl the purl stitches on subsequent rows.

CIRCULAR KNITTING INSTRUCTIONS	CHARACTERISTICS
Alternate knit 1 round, purl 1 round.	Reversible fabric with horizontal ridges, doesn't curl
Knit every round.	Smooth right side, bumpy wrong side, curls
Purl every round.	Bumpy right side, smooth wrong side, curls
Knit 1, then purl 1, alternating around. On the next round, knit the knit stitches and purl the purl stitches.	Reversible fabric with vertical ridges, elastic and resilient, doesn't curl
Knit 2, then purl 2, alternating around. On the next round, knit the knit stitches and purl the purl stitches.	Reversible fabric with vertical ridges, elastic and resilient, doesn't curl
Establish your pattern on the first round, then knit the knit stitches and purl the purl stitches on subsequent rounds.	Reversible fabric with vertical ridges, elastic and resilient, doesn't curl

Q How do you knit or purl "into the back loop?"

A Instead of inserting your needle into the stitch in the normal way, insert it as shown in the illustrations below, catching the back of the loop with your needle. This causes the stitch to twist.

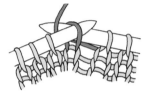

knitting into the back of a stitch

purling into the back of a stitch

Working with Pattern Stitches

Q I like the way pattern stitches look, but the most complicated thing I've done is ribbing. I'm worried anything more intricate will be too difficult for me. Any suggestions for getting started?

A Start with textured patterns made up of knit and purl stitches, where you don't have to worry about increases and decreases and you have the same number of stitches on every row. Look for pattern stitches with a small number of stitches and rows per repeat. They're easier to learn, easier to correct, and look just as good as many more complicated patterns. Once you become confident, try slipped stitch patterns, patterns that involve increases and decreases, and lace patterns (these use yarn overs for the increases). Check the number of stitches at the end of every row to catch mistakes as soon as they happen. Finally, try a pattern stitch where the number of stitches changes from row to row. Try each pattern stitch out on a swatch, then make a scarf, place mat or pillow cover — anything that doesn't require shaping. Once you gain confidence, move on to something larger with shaping, like a shawl or a textured vest. (To learn more about pattern stitches, check Walker's four treasuries of knitting patterns; see Resources, p. 363.)

....

Q **I'm trying to work a very lengthy, complicated pattern stitch and I keep losing my place. Do you have any suggestions?**

A To keep track of your place in the instructions, try the following.

▶ **Notes and holders.** Use sticky notes or a magnetic document holder, and move the notes or horizontal magnet as you work.

▶ **Highlights.** Copy the pattern onto a transparency and use a highlighter to mark each pattern instruction as you complete it. When you get to the last row of the pattern stitch, wash off the highlighter and start over. Note that print from ink-jet printers is water soluble, so make your copy using a laser printer or a copying machine.

▶ **Cards.** Copy each row of the pattern instructions onto a separate file card, punch a hole in the corner of each card, and fasten them together with a ring. As you work each row, turn that card to the back.

To keep track of your place in your knitting, try these tips.

▶ **Markers.** Use markers on your needle to indicate the beginning and end of each pattern repeat across the row. If you lose your place in the pattern stitch, you need only to find the marker at the beginning of the pattern section to get oriented again. If you end up with the wrong number of stitches, markers make it easy to pinpoint the section where the problem lies. Use safety pins or split markers to mark the first row of each pattern repeat as you work it. If you lose track of which row you're on, you need only count the rows from this marker.

▶ **Do-it-yourself chart.** If you work better from charts and have only written instructions, take the time to chart the pattern stitch yourself.

SEE ALSO: *Abbreviations and Charts, p. 170; and Resources, p. 363*

Q **Can I change the pattern stitch that the instructions call for?**

A Yes, but make sure that the new pattern stitch knits up at the same gauge as the old one, and that the fabric is similar. If the fabric is stiffer or looser than the original, the finished product may not please you. For most projects, simply match the stitch gauge and adjust for length as you knit. For projects with mitered corners, raglan sleeves, or any diagonal shaping, however, it's very important to match the row gauge as well. Remember to reserve at least one stitch at each edge for seaming and picking up stitches.

SEE ALSO: *Special Situations, p. 275*

Q **Can I combine pattern stitches in a single piece of knitting?**

A Yes, but you need to allow for any differences in gauge between the pattern stitches. Test this in a swatch before starting on a bigger project. First, knit all your pattern stitches in one swatch, keeping the same number of stitches (or very close to the same number) throughout. The edges of the swatch may be wavy because changing the pattern stitch affects the number of stitches and rows per inch. There are several ways to deal with this.

▶ **Change needles.** Knit the section that would be narrower on bigger needles and the section that would be wider on smaller needles, to balance out the gauge.

▶ **Change the number of stitches** when you change pattern stitches. Decrease just before beginning a wider pattern stitch and increase again before a narrower one. To calculate how many stitches you need, measure the number of stitches per inch in each pattern stitch. Decide how wide your knitted piece needs to be, and multiply this by the stitches per inch for each pattern stitch.

▶ **Blocking.** For minor width changes, use a needle large enough to produce a soft stretchy fabric, and then smooth out the differences by blocking after the knitting is finished.

SEE ALSO: *Blocking, p. 306*

Q Can I modify a pattern stitch?

A Yes, of course, as long as it doesn't change the gauge. For example, if a pattern calls for bobbles and you don't like them, you can leave them out. You may want to replace the bobble with a single purl stitch. Experiment with the pattern stitch in a swatch to be sure you like it with your modifications and to be sure you can work it consistently. Take notes on your version so you can remember what you did.

. . . .

Q **Can I make up my own pattern stitches?**

A Yes. You can create them on the needles or chart them out and then try them. Knit and purl combinations are the simplest to start with. Eyelets are also very effective. Simply place eyelets where you want them by working a yarn over, then work a corresponding decrease somewhere in the same row. Combinations of cables with eyelets or knit/purl patterns are also a great way to get started creating pattern stitches.

Solving Problems

Q **I made a scarf in Stockinette Stitch and now it's curling up. What did I do wrong?**

A Stockinette Stitch always curls. It's usually used in sweaters, vests, and socks that have a noncurling border at the edges. That's why you see ribbing at the edges of sweaters: to keep them from curling. It can help to add a noncurling border (Garter, ribbing, or Seed Stitch) to each edge, but the border may still flip to the front or the back. If you don't want your scarf to curl, use a pattern stitch that doesn't curl. If you really prefer the way Stockinette Stitch looks and feels, try lining the entire scarf, either with a woven fabric or by knitting a second layer. The easiest way to make a double-layer Stockinette Stitch scarf is to knit a tube with a circular needle, flatten it, and use fringe to join the two layers at the ends.

SEE ALSO: *Circular Knitting, chapter 8*

Q **When I knit and purl in the same row, I get messy loops across my needle and lots of extra stitches. What am I doing wrong?**

A When you are knitting, you must always start with the working yarn held behind your needle. When purling, reverse this and hold the working yarn in front of your needle. When you switch between knitting and purling in one row, move the yarn from front to back (or back to front) between the two needle tips before you actually make the stitch. When you fail to do this, an extra strand of yarn falls across the top of the needle, called a yarn over. These yarn overs create extra stitches and make holes in your knitting.

SEE ALSO: *The Yarn Over, p. 81*

Cables

Q **How do you make cables?**

A Cables are formed by simply crossing one or more stitches as you work across the row. They can be very narrow (2 stitches is the minimum) or very wide. Most cables are between 2 and 10 stitches wide and have an even number of stitches, but sometimes uneven cables are worked for visual interest. Usually cables are worked in Stockinette on a Reverse Stockinette or Garter Stitch background. The textured background recedes and the cable stands out, emphasizing it.

WORKING A CABLE

Use a special tool called a cable needle. Work across the row until you come to the cable stitches.

1. Slip half of the stitches onto the cable needle purlwise. Place the cable needle in front of or in back of your knitting. In front it makes a left-slanting cable. In back it makes a right-slanting cable. You don't need to hold onto it: Just let it hang.

SEE ALSO: *Page 118 for cable needles; The Slipped Stitch, p. 75*

2. Knit the other cable stitches from the left needle.

3. Without turning or twisting the cable needle, hold it in your left hand with your left needle and knit the stitches from it, then continue across the row. Work several rows in the knit-and-purl pattern before crossing the cable again. For a two-stitch cable, you may cross it on every right-side row. For wider cables, crossing every fourth, sixth, or eighth row is more attractive.

working a cable

- -

Q Do I have to use a cable needle to make a cable?

A No. You can also rearrange the stitches following these instructions. Throughout, you'll be slipping the stitches purlwise so that they don't twist.

LEFT-SLANTING CABLE WITHOUT A CABLE NEEDLE

HOW TO DO IT:

1. Insert your right needle into the second half of the cable stitches, behind the left needle.

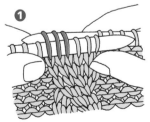

2. Slide your left needle out of all the cable stitches. Half of the stitches will be loose in front of the right needle. Slip your left needle back into the loose stitches.

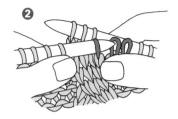

3. Pull your needles apart to twist the cable and separate the stitches, then slip the stitches on your right needle back to your left needle. The cable stitches are now rearranged and back on your left needle. All you need to do is knit across them.

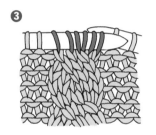

RIGHT-SLANTING CABLE WITHOUT A CABLE NEEDLE

HOW TO DO IT:

1. Insert your right needle into the second half of the cable stitches, in front of the left needle.

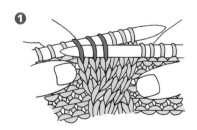

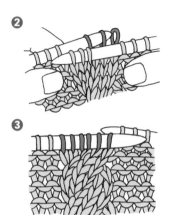

2. Slide your left needle out of all the cable stitches. Half of the stitches will be loose behind the right needle. Slip your left needle back into the loose stitches.

3. Pull your needles apart to twist the cable and separate the stitches, then slip the stitches on your right needle back to your left needle. Knit across the cable.

Q Can I add cables to a pattern?

A Yes. You will need to add extra stitches for each cable; how many depends on how wide the cable is. The wider the cable, the more it pulls in and the more extra stitches you need. Use gauge swatches with and without the cables to calculate the number of additional stitches needed. If you start your cables after working a border, increase the necessary number of stitches at the bottom of each cable when you finish the border to keep it from flaring. Work corresponding decreases at the top of the cable for the same reason when you bind off. It's best to test this in your swatch before you begin your garment. Remember that you'll need extra yarn!

Q There are holes on the sides of my cables where they cross. I keep trying to pull the yarn tighter to get rid of the holes, but it doesn't help. How can I fix this?

A Loosen the yarn. In the case of cables, the more tightly you pull the yarn, the less yarn there is and the bigger the holes. When you cross a cable, the knitting is stretched severely, so a little more yarn is required at this point. Work the cable stitches a bit looser on the row before you cross the cable. When you actually cross the cable, spread the stitches out as you work and knit them loosely.

· ·

Q Can I fix a cable that's twisted wrong, or where I forgot to twist, without ripping out the whole thing?

A Yes, you can. You can unravel just the one cable back to the point of the mistake, correct the mistake, and knit it back up a row at a time, starting with the lowest loose strand and working to the highest. A pair of double-pointed

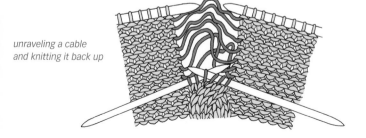

unraveling a cable and knitting it back up

needles the same size as your regular needles makes this process much easier, allowing you to work all rows on the right side without having to turn your work. You'll probably end up with tension problems around the area that you corrected. Use the tip of a double-pointed needle or a cable needle to even out the stitches.

Lace

Q **I'd like to try knitting lace but I'm scared to try because it's supposed to be so difficult. Do you have any hints for getting started?**

A Lace is like any other knitting: It seems much easier once you know how to do it. Lace is made by adding holes using yarn overs and then removing the additional stitches with decreases. The positioning of these in relation to each other makes the pattern. If you can make a yarn over and can work Knit 2 Together (K2tog) and Slip, Slip, Knit (SSK) decreases, you can knit lace. The most difficult thing about lace knitting is "reading" your knitting and correcting mistakes. If the mistake is several rows back, you may find that you need to unravel back to that point to remove the error.

SEE ALSO: *The Yarn Over, p. 81; Decreases, p. 264; and p. 67 for unraveling*

Hints for Knitting Lace

Follow these tips to ease your way into lace.

▶ **Use wood.** Because lace is open, it is looser than regular knitting and tends to slide off the needles, so use less slippery wood needles.

▶ **Get to the point.** Blunt needles make it hard to work the many decreases required in lace, so choose needles with long, tapered points.

▶ **Rely on markers.** To help keep track of wide pattern repeats, place a marker on your needle at the end of every repeat. For narrow patterns, place a marker after every three or four pattern repeats. If you make a mistake, the markers will help you notice it and find your place to correct it.

▶ **Split when needed.** Sometimes you'll need to decrease by working the stitches on either side of a marker together, which is annoying. Use split markers or safety pins fastened to your knitting rather than markers on the needle. Move the marker up closer to the needle periodically.

▶ **Think ahead.** Use stretchy, unbulky cast ons and bind offs. If the knitting will be joined to another piece, cast on leaving a long tail for sewing up. This reduces the number of ends to be hidden in your lace.

(continued on next page)

▶ **Splice.** Start a new ball of yarn by splicing the two ends together. If any tiny ends stick out later, trim them off carefully.

▶ **Conceal.** Hide any ends using duplicate stitch. If there will be fringe on the piece, incorporate the ends into the fringe instead.

▶ **Stretch the lace** while blocking to make it look its best.

SEE ALSO: *Page 29 for casting on lace; p. 99 for binding off lace; p. 146 for splicing; Duplicate Stitch, p. 360; and Blocking, p. 306*

Correcting Mistakes in Lace

Here are two hints for fixing errors.

▶ **Use safety pins.** If you discover a mistake in the middle of your knitting, mark it with a safety pin. You'll notice it as you work back across the row and can stop then to make a correction.

▶ **Dropped yarn overs.** It's easy to accidentally drop a yarn over off your needle. To pick it up again, just insert the tip of your right needle from back to front into the bar between the two stitches or insert the left needle tip from front to back. If the yarn over was originally made on the row below where you are, insert the needle under the second bar down and hook the higher bar through it.

CHAPTER 8

Circular Knitting

Circular knitting is knitting constructed in a tube. Larger tubes, such as sweaters, are made on circular needles. Smaller tubes, such as socks and mittens, are made on sets of double-pointed needles. Almost anything that can be knit flat and sewn together can also be made circularly without seams.

Getting Started with Circular Knitting

Q Why would I use circular knitting?

A Circular knitting allows you to make seamless garments. A seamless sock or mitten is far more comfortable to wear, and a seamless sweater requires no sewing up. Techniques like stranded or Fair Isle knitting are simpler to work in circular knitting because the right side of the fabric is always facing you, allowing you to see the pattern develop and to follow charts more easily.

....

Q Which is better, circular or flat knitting?

A Both are equally good. Flat knitting is preferable when you are making a shawl, scarf, afghan, or place mat in a pattern stitch that doesn't curl. However, circular knitting is useful when you want to make a double-thickness place mat, pot holder, or scarf. Flat knitting is better for more tailored garments, because the seams help the garment to keep its shape. For the same reason, it is also preferred for sweaters made in cotton, silk, or any other fiber that tends to stretch out of shape. But if you want a garment, such as a lace poncho, to stretch and drape, circular knitting is a good choice. Some

knitting techniques, such as intarsia, are more easily per-
formed in flat knitting. You may also find it easier to count
the rows between cable crossings when working flat, because
you know that the cables are crossed only on right-side rows.

SEE ALSO: *Page 248 for intarsia*

Q **What length needles do I need?**

A A circular needle should be, at most, a few inches shorter
than the circumference of the tube you'll be knitting so
that the stitches reach around effortlessly. You can easily fit
on knitting that is twice as long as the needle, but you'll find
it difficult to see whether the knitting is twisted when you
join the beginning and end of the cast on. If your knitting is
three times the length of the needle, you can knit comfortably, but it will be more difficult to slide the stitches around
the needle and to keep track of your pattern stitch.

Double-pointed needles can be any length, as long as they
are not so short that the stitches fall off the ends. Short double-
pointed needles, 5"–6" (12–15 cm), are good for socks and mittens or other narrow tubes. For hats and sweater sleeves,
choose double-pointeds that are at least 7"–8" (19–20 cm).

SEE ALSO: *Knitting Needles, p. 106*

Q How do you use circular needles?

A Cast on as you normally would, then spread the stitches from point to point on the needle. If they don't reach easily around, you need either to use a shorter needle or to cast on more loosely. Take a good look at your cast-on row and make sure it doesn't spiral around the needle at any point: You don't want a twist in your knitting. Make sure that the right side of your cast on (the side you like best) is facing you. Join the beginning and end of the cast-on row using one of the two methods given on pp. 216–217. Knit all the way around, or work in whatever pattern you like. When you get back to the beginning of the round, simply continue to work on the right side, so the knitting grows upward in a spiral.

It's as easy as that. You never turn and work back as you do in flat knitting, so you never work on the wrong side of your knitting.

SEE ALSO: *Twists and Turns, p. 58*

Do You Knit into the Back of Stitches?

When you do flat knitting, if you normally knit into the back of the stitches to prevent them from twisting, you need to knit into the front of them when working circularly.

Q When and how do you use double-pointed needles?

A Use double-pointed needles to knit any tube that's too small to fit comfortably on a circular needle.

DOUBLE-POINTED NEEDLES

HOW TO DO IT:

1. Begin by casting all of your stitches onto one of the needles.

2. Slip about one-third of the stitches onto a second double-pointed needle, and another third onto a third double-pointed needle.

setting up double-pointed needles

3. Lay them on a table or a pillow in your lap and arrange the needles into a triangle as shown in the illustration. Make sure the cast-on row doesn't spiral around any needle at any point. Take a moment at this stage to orient yourself. The needle to the left is Needle #1. Across the bottom is Needle #2. The needle to the right, with the working yarn attached to it, is Needle #3.

4. Join the beginning and end of the round using one of the methods described on p. 216.

5. Using an empty needle, knit across Needle #1. When you are done, you'll have another empty needle in your hand. Use it to knit across Needle #2, which will then be empty. Use the empty needle to knit across Needle #3. You've now completed one round.

6. Continue knitting each needle in succession, using the needle you just emptied as the new working needle.

Note: If you are using a set of five needles, you can divide your stitches among 3 needles and knit with a fourth, keeping the fifth needle as a spare. Or, you can put about one-fourth of the stitches onto each of four needles, arrange them in a square rather than a triangle, and knit with the fifth needle.

Q **Which is better, a set of four or five double-pointed needles?**

A It is really a matter of personal preference. Try knitting with the stitches divided among three needles and four needles to see which you like better. If your stitches are on four, they will be less likely to fall off the ends. If you are working something that calls for a multiple of four stitches, such as pattern repeats, increases, or decreases, you may find your work easier to keep track of on four needles. When working a sock with a set of four, place the front stitches on one needle, divide the stitches for the back evenly between two needles, and work with the fourth needle. When working with a set of five, place one quarter of the stitches on each of four needles and work with the fifth.

CASTING ON AND JOINING

Q **What's the best cast on for circular knitting?**

A All cast ons can be used for circular knitting. However, those that tend to spiral around the needle, like the Cable Cast On and the Loop and Backward Loop cast ons, may twist when you try to join the beginning and end of the cast on.

Q What do I do if my cast-on stitches won't all fit on one double-pointed needle?

A Use regular needles or a circular needle the same size as your double-pointed needles to cast on, then slip the stitches onto the double-pointed needles.

· ·

Q What's the best way to join the beginning and end of a round?

A Each knitter has his or her own preference, but here are two ways to join the beginning and end of a round after you've cast on. I prefer the first.

▶ **Cast on one extra stitch.** Spread your knitting out around your circular needle or divide your stitches among your double-pointed needles, and make sure that the cast-on row isn't twisted. The last stitch you cast on should be on the right needle point. Slip it to the left point. Holding the working yarn and the cast on tail together, knit the first two stitches on the left needle together. This joins the beginning and end of the round and gets rid of the extra stitch. Continue with the working yarn only. When you come to the stitch made with the double strand of yarn at the beginning of the next round, be sure to treat it as a single stitch.

▶ **Cast on the number of stitches needed.** Begin as described for casting on one extra stitch, making sure that the cast-on row is not twisted. Slip one stitch from the left needle to the right needle. Use the left needle to pick up the second stitch on the right needle, and lift it up over the stitch you just slipped, as if you were binding off. Don't drop this stitch, though; keep it on the left needle. The two stitches have simply traded places to join the beginning and end, and your round is now joined.

joining

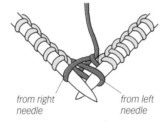

from right needle   *from left needle*

Tighten Up!

The last stitch you cast on (and sometimes the first one as well) will often loosen up while you are working. Pull firmly on your working yarn and the cast-on tail before knitting the first stitch.

SOLVING PROBLEMS

Q I always get a little bump at the bottom edge of my knitting where I joined the beginning and end of the round after I cast on. Is there a way to join smoothly?

A Use one of the methods described on pages 216–217 to minimize the bump, then use the cast-on tail to sew a figure eight across the bump to disguise it.

SEE ALSO: *Solving Problems, p. 318*

Q I find it difficult to get started on double-pointed needles. They fall out of my knitting and flop all over the place. Do you have any suggestions?

A Here are some hints for frustration-free use of double-pointed needles.

▶ **Use wood or bamboo needles** rather than metal; they're less slippery.

▶ **Place a pillow** on your lap to support the needles until you get going. This prevents them from swinging around and from sliding out of the stitches.

▶ **Balance.** Whenever you finish working the stitches on a needle, slide the stitches to the center of the needle and then spread them out evenly. This balances the needle so it doesn't flop to one side.

▶ **Take care.** When you set the knitting down, neatly lay it flat on the pillow so you can pick it up again easily.

Once you have a couple of inches of knitting on the needles, the fabric supports the needles and the whole assemblage is less floppy.

CASTING ON IN SPECIAL SITUATIONS

Q **What's the best cast on for a sock worked from the toe up?**

A Your pattern will usually suggest a cast on. If it doesn't, the one described here is my favorite.

INCREASE CAST ON

HOW TO DO IT:

1. Using double-pointed needles, cast on half as many stitches as you need, using the Long-Tail Cast On (or you can use the Loop Cast On, then knit one row). On the next row, knit into the front and the back of each stitch, doubling the number of stitches.

SEE ALSO: *Basic Cast Ons, p. 12; and Increases, p. 256*

2. Pinch and hold the knitting just below the needle and slide the needle out. The stitches will spring out to the front and the back alternately.

increase cast on

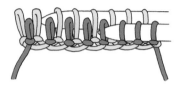

3. Slip one needle into the back stitches.

4. Slip a second needle into the front stitches.

5. Rearrange the stitches onto three needles, or as instructed in your pattern, and begin to work circularly.

. . . .

Q How should I cast on for the center of something, like the top of a hat?

A Use the Loop Cast On, because other cast ons are bulkier and can leave a little bump at the center of the crown. The Loop Cast On is also easily tightened if necessary. There will be a tiny hole at the top of the hat. Close the hole, using a

beginning a hat with i-cord

yarn needle to run the cast-on tail in a loop through all the cast-on stitches on the inside and draw them up snugly.

You can also start the top of a hat with an I-Cord of any length, then increase stitches to the number needed to begin the hat, introduce two more double-pointed needles, and begin working the crown of your hat.

> ## Number of Stitches in I-Cord
>
> Work your I-Cord on a convenient number of stitches. For example, if you need to cast on eight stitches to begin your hat, use a four-stitch I-Cord. If you need six stitches, use a three-stitch I-Cord.

SEE ALSO: *Page 354 for I-Cord*

Gauge

Q I knit a gauge swatch, but when I started working the actual garment circularly, my gauge was different. What caused this?

A You may have a different tension when you knit from when you purl. If you work your gauge swatch flat in Stockinette, for example, you knit half the rows (on the right side) and purl half the rows (on the wrong side). When you began to work circularly, you knit all the rows. If your purl stitches are a little tighter or looser than your knit stitches, then your swatch is smaller or larger, respectively, compared to your circular knitting. You can make an accurate gauge swatch by working it circularly rather than flat.

SEE ALSO: *Blocking, p.306*

Working Circularly

Q **I twisted my knitting when I joined the beginning and end of the round. What do I do now?**

A If you are just a few rows up from the cast on, stop at the end of the round and work the twist around to the point between the two needle tips. Allow the cast on and the rows already worked to twist at that point. Make sure the rest of the knitting is untwisted and continue knitting around.

If you are too far along to twist the first few rounds, you can cut your knitting now, untwist it, and continue working circularly. When the garment is complete, seam the cut area.

If neither of these solutions is practical, you'll have to unravel your knitting and begin again.

correcting a twisted cast on

Two Ways to Make a Circular Swatch

Try either of these methods.

▶ **Swatch only right-side rows.** Work your swatch on two double-pointed needles or a circular needle. Always work across on the right side, never on the wrong side. At the end of each row, slide the knitting back to the other end of the needle, bring the yarn very loosely across the back, and begin knitting again at the first stitch. The stitches at both ends of the needle will be loose and messy; ignore them. When you are done, take the swatch off the needles and measure it. If the yarn across the back isn't loose enough, cut the strands in the middle so the knitting lies flat.

▶ **Swatch in a small circle.** Work your swatch circularly on a set of double-pointed needles or a short circular needle [11"–16" (28–40 cm)]. When you are done, take the swatch off the needles and flatten it before measuring. If you made a very slim tube for your swatch, cut it from bottom to top at the beginning of the round so that it lies flat. If you are worried about it unraveling before you can measure it, then wash it and let it dry before cutting, or steam it gently.

SEE ALSO: *Page 246 for cutting your knitting*

Q When I pick up my circular knitting to work on it again, how can I tell in which direction to go?

A Look for the working yarn. The stitch where the working yarn connects to your knitting is the last stitch you completed. The needle with that stitch belongs in your right hand when you begin knitting.

. . . .

Q My knitting is inside out. Can I fix it?

A Simply push it back through the center of the needle(s) to turn it right side out again. Some people feel more comfortable working with the wrong side out. Experiment to see which you prefer.

. . . .

Q I find it really hard to knit around on circular needles. I'm constantly fighting to get the stitches up to the needle point. What am I doing wrong?

A Your circular needle is probably too long for the tube you're knitting. This forces you to stretch the knitting to get it all the way around the needle, making all the stitches tighter. Get a shorter needle, or switch to double-pointed or two circular needles. If your needle is not too long, then you may need a different style of needle. There may be a bump at the point where the cable joins the needle, or the cable may be too thick to suit you. Look for needles with a smooth, tapered join or a thin cable. If you knit very firmly, you may not find any type of circular needle comfortable.

. . . .

 I have trouble keeping track of the beginning and end of the round. What's the best way to mark it?

 Here are three options.

▶ **Use a marker.** If you are using a circular needle, place a marker on your needle at the beginning of the round. For double-pointed needles, where the beginning of the round is usually at the beginning of a needle, use a split marker or a safety pin in the first stitch.

▶ **Watch the tail.** With double-pointed needles, you know that the beginning of the round is at the beginning of a needle. If the tail of yarn from the cast on is hanging directly below your knitting, then you are at the beginning of the round.

▶ **Weave the tail.** Use the tail of yarn from your cast on to mark your end of round. Weave the tail through your knitting as it grows, draping the tail first to the inside of the tube as you complete a round, then to the outside of the tube after the next round.

Q I have a lot of trouble keeping track of pattern repeats in circular knitting. What's the best way to mark them?

A Any of these methods will help you.

▶ **Use your double-pointed needles** to mark sections of your pattern stitch. For example, if you are working in K2P2 ribbing, set up your needles with a multiple of four stitches on each, with a K2 at the beginning of each needle and a P2 at the end of each needle. You'll know that when you start each needle you'll be knitting two stitches and when you end you'll be purling two stitches.

▶ **Place markers** between pattern repeats on your needles (but not at the ends of the needles).

▶ **Use split markers or safety pins** in your knitting to mark the pattern repeats. Move these up closer to the needles as your knitting grows.

....

Q When I use double-pointed needles, there are loose stitches anywhere two needles come together. How do I avoid this?

A Here are several things you can try.

▶ **Be firm.** Keep a firm tension on the yarn as you knit the first few stitches of each needle.

▶ **Move the gap.** Work two to four additional stitches from the next needle each time you reach the end of the needle. This will move the places where the needles come together around the knitting and make the loose stitches less noticeable.

▶ **Change position.** If you usually start a new needle with the empty needle behind the needle you just finished, try putting the new needle in front instead. If you are purling the first stitch of a needle, put the new needle behind.

new needle in front

▶ **Stay close.** When you start a new needle, don't push the old one out of the way. Instead, keep it as close as possible to the next needle you're just starting.

▶ **Loosen up.** If all else fails, use a needle tip to loosen the stitches on either side of the loose stitches after the knitting is finished. Each will "steal" a little yarn from the problem area, making the knitting look more even overall.

Q I've heard of using two circular needles. Why would I do this, and how?

A If you need to knit a tube that is either too small or too large for a single circular needle, you can divide your stitches between two circular needles. Cast the stitches onto one circular needle, slip half of the stitches onto the second circular needle. Make sure that the cast-on row doesn't spiral around either needle at any point. Join the beginning and end of the round. Knit the first half of the stitches using the needle they are currently on. When you finish with the first needle, pick up both ends of the second needle and knit the second half of the stitches with the needle they're on.

SEE ALSO: *Casting On and Joining, p. 215*

Changing Colors in Circular Knitting

Q You can see where I changed colors at the beginning and end of a round. Is there a way to hide this?

A There are several solutions, depending on how often you change colors.

▶ **For one-row stripes,** break off the yarn at the end of each round and leave a 4"–6" (10–15 cm) tail. When you are finished, turn the piece inside out and Duplicate Stitch these ends across the end of the round and directly behind the stitches of the same color.

▶ **For wider stripes,** knit all the way around in the new color. When you come to the first stitch of the next round, slip it purlwise and then continue knitting the rest of the stripe as usual. When you weave in the ends, use the tails to adjust the tension of the first and last stitch of each color, and use Duplicate Stitch to weave them in across the beginning of the round behind the same color.

▶ **For Fair Isle and stranded patterns,** hide the beginning of the round at a side seam. If the pattern has solid areas between the motifs, shift the beginning of the round to the solid area by starting a motif either a little before or a little after the beginning of the round. When there are continuous motifs, slip the first stitch of the round, if necessary, to prevent breaks in the motifs. When the background color changes, use the method for wider stripes, if possible.

▶ **Make the pattern continuous,** if you can, by adjusting the total number of stitches. For example, if you are working vertical stripes in two colors, use an even number of stitches so the colors always line up, with the correct color on the stitch below when you start a new round. If you are working "salt and pepper" (a checkerboard of two colors), do it on an odd number of stitches, so that the colors alternate from row to row.

SEE ALSO: *Page 231 for helix knitting; Duplicate Stitch, p. 360; The Slipped Stitch, p. 75; and p. 229 for wider stripes*

Pattern Stitches in Circular Knitting

Q You can see where I changed rows in my pattern stitch at the beginning and end of the round. Is there a way to hide this?

A Here are ways to make the changes inconspicuous.

▶ **For garter stitch,** use two balls of your yarn and a circular needle. Cast on using yarn from one ball. Do not join the beginning and end of the round. Instead, slip the stitches back to the other end of the needle and purl across using the second ball of yarn. Your two strands of working yarn should now be dangling at the same edge of the knitting. Make sure your knitting is not twisted, pick up the lower strand of yarn, and knit around with it.

This joins the beginning and end of the round. At the end of this round, pick up the other strand of yarn and purl one round. When you change yarns, be sure that you don't twist the yarns and that you don't pull the new yarn too tight; all the

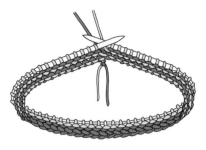

helix knitting

stitches at the beginning and end of each round should be the same tension. The knit rounds and the purled rounds will be continuous. This is called Helix Knitting. It can also be used with two contrasting yarns to make continuous single-row stripes.

▶ **For cables and ribs** (and other strongly vertical patterns), center a group of plain purl or knit stitches at the beginning of the round.

▶ **To make patterns continuous,** adjust the number of stitches. For example, if working K1P1 ribbing, use an even number of stitches. If working K2P2 ribbing, use a multiple of four stitches. If working Seed Stitch, use an odd number of stitches. (At the beginning of each round, a knit stitch will naturally occur above the purl on the previous round, and vice versa.)

Binding Off

Q Is there a way to make the bind off look continuous?

A Bind off all the way around. When you get to the end of the round and the final stitch remains on your right needle, enlarge this stitch so it's about 6" (15 cm) tall and cut it at the top of the loop. Pull the working yarn out. Thread the tail onto a yarn needle and run it around the base of the first bound-off stitch, then back into the last stitch. Adjust the tension to match the stitches on either side before weaving the end in on the wrong side.

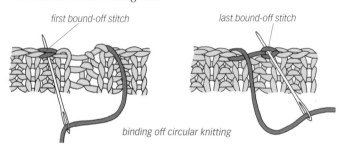

first bound-off stitch   *last bound-off stitch*

binding off circular knitting

. . . .

Q What's the best bind off for the center of a piece of circular knitting, like a hat?

A After you have done the final decreases, break off the yarn and use a yarn needle to run the tail through all the remaining stitches, sliding them off the knitting needle.

Pull the tail firmly to draw the stitches together. If the stitches look a little loose, run the tail through them a second time. Pull the tail to the wrong side and weave it in. Finish the tip or thumb of a mitten in the same way.

SEE ALSO: *At Loose Ends, p. 340*

Converting Flat Knitting to Circular

Q **Can I change a pattern from flat knitting to circular knitting?**

A First, consider whether the project will suffer in any way from the change. If it is knit in wool and the pattern stitch is easy to execute circularly, then it's a good candidate for circular knitting. Follow these steps to make the change.

1. Rewrite any pattern stitches, reversing the wrong-side rows (knits become purls and vice versa; all rows are worked from right to left). If the stitch pattern is not already charted, chart the pattern. If necessary, delete edge stitches so that the pattern repeats seamlessly around the circular garment.

SEE ALSO: *Abbreviations and Charts, p. 170; and Basic Pattern Stitches, p. 190*

2. Decide where the beginning of the round will be (for a pullover, usually a side seam).

3. Determine the order of construction: bottom up or top down? Sleeves sewn in later, picked up and knit down, or knit from the bottom up and joined at a yoke?

4. Determine finishing details. Shoulder seams (if any) sewn or bound off together? Neck ribbing knit as part of the body, or cast off and ribbing picked up afterward?

5. Rewrite garment instructions in rounds rather than rows. For example, a round includes the whole front plus the whole back. If a close fit is important or the yarn is bulky, decide whether you need to delete seam stitches.

Flat or Circular?

Here's a simple ribbing written for flat and for circular knitting.

ROW	FLAT INSTRUCTIONS	CIRCULAR INSTRUCTIONS
	Cast on a multiple of 4 stitches plus 3	*Cast on a multiple of 4 stitches*
1	*K3, P1; repeat from * to end of row, ending K3.	*K3, P1; repeat from * to end of round.
2	*P3, K1; repeat from * to end of row, ending P3. ▶ *Repeat Rows 1 and 2 for pattern.*	▶ *Repeat Round 1 for pattern.*

CHAPTER 9

Color

Color plays a major role in your knitting, whether it's the creamy natural wool in a cabled sweater; the vibrant stripes in a scarf; hand-painted novelty yarn in a shawl; the fine gradation of patterns in a Fair Isle sweater, or the intricate tapestries produced by intarsia. Color is highly personal. Choose the colors you like and combine any that please you. Once you've picked the colors, this chapter will help you combine them in your knitting.

Stripes

Q How do I make stripes?

A At a minimum, you need two balls of yarn in different colors. The two yarns should be the same thickness, but they don't need to be the same yarn. When you're knitting back and forth, let go of one yarn at the end of the row and knit the next row with the other yarn. When you're knitting circularly, simply begin knitting with the new color at the beginning of the round. There's no need to tie on the new yarn; just leave a 6"-long (15 cm) tail dangling to be woven in later. If the fabric gets annoyingly slack at the edge, temporarily knot the ends loosely together by tying one strand around the other. Untie the knot before weaving the ends in when you finish the item.

....

Q Should I cut the yarn every time I end a stripe, or should I just pick up the yarn again when I need it?

A That depends on how far the yarn must travel between stripes. If you are using the yarn again in the next row or two, then you don't need to cut it. When you begin to use it again, carry it up to where it's needed loosely enough so that the edge of the knitting doesn't pucker. If the distance is longer, cut it. The behavior of your knitting should be your guide. For example, if you're making a long, narrow scarf, then carrying the yarns up the edge may make one edge less stretchy than the other so that the scarf curves instead of hanging straight. If you decide to carry the yarn up more than a few rows, prevent loose loops by knitting it together with the working color occasionally on the first stitch of the row or twisting the unused yarn together with the working yarn between rows.

SEE ALSO: *Changing Colors in Circular Knitting, p. 228; and At Loose Ends, p. 340*

Q When I change colors in Garter Stitch, I get little bumps of the old color on the first row. Is there a way to avoid this?

A If you don't want the color from the previous row to show, then you must do two rows in each color before changing. This creates an obvious right and wrong side to the fabric, and you change colors only on right-side rows. The illustration below shows changing colors every row and every second row.

garter stitch

Q When I put stripes in ribbing, the old color shows through on the purled part of the rib. Is there a way to avoid this?

A The old color shows only when you purl, so knit the entire first row of the new color. On the next row go back to ribbing as usual. Your ribbing will still look like ribbing as long as you aren't changing colors too frequently. Obviously, this won't work if you are changing colors on every row. This creates a very definite right and wrong side to the fabric, so it won't work for reversible items like scarves.

knit 1 purl 1 ribbing

Q Can I add stripes to pattern stitches besides ribbing?

A Yes, but it's difficult to give strict rules for this. If you don't want bumps of the old color to appear when you change colors, start the new color on a right-side row that is plain knitting or a wrong-side row that is plain purling. Look for a point in the pattern stitch, for example, at the end of a repeat, where it seems logical to change colors. Using several colors may result in unexpectedly satisfying results. Experimentation is the key; make a swatch and try all the possibilities.

....

Q If I knit a garment in stripes, is there a way to make them match exactly at the seams?

A Yes. The first step is to knit the garment pieces so the number of rows and the arrangement of stripes are exactly the same on corresponding pieces. Sew the pieces together using Mattress Stitch, and make sure that the stripes match as you work the seam.

SEE ALSO: *Side Seams, p. 312*

Stranded Knitting

Q What's the difference between stranded and Fair Isle knitting?

A In stranded knitting, yarns of different colors are carried continuously across the row as you knit, allowing you to work patterns using any color at any point in the row. Traditional Fair Isle knitting is stranded knitting in which just two colors are used per row. The color patterns in stranded knitting are usually represented in charts, with a different symbol for each color. (For more on Fair Isle knitting, check *Alice Starmore's Book of Fair Isle Knitting*; McGregor's *Traditional Fair Isle Knitting*; and Feitelson's *The Art of Fair Isle Knitting*; see Resources, p. 363.)

SEE ALSO: *Abbreviations and Charts, p. 170; and Changing Colors in Circular Knitting, p. 228*

Q **Stranded knitting looks very complicated. What's a good way to get started?**

A You can begin very simply with just two colors of yarn (Fair Isle knitting) that are the same thickness. It will be easier to see what you're doing on the knit side of the fabric, so work circularly. Cast on a multiple of four stitches with the main color and knit a few rounds. Now begin working with both colors. Knit three stitches with the main color, then one

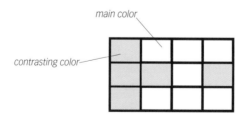

main color

contrasting color

with the contrasting color. Keep alternating colors, knitting three stitches with the main color, then one stitch with the contrasting color, all the way around. When you switch from one color to the other, make sure you spread the stitches out on the right-hand needle and carry the yarn loosely across the back of the knitting. Try another round, this time centering three contrasting color stitches over the one stitch in this color on the previous round. When you finish this round, work one more round just like the first one, and you'll have created diamonds. Now you can make up your own patterns. The possibilities are limitless. If you want to use a third color, simply swap it for one of the other colors for the entire round. You can also change both colors at the beginning of the round. If you'll be using the original colors again soon, leave them hanging behind the knitting until wanted.

SEE ALSO: *Page 278 for working an increase in two colors*

Q My pattern requires that I carry one color a long way before it is used again. Is it okay to leave the long strand on the back?

A No, you need to weave it in every few stitches when it's not in use, in the same way that you weave in tails of yarn as you knit.

SEE ALSO: *Page 147 for weaving in the ends as you knit*

Q What should I do if I need to work stranding on the purl side?

A Work across, purling every stitch and making sure you keep the unused yarn in front of the work (that is, on the side closest to you).

....

Q I don't like the way the yarns twist when I work stranded knitting. How can I prevent this?

A When you drop one yarn and pick up the next, make sure you don't twist them. Some knitters and knitting instructions tell you to twist the yarn when you change colors or there will be holes in your knitting. While this is necessary for some color techniques, it doesn't apply to stranded knitting.

....

Q I find it tedious to keep changing yarns. Is there a more efficient way to do this?

A You can hold both yarns in the same hand and just knit the strand you need. This also prevents you from twisting the yarn unnecessarily, and it usually results in a more even tension. Some people like to hold one yarn over the index finger and a second over the middle finger. There is also a tool called a yarn guide ring that fits onto your finger, with channels in the top for several yarns to run through. This may make it easier for you to keep the strands of yarn in position on your finger. Or, you can hold one or more strands of yarn in each hand.

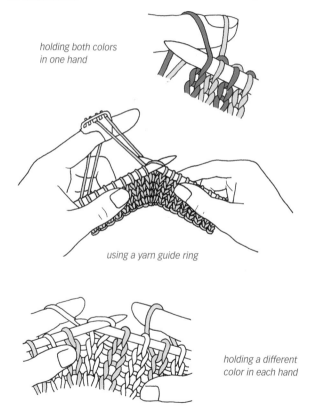

holding both colors in one hand

using a yarn guide ring

holding a different color in each hand

SOLVING PROBLEMS IN STRANDED KNITTING

Q The pattern stitches look much bigger in some sections than in others. Why does this happen?

A The stitches made with yarn carried below the other color are taller. If you switch the position of the two yarns in the course of your knitting, the change may be noticeable. Also, if you are holding one yarn in each hand, you may be knitting more tightly with one hand than the other. In this case, when you switch hands, the difference is even more noticeable, because the looser stitches are larger and puffier.

....

Q Why is my stranded knitting puckered, and what can I do about it?

A Pulling the yarn snugly when you change colors causes the strands on the back of the fabric to be too tight, drawing in the knitting. To prevent this, spread your knitting out on the right needle just before you knit the first stitch of a new color. If your needle is too short, making it difficult to spread out, change to a longer needle. If you are working circularly, turn the knitting inside out so that the purl side is on the outside of the tube. Continue knitting in the same direction as before. Because the strands of yarn run around the outside of the tube, their path will be just a bit longer.

....

Q **My stranded knitting is too loose. Individual stitches puff out and the knitting looks uneven. How can I fix this?**

A Use smaller needles, or increase tension on the yarn by wrapping it an extra time around your index or little finger. Don't stretch the knitting too much: Smooth it out just enough to lie flat as you knit the first stitch of the new color. If you're working in the round on a circular needle, make sure the needle is short enough. It should be a little shorter than the knitting so that the knitting is relaxed, not stretched around the needle.

....

Q **The stitches in my stranded knitting aren't even. Is there a way to fix them?**

A Some unevenness is natural in stranded knitting. When you're finished, block the piece under tension to create a smooth surface and more even stitches.

SEE ALSO: *Blocking, p. 306*

SPECIAL SITUATIONS
IN STRANDED KNITTING

Q **What is corrugated ribbing and how is it done?**

A This is ribbing where the knit stitches are one color and the purl stitches are another. If you change colors on subsequent rows, you can achieve very complex-looking ribbing. Work corrugated ribbing the same way you would work any stranded knitting, but be especially careful to keep the yarn not in use on the wrong side of the fabric. Note that corrugated ribbing doesn't behave like single-color ribbing. The stranding prevents it from being as elastic or resilient as regular ribbing. (For examples of color placement in corrugated ribbings, check Feitelson's *The Art of Fair Isle Knitting*; see Resources, p. 363.

. . . .

Q **I've been told that I need to work "steeks" when I do stranded knitting. What are these and why would I use them?**

A Steeks are extra stitches added in areas that will be cut open later, such as armholes, neck openings, and the fronts of cardigans. If you have some sewing experience, you'll recognize these as seam allowances. Steeks allow you to make the entire garment circularly, so that you can work the color pattern from the knit side throughout. Steek stitches are usually knit in stripes or a tiny checkerboard rather than the pattern stitch of the garment, making it easy for the knitter to distinguish them. After knitting is completed, join the shoulder seams and block the body. Before cutting, secure the stitches with machine- or hand-stitching along each side of the cutting line (this is optional in wool but required in other, more slippery fibers). Cut the steeks down the center between the lines of stitching. Pick up and knit the borders or sleeves. Trim the cut edges and overcast them on the inside of the garment to prevent them from unraveling. Steeks work best in garments of natural wool, because the cut ends will felt, preventing eventual unraveling.

SEE ALSO: *Page 296 for cutting your knitting*

Mosaic Knitting

Q **What is mosaic knitting and how do you do it?**

A Mosaic knitting is a method of working with multiple colors in which only one color is used at a time. Work a right-side row and then a wrong-side row, knitting the stitches in one color while slipping the stitches that will be worked in the other color. Then work two rows in the second color, knitting the stitches in the second color and slipping the ones already knit in the first color. Mosaic knitting does not have the long strands across the back of the fabric that characterize stranded knitting. Because only one yarn is used at a time, more complicated textures combining knit and purl stitches are easier to execute. (For more on mosaic knitting, check Walker's *Mosaic Knitting* and Bartlett's *Slip-Stitch Knitting*; see Resources, p. 363.)

Intarsia

Q What is intarsia and how is it done?

A Intarsia knitting features multiple colors, but the colors are never carried across the back of the fabric to be used elsewhere in the row. The difference between stranded knitting

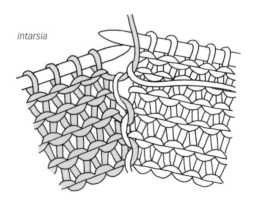

intarsia

and intarsia is clear when you look at the wrong side. You must have a separate ball of yarn or bobbin for each occurrence of a color. When working intarsia, knit as many stitches as are needed in one color, then drop the yarn on the purl side of the knitting, to the left of the stitch just completed. Pick up the next color to be used under and to the right of the dropped strand. (For inspiration, turn to any books by the master of intarsia design, Kaffe Fassett, especially *Glorious Inspiration for Needlepoint and Knitting*; see Resources, p. 363.)

••

Q **When I work intarsia, how can I keep the balls of yarn from getting tangled?**

A Wind a small amount of each yarn into a butterfly or onto a bobbin. Release just enough yarn to knit each color section, leaving the butterflies and bobbins dangling by short strands so they can't tangle around each other. Another approach to "multiple yarn management" is to break off an arm's length of yarn and simply leave it dangling. When you need to use a strand, pull it free from the other yarns. When a strand runs out, break off another arm's length of that color, splice the ends together and continue knitting. Splicing minimizes the number of ends to be woven in later.

SEE ALSO: *Page 146 for splicing*

Q I have holes in my intarsia where I start or end a color. What am I doing wrong?

A At the point where you begin or end a color, you must weave in the end on the wrong side of the fabric to close up the hole.

· ·

Q My knitting is normally smooth and even, but when I work intarsia there are uneven, lopsided stitches. How can I correct this?

A Here are some tips for making your color work more even.

▶ **Check as you go.** Check the stitches for consistency at each color change. When you pick up the new color, pull on the yarn gently to correct any looseness in the last stitch worked with this strand before working the first stitch on the current row.

▶ **Avoid angles.** If you are working an irregular area of the color or a diagonal, the first and last stitches may be distorted because the yarn is coming to the stitch at an angle, rather than straight across the row. You can adjust this angle by wrapping the working yarn around the yarn in the adjacent color block a stitch or two before you begin using it.

▶ **Weave in.** Adjust the first and last stitch of an area during finishing by weaving the end in diagonally so that it doesn't distort the stitch on the right side of the fabric.

▶ **Fix tension.** When the knitting is complete, adjust the tension by inserting the tip of a knitting needle into the backs of the stitches. Stretch the knitting from top to bottom to even out the stitches along a vertical color change.

▶ **Block the pieces.** To a certain extent, inconsistencies can be smoothed out by blocking. When working intarsia, it's best to block all the pieces to the proper size and shape before sewing together.

(For detailed information on perfectly executing and finishing intarsia, check the Stuevers' *Intarsia*; see Resources, p. 363.)

Variegated Yarns

Q I love hand-painted and multicolor yarns. How can I make them look as good knit up as they do in the ball or skein?

A The lovely interplay of colors in the ball or skein is very difficult to reproduce in the final knitted product. Hand-painted, multicolor, or variegated yarns have such a wide range of characteristics that generalizations are impossible. Some yarns have very long sections of each color, long enough to make solid stripes of color in the body of a sweater. Other yarns have short lengths of color that change after just one or two stitches. The range of hue and intensity in each yarn varies a great deal, too. Some have shades of a single color; others combine multiple colors and intensities. The key to success is to experiment. Remember that the length of the color repeats in your yarn works in conjunction with the number of stitches and needle size to create stripes and blocks of color. Experiment with swatches of different widths to see what effect you like best. Incorporate the characteristics of the swatches into your garment by knitting it in narrow blocks or strips. Here are some ideas for getting the best from these yarns.

▶ **Use textured stitches.** Slipped stitches, knitting into the row below, increases, and decreases all help to prevent the striping that is so often a problem with variegated yarns. Using bands or blocks of several different textured stitches in a garment can keep it interesting, masking obvious color repeats and highlighting the various qualities of the yarn.

▶ **Try lace.** Lace is made up of holes and decreases, both of which break up stripes.

▶ **Use two strands of yarn.** Knit with a double strand of yarn, using two balls of the same variegated yarn or working with both ends of the skein or ball at the same time. You can also use one strand of solid yarn and one strand of variegated.

▶ **Alternate two strands of yarn.** Using a circular needle, knit one round with each yarn or, using straight needles, knit two rows of each yarn. Use two balls of variegated, both ends of the same skein or ball, or a strand of solid alternately with the variegated.

▶ **Add several solid yarns.** Pick coordinating and contrasting colors. Consider working the variegated in a different textured stitch than the solids.

▶ **Emphasize or de-emphasize a color.** When you come to a stitch in a particular color, or when it appears in your working yarn, purl or slip the next stitch. Decide whether you prefer the effect when you slip with the yarn in front or in back. If the lengths of color are long enough, work a textured stitch on a Stockinette background whenever you come to this color. Seed Stitch is effective when used this way.

▶ **Flat versus circular.** Flat knitting tends to create repeating pools of color, alternating diagonally, left-right-left-right up the fabric. Circular knitting tends to create spirals that change angle as the knitting becomes wider or narrower.

▶ **Use geometry.** Knitting triangular or circular units makes each row a different length, preventing repetitive striping or blotching. Knitting in small or large squares or rectangles turned at right angles to each other breaks up any striping, as does working with small motifs.

SEE ALSO: *Page 129 for dye lot*

(For designs using hand-painted yarns, check Potter's *Hand-paint Country*; Nobel and Potter's *Lavish Lace*; and Burns, Kaisler, and Tosten's *Knitting With Hand-Dyed Yarns*; see Resources, p. 363.)

∨∨∨∨∨∨∨∨∨∨∨∨∨∨∨∨∨∨∨∨∨∨∨∨

CHAPTER 10

Shaping

∨∨∨∨∨∨∨∨∨∨∨∨∨∨∨∨∨∨∨∨∨∨∨∨

Knit and purl stitches are the basic building blocks
of knitting. Increases and decreases let you stretch,
compress, and shape these building blocks to create
everything from lace shawls to tailored garments.

Increases

Q What is an increase and how do I do one?

A Increases (inc) make your knitting wider by adding stitches. You may decide to shape a garment so that it fits better. For example, sleeves fit better if they are tapered. Sleeves are usually begun from the bottom, with increases worked periodically along the seam line so that the wrist is narrower than the upper sleeve.

There are many ways to increase. Here are the ones that I find most useful.

▶ **Knit into Front and Back.** Knit into the stitch as usual, but leave it on the left needle. Bring the tip of the right needle around to the back, knit into the back loop of the same stitch, and slip it off the needle. This increase

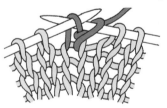

leaves a small bar or bump at the base of the second stitch, so it is sometimes called a bar increase. Some people find the bump unsightly, but it can be an effective decorative detail.

knit into front and back

▶ **Make 1 (M1).** I first encountered this increase in Elizabeth Zimmermann's *Knitting Without Tears* (see Resources, p. 363. Simply make a half hitch, as for a Loop Cast On, with the working yarn on the right needle. You can twist this either to the right or to the left to control the slant that appears at the base of the increase. If it seems a little loose, knit into either the back or front to twist it more on the following row.

right-slanting make 1

left-slanting make 1

SEE ALSO: *Page 194 for knitting into the back loop*

▶ **Lifted Make 1.** This makes an increase identical in structure to Make 1, but it is slightly tighter and appears one row lower. Insert the left needle under the strand between two needles from the back to lift this strand onto

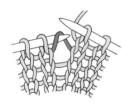

make 1, right slant

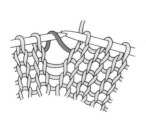

make 1, left slant

the left needle. Knit into the front of the strand to twist it. To reverse the twist, insert the left needle from the front and then knit into the back of the loop.

▶ **Row below.** Knit the stitch normally. Then, from the back, insert the left needle into the left half of the stitch on the row below. Knit into this stitch. To reverse the slant of this increase, reverse the order: Lift up the stitch from the row below and knit it, then knit the stitch normally. You may find it easiest to lift with the right needle and slip to the left needle before knitting.

row below increase, left slant   row below increase, right slant

▶ **Yarn over (YO).** This forms a hole in your knitting and is used in lace patterns or to make eyelet embellishments. Simply wrap the yarn around your right needle as if you were knitting a stitch. On the next row, knit or purl into this loop as you would any other stitch.

SEE ALSO: *The Yarn Over, p. 81*

▶ **Eyelet.** This makes a smaller hole than a yarn over and forms it one row lower. Insert the left needle under the strand between two stitches from the front, then knit into it normally so it does not twist.

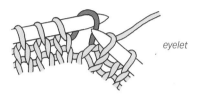

eyelet

....

Q What are paired increases? Why do you do them and how?

A These are increases done two at a time (in pairs) that are mirror images of each other. They are done to create decorative effects within pattern stitches or to make two edges of a knitted piece symmetrical, such as the two sides of a V-neck sweater. To work them, use an increase that can slant in either of two directions, such as the Make 1, the Lifted Make 1, or the row below. Work the first increase in the pair in one direction and the second in the opposite, reversing the twist of the Make 1 increases or the order of the steps in the Row Below Increase.

Q What are double increases? How do you do them and why?

A The increases described previously are all single increases; they add just one stitch at a time. A double increase adds two stitches each time you work it. Like the single increase, there are many ways to work a double increase.

▶ **Knit into the Front-Back-Front.** Knit into the stitch as usual, but leave it on the left needle. Bring the tip of the right needle around to the back, knit into the back loop of the stitch, and still leave it on the left needle. Bring the tip of the right needle to the front and knit into the stitch again. Finally, slip it off the needle.

▶ **Knit-Purl-Knit.** Knit into the stitch as usual, but leave it on the left needle. Bring the yarn to the front and purl into the stitch. Bring the yarn to the back and knit into the stitch again. Finally, slip it off the needle. This leaves a small hole below the increases, which fan out above, and may be used as an embellishment.

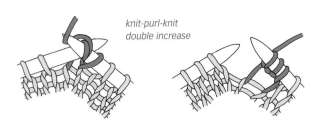

knit-purl-knit double increase

▶ **Make 1.** Work two Make 1 increases, reversing the twist on the second. If you are familiar with knots, you'll recognize this as a double reverse half hitch. This tends to leave a hole at the base of the increase.

▶ **Row below.** Work two row below increases, reversing the order on the second. This is the least noticeable of the double increases, leaving no bumps and no holes.

....

Q Is there a way to work more than two increases together?

A Yes. You can knit into the front and back of a stitch as many times as you like. You can also alternately knit and purl into a stitch multiple times. These multiple increases are frequently used in bobble or popcorn patterns.

....

Q I know there are different ways to work a Make 1. Is one better than the others?

A The Lifted Make 1 "steals" a little bit of yarn from the two stitches on either side when it is lifted and twisted to form the new stitch. If you are a loose knitter, this may be a benefit because it prevents a hole from appearing when you increase. If you are a tight knitter, are using a yarn that doesn't stretch, or find that the Lifted Make 1 noticeably distorts the stitches on either side, it's better to use Make 1.

Q When I use paired Make 1 increases, one twists more than the other. Why does this happen?

A When you knit a Make 1 that was twisted clockwise, it doesn't add any more twist; but when you knit a Make 1 that was twisted counterclockwise, it adds another half turn. In order to make them identical, you can twist the counterclockwise Make 1 less, by working into the back of it when you knit (or purl) it. Or, you can add more twist to the clockwise Make 1 by working into the back of it.

....

Q My pattern says to increase. How do I know which increase to use?

A Check the introduction and any explanatory material, such as the abbreviations, to see if the pattern explains which increase to use. If you can't find it, you'll need to do a little math to see whether to use the type of increase where you work twice into a stitch (Knit into Front and Back), or whether to use one of the increases that is done between stitches (Make 1, Lifted Make 1, or Row Below).

SEE ALSO: *What Does It Mean When It Says . . . ?, p. 270*

Q Why are most increases worked on the knit side?

A It's easy to see how they'll look in the finished knitting when worked on the knit side.

....

Q Is it possible to increase on the purl side?

A Yes. All of the increases described earlier can be easily done on the wrong side. Knitting and purling into one stitch results in what looks like two purl stitches on the right side of the fabric, but you can mimic the same increase on the right side by purling and then knitting. When working the row below increase from the purl side, be careful to lift up the correct strand of the stitch.

....

Q Why would I increase rather than cast on?

A Increases are worked when only one or two stitches need to be added at a time or when they must be done in the center of the knitting. Casting on is done at the beginning of a row and is used to add more than one stitch at the edge of the fabric.

Decreases

Q What is a decrease and how do I do one?

A Decreases (dec) make your knitting narrower by removing stitches. They are done as part of a pattern stitch or to shape a piece of knitting. Here are various ways to decrease.

▶ **Knit 2 Together (K2tog).** Insert the right needle into the first two stitches and knit them together. This is the most basic decrease and can be used any time you are knitting. It makes a decrease that slants to the right.

knit 2 together

▶ **Purl 2 Together (P2tog).** Insert the right needle into the first two stitches and purl them together. This can be used any time you are purling. When worked on the wrong side of the fabric it looks identical to a K2tog worked on the right side of the fabric.

purl 2 together

▶ **Slip 1, Knit 1, Pass Slipped Stitch Over (SKP or Sl1, K1, PSSO).** Slip the first stitch knitwise, knit the next stitch, pass the slipped stitch over the knit one and off the needle (as you would when binding off). This makes a decrease that slants to the left, the opposite of K2tog, although it has a tendency to look less even.

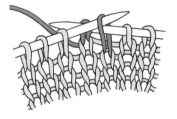

slip 1, knit 1, pass slipped stitch over

▶ **Slip, Slip, Knit (SSK).** Slip the first stitch knitwise, slip the second stitch knitwise, insert the left needle into these two stitches and knit them together. This also makes a decrease that slants to the left, the opposite of a K2tog, but it is more even and pairs better with the K2tog than does SKP.

slip, slip, knit

▶ **Knit 2 Together Through the Back Loop (K2tog tbl).**
Insert the right needle into the back of the first two
stitches knitwise and knit them together. This forms a
left-slanting decrease by twisting the stitches. This is a
very uneven decrease, but it's a quick substitute for SSK
when worked in a yarn that is dark or textured, where it
won't show as much.

*knit 2 together
through back loop*

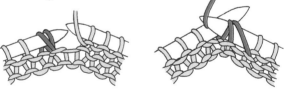

▶ **Slip, Slip, Purl (SSP).** Slip the first stitch knitwise, slip
the second stitch knitwise, insert the left needle into
these two stitches knitwise and slip them back to the left
needle together.

slip, slip, purl

Reinsert the right needle and purl the two stitches
together. This makes a decrease that slants to the left,
and it is identical to SSK when worked on the wrong
side of the fabric.

▶ **Purl 2 Together Through the Back Loop (P2tog tbl).**
Insert the right needle into the back of the first two
stitches purlwise and purl
them together. This forms
a left-slanting twisted
decrease. It is much quicker
than SSP and is identical to
K2tog tbl when worked from
the wrong side of the fabric.

*purl 2 together
through back loop*

Notes for Nonstandard Stitches

If your stitches don't face the standard way on the needle,
then you'll need to adjust for this when working decreases.

▶ **Left-slanting decrease.** K2tog working into the back
loops as you normally do. The results are identical to SSK
worked on standard stitches.

▶ **Right-slanting decrease.** Slip two stitches, one at a time,
to the right needle, inserting the needle knitwise into the back
loop. Slip these stitches back to the left needle, one at a time,
knitwise. This changes the orientation of the stitches. Finally,
K2tog through the *front* of the loops.

SEE ALSO: *The Slipped Stitch, p. 75; and Twists and Turns, p. 58*

Q What is a double decrease? When would I use it?

A The decreases just described are all single decreases, eliminating just one stitch at a time. Double decreases (DD) remove two stitches at a time. Use them to decrease more rapidly than is possible using single decreases (such as when making a ruffle), to work decreases in a pattern stitch with a two-stitch repeat (such as K1P1 ribbing), or as part of a decorative pattern stitch. They are frequently used where decreases for shaping are done in pairs, such as at the shoulders of a raglan-sleeved sweater or the top of a beret.

▶ **Knit 3 Together (K3tog).** This is the most basic of

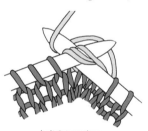

knit 3 together

double decreases. Simply insert the right needle into the first three stitches and knit them together. This makes an asymmetrical decrease that slants to the right and is noticeably thick because of the three overlapping stitches.

▶ **Purl 3 Together (P3tog).** Insert the right needle into the first three stitches and purl them together. Like the knit version, it is thick and asymmetrical.

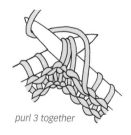

purl 3 together

▶ **Slip 1, Knit 2 Together, Pass Slipped Stitch Over (SK2P).** Slip the first stitch knitwise, knit the next two stitches together, then pass the slipped stitch off over the knit stitch, as if you were binding off. This makes a decrease that is more symmetrical than K3tog, because it is centered over the middle stitch. However, it has a definite slant to the left.

slip 1, knit 2 together, pass slipped stitch over

▶ **Raised Double Decrease.** Insert the right needle knitwise into the first two stitches, as if to knit them together, but instead simply slip them to the right needle. Knit the next stitch, then pass the two slipped stitches over it and off the needle. This results in a decrease that is centered, with the middle stitch on top, so there is no slant.

raised double decrease

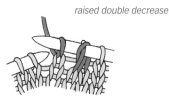 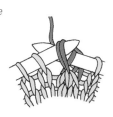

What Does It Mean When It Says…?

▶ **Increase 1 stitch at each edge every 6 rows 12 times, then every 4 rows 7 times.** This is used to slope both sides of your knitting, for example, on a sleeve. "Increase 1 stitch at each edge" means to increase 1 stitch at the beginning and 1 at the end of the row. "Every 6 rows 12 times" means to work the increases on 1 row, then work 5 more rows without increasing. This pattern is repeated 12 times, resulting in an increase of 24 stitches (2 stitches x 12 times) in 72 rows (6 rows x 12 times). At this point, you step up the frequency of the increases by working only 3 rows between increase rows ("then every 4 rows 7 times": another 14 stitches in just 28 rows).

▶ **Increase 8 stitches evenly spaced across row.** This is done at the end of a ribbed border. To do it, increase a total of 8 stitches (or however many are specified), spaced as evenly as possible across the row. Place a safety pin or split marker for each increase stitch at the points where you want to increase. To determine the placement, divide your knitting in half, then in quarters, and place one-quarter of the markers in each section. Or, calculate the placement mathematically. From your total number of stitches on the needle, subtract 2 to allow for edge stitches, and then divide by 1 fewer than the required increases to get the number of stitches between increases. If your numbers don't work out evenly, simply divide the extra stitches between the 2 end sections. When you work your increases, remember that a Knit-into-Front-and-Back increase uses one of the stitches, so be sure to count it as the first stitch in each group. On the other hand, if you use a Make 1 or a Lifted Make 1 increase, these are done between stitches, so you'll have all the stitches of each group between the increases.

▶ **Reverse shaping.** Do this when a section of a garment needs to be a mirror image of another section, for example, the 2 fronts of a cardigan, on which the armhole and neck shaping must match. Say you worked the left front first, and bound off for the armhole at the beginning of a right-side row. To reverse shaping for the right front, simply work 1 row extra before beginning the arm-hole, and bind off for the underarm on the next row, this time at the beginning of a wrong-side row. To reverse the

two fronts of a cardigan form a mirror image

shape of the neck, which was bound off at the beginning of a wrong-side row on the left front, again work 1 row more than the left front, and bind off at the beginning of a right-side row.

▶ **Work both sides at the same time with separate balls of yarn.** This is done when working the shoulders of a sweater or vest, after you bind off the center neck. Use 2 balls of working yarn (or knit from both the center and the outside of a center-pull ball or skein). With the stitches for both shoulders still on the needle, separated by the gap for the neckline, work across 1 shoulder toward the center, using the original ball of yarn, until you reach the bound-off area. At the gap, leave that yarn dangling, and use the yarn from your second ball to work across the second shoulder. When you reach the end of the row, turn and work back toward the neck with this second ball of yarn. When you reach the neck opening again, switch to the ball of yarn attached to the other shoulder. Continue working across both shoulders (each with its own ball of yarn) on every row.

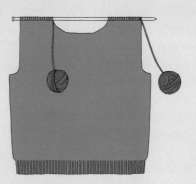

work both sides at the same time

▶ **Bind off 2 stitches at each neck edge every other row 3 times.** Do this after you've bound off the center stitches to create a neck opening and joined a second ball of yarn (see above); groups of bound-off stitches are used to make a curved edge. Because you can bind off only at the beginning of a row, you'll bind off at 1 neck edge on right-side rows and at the other on wrong-side rows. Starting from the armhole edge, work across to the neck opening. Leave the yarn dangling, and pick up the yarn for the other side of the neck. In this example, bind off 2 stitches and work to the end of the row. Turn and work the next row back to the neck edge. Leave this yarn dangling and pick up the other yarn. Bind off 2 stitches and then work to the end of the row. You've completed 2 rows, and you've bound off the first 2 stitches at each neck edge. For this example, repeat all of this twice to complete the process.

▶ **Decrease 1 stitch at each neck edge every other row 3 times.** This is usually the last step after binding off the center of the neck and then binding off groups of stitches at each side of the neck, as in the previous direction. The decreases finish the shaping to make a neat curve. They are also used to create the diagonal of a V-neck. As above, work with 2 balls of yarn, 1 for each side of the neck opening. When working decreases every other row, it's easiest to do them on the right side of the fabric, so you can see how they look. Starting from the armhole edge on a right-side row, work across until 3 stitches remain before the neck opening, K2tog, then knit the last stitch. Leave the yarn dangling and pick up the yarn for the other side of the neck. Knit 1, work a SSK decrease, then work to the end of the row. Turn, and work the next row back to the neck edge. Leave this yarn dangling and pick up the other yarn. Work to the end of the row. You've completed 2 rows, and you've decreased 1 stitch at each neck edge. Repeat all of this twice. For this example, the decreases are worked 1 stitch in from the edge, which makes it easier to pick up stitches for the border later. The reason for using the K2tog decrease on 1 side of the neck and the SSK decrease on the other side of the neck is that they are mirror images of each other and this detail makes the 2 sides of the neck look symmetrical. You may prefer to reverse their positions for a slightly different effect.

▶ **Increase, decrease, or bind off on the next right-side row and all alternate rows.** Do this when you want to make a diagonal or sloped edge. Work to the end of a wrong-side row. When you work the next right-side row, do whatever shaping the pattern indicates. After this, shaping continues on all alternate (right-side) rows. Another way to say this is "every other row."

SEE ALSO: *Decreases, p. 264; Binding Off, chapter 3; and Increases, p. 256*

Special Situations

Q If a pattern says to increase or decrease at the beginning or end of the row, should I do it at the very edge of my knitting?

A It's best to do all increases and decreases at least one or two stitches away from the edge, because these procedures tend to make the edge looser or tighter. They can also make it very confusing to pick up stitches or seam along the edge later. For example, to work decreases two stitches in from both edges of a sleeve, knit the first two stitches, SSK, then work across the row until there are four stitches left, K2tog, using the next two stitches, then knit the final two. The two decreases mirror each other and there are two stitches in Stockinette at each end of the row. Repeating this procedure for the length of the sleeve edges ensures a neat, even, easy-to-see edge when you sew it up.

The exception to this rule is when a yarn over is to be worked at the beginning of the row, before the first stitch. The resulting row of loops along the edge may be used decoratively, or it may be used later for joining.

SEE ALSO: *Knitting Instructions, p. 175*

Q The instructions say to work "in pattern as established" while shaping the armholes and neck, but I'm having trouble doing this because of increases and decreases in the pattern stitch. I keep ending up with the wrong number of stitches. What should I do?

A Shaping can be very confusing when you're working a pattern stitch that already involves increases and decreases. As the piece becomes narrower or wider, one option is simply to work the incomplete pattern repeat at the edge in Stockinette or a very simple pattern stitch like Seed Stitch. Markers between pattern repeats make it easy to see where the pattern stitch begins and ends. Whenever you have enough stitches at the edge, work a full pattern repeat. This works well if the pattern repeat is narrow, but it can look terrible if it is wide. For wider patterns, you'll need to maintain the pattern stitch as close to the edge as you can. One solution is to make half of a pattern repeat in pattern stitch and the other half in Stockinette.

When you are working a pattern stitch with increases and decreases, it's important to understand how they interact. For each increase there is a corresponding decrease; otherwise, the total number of stitches would change. In some pattern stitches, corresponding increases and decreases are worked on the same row, so that you always have the same number of stitches in a row. The rule of thumb when doing shaping in these stitches is to work the corresponding increase and decrease only if there are enough stitches for both of them.

In cases where there is a double decrease at the center of a pattern, you may need to substitute a single one when the corresponding increase falls beyond the edge of the fabric. You may encounter situations where you need to work a shaping decrease or increase close to where one would naturally fall in the pattern stitch. When this happens, you can continue the pattern to the edge.

In other patterns, the corresponding increases and decreases may be several rows apart, so you'll have more stitches on some rows and fewer on others. In these cases, you'll need to keep track of the corresponding increases and decreases over several rows.

Making a Shaped Swatch

Test the shaping on a swatch before you begin the garment. Once you have knit a swatch big enough to measure, bind off about 2" (5 cm) of stitches at the edge, then decrease one stitch on each right-side row for about 2" (5 cm). Work straight for another 3 or 4 inches before binding off. This produces the same shaping as an armhole and is very similar to one side of a neck opening. It's also extremely useful for picking up stitches and testing the border.

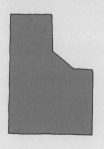

Another helpful exercise is to graph the pattern stitch in relation to the shaping. It's not necessary to graph the whole garment, just the section where the shaping takes place. For instance, chart a sweater from the armhole up to the shoulder and over to the center to include neck shaping.

SEE ALSO: *Pattern Stitches, chapter 7*

Q I'm working a pattern with a two-stitch repeat. When I do increases or decreases, it messes up the pattern. Is there a way to avoid this?

A Yes. Work double increases or double decreases instead of single ones. For example, if you are supposed to increase eight stitches evenly spaced, work four double increases instead. This way, you'll add a full repeat of the pattern stitch at each increase point.

. . . .

Q Is there a good way to work an increase when I'm working with two colors in stranded knitting?

A Yes. When it comes time to increase, knit a stitch with both strands held together. On the next row or round treat the two strands as separate stitches.

CHAPTER 11

Fitting

Several factors affect the fit of a garment. Some of these are obvious: the measurements of the body, the measurements of the finished garment, and the differences between these two. Other factors are less obvious: the thickness, drape, and stretch of the fabric; and the silhouette and structure of the garment. When you are knitting from a pattern, you can't control all of these factors, but you can make informed choices to help ensure success.

Before You Begin

Q How do I take body measurements to guarantee a good fit?

A If the garment is for you, get someone else to take the measurements. Wear whatever clothing you expect to wear under the garment and use a flexible tape measure. Make circumference measurements at the widest points of the chest/bust and hips, and at the narrowest point of the waist. Be sure to hold the tape measure horizontally, untwisted, and a bit loose. For accurate length measurements, let the tape measure hang loosely from the top. The most important measurements for sweaters are around the chest/bust (because this measurement is used to select the correct size) and across the shoulders (because the sweater hangs from the shoulders). Fit in these areas also affects the fit of the sleeves.

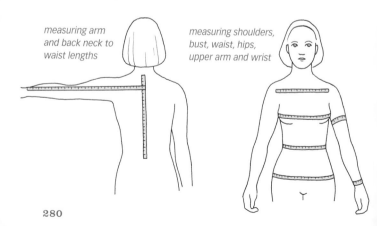

measuring arm and back neck to waist lengths

measuring shoulders, bust, waist, hips, upper arm and wrist

Q **What does "ease" mean, and how do I know the right amount to allow?**

A Ease is the difference between the measurement of a garment and the body it is supposed to fit. The amount of ease required depends on the thickness of the fabric and the silhouette of the garment. In a very close-fitting, stretchy garment, such as a leotard, the garment may actually be smaller than the body because it is made of very thin fabric that is designed to stretch when worn. A bulky sweater requires more ease to fit comfortably than a sweater knit in a thinner yarn. A slim, fitted garment silhouette needs less ease than an oversize one.

Ease Guidelines

The Craft Yarn Council of America suggests these guidelines for ease in hand-knit garments.

STYLE	DIFFERENCE BETWEEN BODY & GARMENT SIZES
Very-close fitting	Actual chest/bust measurement or less
Close-fitting	1–2" (2.5–5 cm)
Standard-fitting	2–4" (5–10 cm)
Loose-fitting	4–6" (10–15 cm)
Oversize	6" (15 cm) or more

Q How do I choose the right size from the pattern?

A Select the size in the pattern that is closest to your body measurement plus the appropriate ease. If the sweater extends below the hips, it must be large enough to clear the hips with some ease as well. Some patterns state the finished garment measurement, but you should still check your calculations and your desired measurement against those given in the pattern. Keep in mind, though, that the finished garment will be the correct size only if your knitting matches the gauge exactly.

SEE ALSO: *Sizing, p. 160; Gauge, p. 162; and Measurements and Schematics, p. 168*

Q How can I control the qualities of the fabric?

A When knitting from a pattern, your goal is to recreate the fabric of the original garment as closely as possible. To do this you need to match the yarn and the gauge. Choosing the same weight yarn with the same fiber content is very important. If you substitute a worsted-weight cotton for a worsted-weight wool, or vice versa, the fabric you knit will be very different. You must also make sure that your knitting matches the gauge specified in the pattern. If you use the same kind of yarn and match the gauge perfectly, then your fabric will have the same thickness, drape, and stretch as the original.

. . . .

Q **What does "silhouette" mean, and how do I go about choosing it?**

A The silhouette of a garment determines how closely it fits the body and how it hangs. Choose silhouette depending on current fashion and personal preference. Take a look at the clothes you already own. Try on a sweater or sweat-shirt that is comfortable and looks good on you. Measure it and compare the ease in the chest/bust and hips to your body measurements. Then take a look at the Ease Guidelines (p. 281) to see which silhouette you prefer. (For more on silhouette, check Newton's *Designing Knitwear;* see Resources, p. 363.)

. . . .

Q **What difference does garment structure make?**

A Generally, the simpler the garment structure, the less well it fits. The simplest of sweaters can be knit in rectangles to make a basic T, leaving a slit at the top for a boatneck. Unfortunately, this type of garment doesn't fit well unless it is knit in a very thin, loose fabric that stretches to conform to the body. This is because excess fabric forms folds under the arms and in front and back of the shoulders, and the untapered sleeves have extra bulk at the wrists. If the sweater is bulky, these problems can be both unsightly and uncomfortable. Shaped neck openings, sloped shoulders, and tapered sleeves make for a better fit.

Seamless sweaters knit circularly can still be shaped effectively in the shoulder area if you make raglan sleeves or a circular yoke.

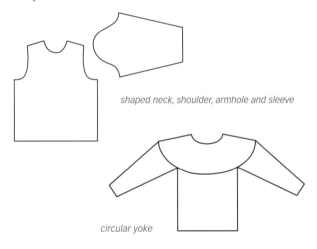

shaped neck, shoulder, armhole and sleeve

circular yoke

SEE ALSO: *Adjusting Sleeve Length, p. 288*

Start with a Sweater You Like

Use a sweater you already like as a model for your knitting. Choose a sweater of the same weight and style as the one you plan to make. If your yarn is thicker, be sure to allow a little extra ease; if it is thinner, allow a little less.

Lay the sweater out on a flat surface and take accurate measurements. Compare these to the finished measurements of the sweater in the pattern. If the garment is knit from either the bottom up or the top down, decide on the size to make based on the width of the body; if the sweater is knit sideways (cuff-to-cuff), determine the size based on the length you want. Next, compare the measurements of other key areas to the pattern instructions. These include the length from bottom to armhole, the depth of the armhole from underarm to shoulder, the width of the front or back between the two armholes, the width of the neck, the depth of the neck opening in front and back, and the shoulder slope. Also compare the sleeve length, the sleeve width at the underarm, and the width at the cuff.

You can easily adjust the body length of the knitting as you work. Sleeve length can also be adjusted (see Adjusting Length, later in this chapter). Adjusting the body length and width above the armhole and the width and shape of the sleeve cap is a little more difficult because the two must fit each other. You may find it easier to make a full-size pattern on knitter's graph paper with a grid that matches your gauge.

Q Do you have any general suggestions to improve fit?

A Here are some tips that should help.

▶ **Make fitted garments** (not drop-shoulder styles). They require a little more attention while you work the shaping, but you'll be knitting less fabric and the garments fit much, much better.

▶ **Avoid loosely knit garments** made from bulky yarn. No matter how well they fit to begin with, they tend to stretch out of shape.

▶ **Seams,** especially shoulder seams, help keep garments from stretching out of shape. Avoid garments where the front and back or the body and sleeve are knit in one piece.

▶ **Choose wool or wool blend yarn** because wool is less dense than other fibers. It is also naturally elastic, so it tends to hold its shape better. If you do choose to make drop-shoulder garments, for best results use wool and avoid bulky yarns.

While You Work

Q Is there a way to see if my sweater will fit before it's completely sewn together?

A Check the measurements of the pieces against the planned measurements as you knit. If they don't match, investigate the problem. Hold the pieces up to your body or against an existing sweater to see if they look the right size. If the body length to the underarm or the sleeve length isn't right, simply knit it longer or shorter. (To check the sleeve length accurately, see Fitting Sleeves, p. 289.)

....

Q How do I measure my knitting accurately?

A Lay it down on an even surface, smooth gently to flatten it, then measure it with a flexible tape measure. The knitting must lie flat while you measure it. If the knitting is bunched up tightly on a straight needle, work halfway across the row before laying it down. If it is still too gathered to get an accurate measurement, you may need to transfer it to a circular needle, or divide it between two circular needles if you are already working in the round. Do this, too, if you are using a circular needle that is too short to allow the knitting to be laid flat. If the knitting curls at the edges, gently unroll it and hold it flat with a book or a yardstick while you measure. Be careful not to stretch the piece.

Adjusting Sleeve Length

1. Determine the length you want between the top of the cuff and the underarm.

Ex: *Cuff to underarm length = 16" (40 cm)*

2. Multiply this times the row gauge to get the number of rows during which you shape the sleeve.

Ex: *16" (40 cm) x 7 rows per inch (2.5 cm) = 112 rows*

3. Determine the width at the cuff and the width at the underarm. Subtract the cuff width from the underarm width to find the difference.

Ex: *16" (40 cm) armhole width – 8" (20 cm) cuff width = 8" (20 cm)*

4. Multiply the difference times the stitch gauge to get the number of stitches added in the shaping.

Ex: *8" (20 cm) x 5 stitches per inch (2.5 cm) = 40 stitches*

5. Divide this number by 2 for the number of rows that must contain increases (because you increase 1 stitch at both ends of the row). If this number is a fraction, round up.

Ex: *40 stitches / 2 = 20 rows of increases*

6. Divide the total number of rows in the sleeve length by the number of increase rows to calculate the number of rows between increases.

112 rows / 20 rows of increases = 5.6 rows betw. increases

Note: To accommodate the fractional number, it's best to increase a little more frequently at the bottom of the sleeve. In this example, you can increase at the ends of every fourth row 5 times (4 x 5 = 20), then change to increase every sixth row 15 more times (6 x 15 = 90). Alternatively, for an even slope along the entire sleeve, you can intersperse the 2 frequencies. Work increases every sixth row 3 times, then work increases in the fourth row. Repeat this sequence 5 times to complete all the required increases. Work the extra 2 rows even to get to the correct length (20 + 90 + 2 = 112 rows). If your sleeve is worked from the top down, simply substitute decreases for increases.

Fitting Sleeves

To ensure that your sleeves are the correct length, first complete the back and front of the sweater, then join them at the shoulders and work the neck ribbing or border. Now try on the partially completed sweater and measure the length of your arm from the edge of the shoulder to the point on your wrist where the cuff should end. This is the length your sleeve should be.

If you need to end each sleeve at a certain point in a pattern stitch and can't match the length exactly, you may want to make the sleeves a little shorter, because the weight of the sleeves tends to stretch the shoulders when they are attached.

Q I'd like to make the sleeves on my sweater shorter than the pattern indicates. Does this change the way I should increase along the sleeve seam?

A When you shorten the sleeves, you'll probably need to make your increases closer together than the pattern indicates. Instructions to help you recalculate the spacing of the increases appear later in this chapter. For longer sleeves, you may also want to change the spacing of the increases. The same formula works for either.

Q How can I tell what size to make for someone else?

A The Craft Yarn Council of America has developed charts of standard sizes. You can also base sizing on a garment the recipient already has and likes.

SEE ALSO: *Resources, p. 363*

Q Which is better: knitting a sweater from the bottom up or from the top down?

A Neither is better than the other. Working from the bottom up is the method most frequently used, but proponents of top-down knitting advocate it because you can complete the shoulder area and fitting first, then go on to make the garment exactly the length you want. If it needs to be lengthened or shortened later, it's simple to unravel from the bottom and rework to the correct length. (Check Walker's *Knitting from the Top*; see Resources, p. 363.)

. . . .

Q Can I tell ahead of time if my sweater will stretch out of shape?

A Sometimes you can get an idea by hanging the pieces up as you finish them. Before hanging each piece, measure its length and make a note of it. Use a skirt or pants hanger, or clothespins, to hang the back and front upside down. (Don't hang from the shoulders; without any ribbing or seaming, the shoulders will stretch excessively.) Leave them for a few days, then measure again. Garments that have no seams or are loosely knit from very bulky yarn or fibers other than wool are more prone to stretching.

After You're Done

Q What should I do if my sweater doesn't fit when it's finished?

A Try it on to figure out exactly where and by how much it doesn't fit. If it's too big, pinch the excess fabric and secure it with safety pins until it hangs correctly. (Get a friend to help.) Remove the garment and note the measurements, so that you can determine how much needs to be removed. If it's too small, lay it on top of a similar garment that fits correctly to see what areas need to be expanded. Make notes and sketches to document the changes you plan to make.

ADJUSTING LENGTH

Q How do I correct the length of the body?

A If your garment is seamed, remove the seams in the area to be changed. See the chart (opposite page) for instructions on how to proceed. Note that to lengthen the body you can always pick up stitches at the bottom edge and simply widen the border. When you are done adjusting the length of both the front and back, sew the seams back up.

SEE ALSO: *Kitchener Stitch, p, 321*

Q My sleeves are too long/short. Is there any way to shorten/lengthen them?

A Yes. Follow the suggestions for lengthening or shortening the body above. To shorten tapered sleeves, be sure to work decreases across the new bottom edge of the sleeve so that the number of stitches matches the cuff before

How to Adjust Body Length

	IF YOU KNIT FROM THE BOTTOM UP	IF YOU KNIT FROM THE TOP DOWN
GET READY	*Carefully snip a single strand of yarn at the center of the garment, where the bottom border should begin. Working from the center out, unravel the 2 ends to the edges of the piece.*	*First unravel the bound-off edge and the bottom border.*
TO LENGTHEN	*If the body was worked in Stockinette, you will be able to extend it seamlessly simply by knitting down from this point. Then work the bottom border or reattach it using Kitchener Stitch. If the body is in a pattern stitch, this won't work. Instead, put the bottom border on a needle and work the pattern stitch upward. When it is long enough, use Kitchener Stitch to join it to the body. Alternatively, you may find it easier to simply knit a longer border down from the body.*	*Put the stitches back on the needle and work until the desired length to the bottom border. Reknit the bottom border.*
TO SHORTEN	*Put the stitches at the bottom edge back on the needle. You can either knit the border down from this point and bind off or unravel the detached section down to the top of the border and weave the 2 sections together using Kitchener Stitch.*	*Continue unraveling back to the point where the bottom border should begin, put the stitches back on the needle, and reknit the bottom border.*

reknitting or rejoining it. If you lengthen the sleeve and decide to continue tapering it down to the new cuff, make sure the sleeve doesn't get too narrow. **Hint:** When lengthening a sleeve, you can also simply pick up stitches across the bottom of the cuff and widen the border.

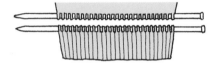

lengthening a sleeve

Q **I made a cuff-to-cuff sweater and it stretched. The sleeves end way below my hands. What do I do?**

A You have two options. You can either add support to the shoulder line and to the sleeves to hike them up and prevent further stretching, or you can shorten the sleeves. To add support, turn the garment inside out and try to unobtrusively crochet a chain across where the shoulder seam should fall, and down the center of the sleeve. You'll need to experiment to determine how tightly to work the chain. If this doesn't work, try on the sweater and use safety pins to mark the point on the sleeves where the top of the cuff should be, then shorten the sleeves as described in the preceeding answer.

ADJUSTING WIDTH

Q The neck of my sweater is too loose. What do I do?

A If it is only a little loose, unravel the bind off and work it again more tightly. If it is much too loose, try on the sweater and pinch up the neckline border in sections until it fits. Use safety pins to secure these tucks. Take off the garment and count the number of stitches that have been taken up in the tucks. Subtract this from the original number in the border to determine the approximate number of stitches for a new border. Unravel the original border, pick up the correct number of stitches and work a smaller border. If the neckline looks gathered, you may need to work a shaped border. In this case, pick up a larger number of stitches and work a row or round of Reverse Stockinette. Work another row or round of Reverse Stockinette, decreasing about half the number of extra stitches evenly spaced around the neck. Work the border. On the last row, decrease to the desired number of stitches, then bind off.

. . . .

Q The neck of my sweater is too tight. What do I do?

A Unravel the bound-off edge and work it again as loosely as you can. If it is still not loose enough, put a string or piece of yarn around your neck where you want the neck opening to fall. Measure the string or yarn to determine the correct size of the opening. Measure the opening as it is now and calculate how much larger it needs to be. Based on the number of stitches per inch (2.5 cm) in the border, calculate how many more stitches you need. Add this to the original number of stitches in the border to determine how many stitches you need. Unravel the whole border, pick up this number of stitches, and work the border again.

. . . .

Q **The shoulders of my sweater are too wide. Can I adjust them?**

A Many times, too-wide shoulders in a sweater are actually caused by a neck opening that's too loose. First, determine whether making the neck opening smaller will solve the problem. Next, consider the fit of the sweater. If it is an oversize sweater, the shoulder line may intentionally be wider than the natural shoulder line of your body. In this case, it is best to leave the shoulders alone and shorten the sleeves. If it is a fitted sweater, decide where the shoulder line should fall. How many stitches away from the armhole edge is this? To make the shoulders narrower, you have two choices. You can unravel the sweater back to the underarm and reknit, making the armhole opening wider. Or, you can remove the sleeves and cut away some of the fabric at the armhole using the following technique.

Mark the desired armhole opening edge (contrasting color basting thread works best). Using a sewing machine set for very small stitches, make two rows of stitching to the outside of the marked edge. You can also use hand sewing to secure the knitting before cutting. Be careful to sew through each strand of yarn along the length of the cut, or you can crochet a chain firmly through each stitch. Cut the knitting beyond the stitching. Pin the sleeve to the new armhole opening to see if it still fits. If it is too small and the armhole puckers when it is joined, then unravel the sleeve cap and make it a little taller or wider. If the cap is too big, you can either gather it as you sew it in or reknit it a little shorter or narrower.

....

Q My armholes are too tight. Is there a way to make them bigger?

A Undo the sleeve seam for a few inches on both sides of the underarm. Knit a diamond-shaped insert and sew it in to form a gusset, aligning the widest point at the underarm seam.

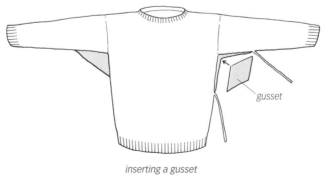

gusset

inserting a gusset

Q My sleeves are too tight. Is there a way to make them bigger?

A Undo the sleeve seam from cuff to underarm and the body seam for a few inches beyond the underarm. Knit a diamond-shaped insert and sew it in to form a gusset, with the widest point at the underarm seam.

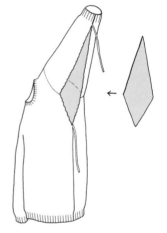

altering a too-tight sleeve with gusset

Q My sweater's too narrow. Is there any way to make it bigger?

A If the body is too narrow but the sleeves fit properly, open up the side seam all the way to the underarm, plus a few inches down the sleeve seam. Knit a long strip tapered at one end, and sew it in to form a gusset, with the tapered end at the sleeve. Note that the insert enlarges the body, but then tapers at the underarm as it fits into the sleeve.

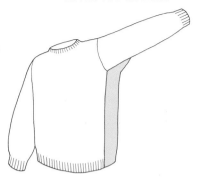

altering a too-narrow body with a gusset

. . . .

Q Both the sleeves and body of my sweater are too tight. Is there a way to make them bigger?

A Undo the sleeve and side seams, from top to bottom. Knit a strip and sew it in along the body and sleeve seams. Or, pick up stitches along one edge, knit until the addition is the desired width, then sew to the other edge, either before or after binding off. A combination of Mattress Stitch and

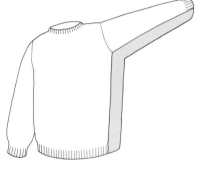

altering a too-tight body and sleeve with an insert

weaving or Kitchener Stitch allows you to join the addition to the edge of the existing knitting, just as you join a sleeve to an armhole. Another option is to pick up along both edges, knit to the center of the area to be added, then use Kitchener Stitch or Three-Needle Bind Off to join the two halves. The insert enlarges both body and sleeve. Work a noncurling pattern where the insert meets the ribbing.

SEE ALSO: *Sewing Up, p. 311; Kitchener Stitch, p. 321; and Three-Needle Bind Off, p. 101*

 My sleeves are too loose. Is there a way to make them smaller?

First decide whether simply making the cuff smaller will solve the problem. Pinch in the cuff and secure it with a safety pin. If you like the way it looks, note the number of stitches you need to make a cuff the proper size. Remove the cuff as described in the instructions on lengthening and shortening garments previously explained in this chapter. Put the stitches back on the needle. On the first row, decrease to the desired number of stitches and reknit the cuff.

To make the whole sleeve narrower, try on the sweater and pinch the sleeves along the seam line to remove the excess fabric. Use safety pins to hold it in place. Remove the sweater and mark the desired seam line. Unstitch the original sleeve seam. Using a sewing machine set for very fine stitches, stitch twice just to the outside of the marked seam lines. Cut off the

excess fabric just beyond the stitching and sew the sleeve
seam up again.

....

Q My sweater's too wide. Is there any way to make
it smaller?

A If just the body is too wide, you can make it narrower
by cutting and reseaming below the armholes as
described in the previous answer. If the shoulders are also
too wide, however, it would be best to unravel the sweater
and make a smaller size. You may decide instead to find a
recipient who can wear it!

Solving Other Problems with Fit

Q My sweaters and vests ride up in the front. How can
I prevent this?

A This happens when there is no back neck shaping. Look
for patterns where the back of the neck is shaped, not
straight.

Q My sweater shifts from side to side and hangs off-center. What's wrong?

A It's possible that the neck opening is too wide, which allows it to shift back and forth. On the other hand, in some designs the neck is supposed to be wide, with the shoulder shaping holding the garment in place. You can usually correct this problem by making the neck border with fewer stitches or by making the neck border wider in order to fill in the neck opening more. You can also add shoulder shaping as described in the next answer.

Short-Row Shaping

Q What are short rows? When would I use them?

A Short rows are a way of shaping knitting that involves working partway across a row and then turning back before finishing the row. Working a series of knitted short rows makes it possible to work sock heels, add darts, or make a round shape like a ball seamlessly. (For more on short-row sock heels, check Gibson-Roberts' *Simple Socks: Plain and Fancy*, and for how to add darts, check Newton's *Designing Knitwear*; see Resources, p. 363.)

How to Wrap and Turn

Failure to wrap when you turn causes holes! To avoid this, when you reach the turning point, slip the next stitch, bring the yarn from back to front (or front to back if you've been purling), then slip the stitch back to the left needle, and turn your work. Make sure the yarn is in the correct position (in front or in back, depending on whether you now need to knit or purl), and continue back across the row.

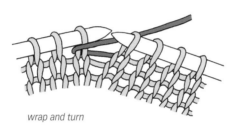

wrap and turn

The next time you work each wrapped stitch, pick up the wrap on the tip of your needle and knit it together with its stitch. This will make it disappear.

Q How can I use the Three-Needle Bind Off to join
shoulder seams when the shoulder is shaped by
binding off in steps?

A If you use short rows to shape the shoulders, then all of
the stitches will still be active when you join the shoulders. Follow the instructions for binding off your shoulders,
but instead of binding off, just don't work these stitches on
subsequent rows. For example, if the instructions say to bind
off 5 stitches at the armhole edge 5 times, stop working 5
stitches away from the armhole edge, slip and wrap the next
stitch, then work back to the neck edge. On the following
row, stop 10 stitches from the edge and turn, then 15, and so
on. When your shaping is complete, work back across the
whole row, picking up all the wraps. Do this on both left and
right sides, front and back, then join the shoulders using the
Three-Needle Bind Off.

> *Note: If you have trouble keeping track of where you should
> turn, work across the stitches the pattern directs you to bind
> off, then place a marker. When you turn and work back to the
> marker on the next row, remove the marker, slip and wrap the
> next stitch, then turn back. Work across the next group of
> stitches that the pattern directs you to bind off, and again
> place the marker. Continue in this manner until you've
> worked all the stitches.*

SEE ALSO: *Three-Needle Bind Off, p. 101*

CHAPTER 12

Finishing

Finishing embraces all the steps you must go through after you complete the knitting itself. This includes blocking, sewing up, adding borders, picking up stitches, and adding buttonholes and buttons. Perfect finishing requires practice and attention to detail, but it makes a garment look handcrafted rather than homemade.

Blocking

Q What is blocking?

A The knitted fabric is wet, stretched, and smoothed to shape, and then allowed to dry — but not necessarily in that order.

· ·

Q Why should I block my knitting?

A You can accomplish many things by blocking.

▶ Reduce curling, straighten edges, and make sewing up easier.

▶ Get rid of slight variations in length or width between two pieces that should match.

▶ Open out a fabric, such as lace, to show off the patterning.

▶ Smooth the surface of the knitting and make the stitches more even.

▶ Adjust the shape of the finished garment or reshape it after washing.

Q What equipment do I need to block my knitting?

A You'll need just a few things.

▶ **Something to block it on.** It can be as simple as a towel on a bed, table, or counter. Sweater drying racks have the advantage of supporting your knitting on a nylon screen, allowing for air circulation. For quicker drying, prop up your knitting in front of a fan or place it near a heating or air-conditioning vent.

▶ **Something to hold it in place,** like rustproof pins, if it needs to be stretched. Blocking wires are sold in sets that include stiff, straight, and bendable curved wires; a yardstick; and pins. They simplify the process of pinning out and stretching both knitted pieces and finished garments.

▶ **Something to wet it with.** You can wash your knitting gently in a basin, mist it with a spray bottle, steam it with a steamer or iron, or lay a damp towel on it to moisten it.

Q When should I block?

A Individual pieces may be blocked before sewing up, and whole garments may be blocked after they are completed. Use blocking to reshape after washing, or to open out lacy or ribbed fabrics.

....

Q How do I block my knitting?

A There are several different ways to block knitting.

▶ **Misting.** Pin out the garment (or pieces) to the correct dimensions and shape. You may use blocking wires or many pins to hold the edges. If you use blocking wires, run these through the edges of the garment or the individual pieces. The wires hold the edges even and can be

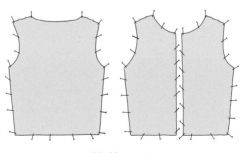

blocking a vest

secured with just a few pins. A blocking board marked in squares may make matching the correct measurements easier. Mist your knitting with water using a spray bottle; let it dry. If you don't have a spray bottle, wet a towel and lay it over the knitting to moisten it slightly.

▶ **Steaming.** Pin out the dry garment as for misting. Use a steam iron or steamer to spray the garment with steam. Do not actually touch the iron to the fabric, because the fibers may burn or melt. Acrylics and other synthetic fibers should not be blocked this way because too much heat can cause them to lose their resilience as well as make the surface shiny.

▶ **Wet blocking.** Soak the garment (or pieces) in water, or hand wash. Garments can become very heavy when saturated with water, so support the knitting from the bottom when you lift it from the water. Squeeze gently; never wring or twist. Roll it in a towel or spin it in your washing machine to remove excess water. Lay it out flat, pat or gently stretch it into the shape or dimensions you want, and let it dry. If you place it on top of a towel, there's usually enough friction for it to hold its shape as it dries, or you may prefer to pin it in place. If you need to pin a heavy garment out to specific dimensions, misting or steaming is preferable to wet blocking, because the garment is much easier to handle while dry.

SEE ALSO: *Wash and Wear, p. 344*

Q Does it matter what fiber the yarn is made of when you're deciding which blocking method to choose?

A Yes. Acrylic, polyester, and other synthetic fibers do not block well: They hold their shape only for a short time. Animal fibers such as wool and mohair block well and require only a little moisture, for example, from steaming or misting. Slippery, nonstretchy fibers such as linen, cotton, and silk respond better to more moisture, making them good candidates for wet blocking.

Q I've been told that I should never block ribbing. Is this true?

A This warning is against stretching the ribbed borders on a garment when you block it. For ribbed borders to remain elastic, they should dry in a relaxed position during blocking. On the other hand, there are times when blocked ribbing is appropriate. For example, if you have a scarf made in ribbing and you prefer it flat rather than scrunched up by the natural elasticity of the rib, then it's perfectly all right to stretch it while blocking. If you have a wide band of ribbing at the bottom of a sweater that hugs your hips and you want it to be looser, blocking to stretch the ribbing slightly will do the trick.

Sewing Up

Sewing the pieces of your sweater together can be daunting. Joining the shoulders, the side seams, and attaching the sleeves to the body each require different techniques. Once you learn these, you'll be able to seam flawlessly.

....

SHOULDERS

Q How do I sew together the shoulders of a sweater?

A Weave the two edges together. If you've ever done Kitchener Stitch, this will seem familiar, except that it is done along two bound-off edges. Using a yarn needle, weave the yarn between the two pieces of knitting to form a new row of knit stitches.

GET READY: Lay the pieces on a flat surface, right side up, with the edges to be joined next to each other.

HOW TO DO IT:

1. Find the place in the first row where a stitch comes together to form a point and insert your needle under those two strands.

2. On the opposite side of the seam, find the first stitch where the two strands come together to

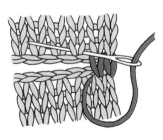

sewing shoulders together

form a point at the edge of the fabric and insert the needle under these two strands.

3. Go back to the first side, and insert the needle under the V of the next stitch. **Hint:** Go back into the same spot you last came out of in Step 1. Alternate from side to side until the seam is finished.

. . . .

Q Is there a way to join shoulders without sewing?

A Yes. The Three-Needle Bind Off is a great way to join shoulders, if you have not yet bound them off.

SEE ALSO: *Three-Needle Bind Off, p. 101; and Short-Row Shaping, p. 302*

SIDE SEAMS

Q How do I sew together the sides of a sweater?

A To join the sides of two Stockinette Stitch pieces, use Mattress Stitch. Lay the two pieces side by side on a flat surface. Always work with the right side of the fabric facing you. Work a full stitch in from

working mattress stitch under one strand for side seam

the edge. To make a firm, strong seam, sew under just one strand on each side with every stitch, working from bottom to top. To make a less bulky seam, sew under two strands on each side with every stitch. Work alternately on one side of the seam and then the other. As you sew, pull the yarn tight enough to draw the two edges together, but loose enough that the seam still stretches a little.

mattress stitch under two strands

<hr />

Q How do I sew together Garter Stitch?

A It's actually easier to sew up Garter Stitch pieces than Stockinette ones. Simply work Mattress Stitch from side to side as described previously, sewing through the bumps at

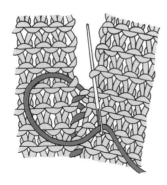

sewing garter stitch pieces together

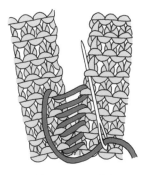

the edge. For a slightly neater and more substantial seam, sew through the top of a stitch just in from the edge. The tops of the stitches are curved, like little frowns. Pull the yarn tight enough that the sewn lengths look about the same as the knit stitches on either side.

working mattress stitch to assemble garter stitch

Q **The seams in my ribbed borders never look neat. How can I fix them?**

A When you are working in K1P1 ribbing, always use an odd number of stitches and make sure that each edge ends with a knit stitch when you look at the right side of the

sewing a k1p1 ribbing seam

fabric. When you sew up, work just one-half stitch from the edge. This will look like one knit stitch between two purl stitches at the seam when it is complete. When you are working in K2P2 ribbing, use a multiple of four stitches plus two more, and

314

make sure that you have two knit stitches at each edge. Work a full stitch in from the edge in K2P2 ribbing. This should look like two knit stitches, with two purl stitches on either side when the seam is completed.

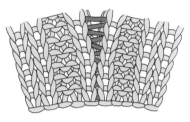

sewing a K2P2 ribbing seam

SLEEVES

Q How do I sew the sleeve seam?

A Join it with Mattress Stitch just as you would the two sides of the sweater.

Q How do I sew in the sleeves of a sweater?

A For a drop-shoulder sweater, where the sleeves have no shaping at the top, use a combination of Mattress Stitch along the armhole edge (sewing under a strand between two stitches) and weaving at the top of the sleeve (sewing under the V of a stitch) to attach the sleeve to the body. Because knit stitches are wider than they are tall, you will sometimes need to sew under two strands along the body to make the edges come out even.

For a shaped sleeve cap, lay the pieces on a flat surface, right-side up. Match the edges of the sleeve with the edges of the armhole and use safety pins to hold in place. Match the center of the sleeve cap with the shoulder seam and secure it with safety pins. Smooth the sleeve cap into the armhole and use safety pins to hold it in several places while sewing up. At the underarm, where you are joining stitches to stitches, use weaving as described for joining shoulders. Along the shaped sides of the sleeve cap, you'll be joining one row to another like the side seam of a sweater, so change to Mattress Stitch for this section. At the top of the sleeve cap, you'll be joining stitches to rows, so use the method described in the previous paragraph and illustrated below.

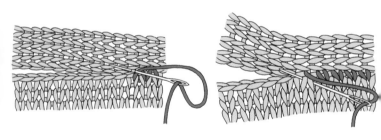

attaching sleeves to body

SEE ALSO: *Page 315 for weaving where the sleeve joins the underarm; and p. 312 for Mattress Stitch*

Q **Is there a way to join the sleeve to the body without sewing?**

A Yes. Use the Three-Needle Bind Off. You must have live stitches across the sleeve cap and along the armhole edge. If your sleeve cap isn't shaped, don't bind it off before joining it to the body. If the sleeve cap has been shaped, pick up stitches all along the edge. If it's a drop-shoulder sweater with no defined armhole, mark the beginning and end of the armhole area with safety pins. Pick up exactly the same number of stitches along the armhole edge as there are along the sleeve cap. Now use the Three-Needle Bind Off to join the two pieces. This is not an invisible join, so you may want to make it a decorative element by binding off on the right side of the fabric or by using contrasting yarn.

SEE ALSO: *Three-Needle Bind Off, p. 101*

Q **I knit a sweater sideways, in one piece from cuff-to-cuff. How do I sew together the sleeve and side seams?**

A The sleeves were knit in the same direction they normally are. Sew as usual using Mattress Stitch. The body was knit sideways, so the side seams are actually the top or bottom of the pieces. Join these by weaving, just as for shoulder seams.

Solving Problems

Q How do I get rid of the gap at the bottom of a seam?

A When you start the seam, sew a figure eight across the beginning of a sleeve or body seam, to even it off.

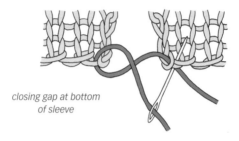

closing gap at bottom of sleeve

....

Q I sewed up the seam, but the ends didn't come out even. Why did this happen and how do I fix it?

A No matter how hard you try to make pieces identical, sometimes you end up with a few more rows in one piece than in the other. Even when pieces are identical, it can be very difficult to sew consistently up both sides of the seam. Control this problem before you begin to sew by fastening together the top and bottom edges using safety pins placed horizontally between the two pieces. Also place safety pins at the center and every few inches along the seam. As you approach each safety pin, check to make sure that it's still horizontal. If not, then work under two strands on the side that's too long and under only one strand on the side that's too short to ease in the extra fabric.

Begin at the Bottom

Sew from the cast-on edge up toward the underarm on both the sleeve seam and the side seam. Any unevenness is then hidden at the underarm.

Q I can't sew with the yarn I used for the knitting. What do I do?

A It can be very difficult to sew with heavily textured yarns (bouclé, eyelash, chenille, and other novelty yarns), yarns that are loosely spun, or yarns with plies that stretch at different rates. Luckily, you have lots of options.

▶ **Pick up stitches** along each piece and then use the Three-Needle Bind Off to join them.

▶ **Crochet the two pieces together.** Begin with a slip knot on your crochet hook and work with the two pieces of knitting placed right sides together. Insert the crochet hook through both layers, and hook up a new loop through both layers of fabric and through the loop on the crochet hook. You may need to experiment to get the proper tension along the seam, which will be rather bulky.

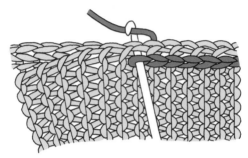

crocheting two pieces together

▶ **Substitute a smooth yarn** in a matching color for the yarn you used in your project. It's best to choose a yarn with similar fiber content. If you can't find a knitting yarn that works, try cotton embroidery floss or wool tapestry yarn, both of which come in a wide variety of colors. Be careful to stretch the seam and work loosely enough so that the cotton floss doesn't break when the sweater is stretched. (For more on crocheting, check Eckman's *The Crochet Answer Book*; see Resources, p. 363.)

Kitchener Stitch

Q **What is Kitchener Stitch and how do I do it?**

A Kitchener Stitch (or grafting) is a method of sewing two pieces of knitting together seamlessly. It is always done on live stitches.

KITCHENER STITCH IN STOCKINETTE

GET READY: Hold the two pieces of knitting with wrong-sides together and the needles at the top. If you are right-handed, point the needles to the right; if you are left-handed, reverse them. Use a yarn needle threaded with matching yarn. If the working yarn is hanging at the edge, use a length of it for this purpose.

HOW TO DO IT:

1. Put the needle into the first stitch on the front needle as if to knit and slip it off the knitting needle.

2. Put the needle into the second stitch on the front needle as if to purl and leave it on the knitting needle. Pull up the slack in the yarn.

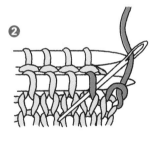

3. Put the needle into the first stitch on the back needle, as if to purl, and slip the stitch off the needle.

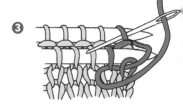

4. Put the needle into the second stitch on the back needle as if to knit. Leave it on the knitting needle and pull up the slack in the yarn.

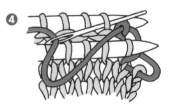

Repeat steps 1 through 4 across the needles, always working with the yarn under the tips of the knitting needles, so that you don't confuse the sewing yarn with the knitted stitches.

Now that you know how to do it, here's the short version. Memorize this and repeat it as you work, so you won't get mixed up:

> **Front:** Knit off, purl on.
> **Back:** Purl off, knit on.

KITCHENER STITCH IN GARTER STITCH

GET READY: Hold the two pieces of knitting together with the needles at the top. If you are right-handed, point the needles to the right; if you are left-handed, reverse them. To be sure that you are joining the pieces correctly (so that there aren't two purl rows or two knit rows together), the tail of yarn from the last row should be hanging down from the same edge of both pieces. Use a yarn needle threaded with matching yarn. If possible, use the yarn attached to one of the pieces.

HOW TO DO IT:

1. Put the needle into the first stitch on the front needle as if to knit and slip it off the knitting needle.

2. Put the needle into the second stitch on the front needle as if to purl and leave it on the knitting needle. Pull up the slack in the yarn.

3. Repeat Steps 1 and 2 on the back needle. Repeat these 3 steps, alternating the front and back, across the needles. In this case the short version is the same on both front and back needles: Knit off, purl on.

Borders

Borders around the neckline and armholes support the garment and prevent the edges from curling. They're also a great opportunity to embellish, either by using a knock-out yarn or a decorative pattern stitch.

....

PICKING UP STITCHES

Q I'm never sure where to insert my needle when picking up stitches for a neckline or armhole border. What's the right method?

A Work one full stitch in from the edge. If you are working in anything but Stockinette Stitch, this will be easier if you keep one or two edge stitches in Stockinette and work any increases, decreases, and pattern stitches farther in, so they don't interfere with picking up. Insert the tip of your needle through the fabric to the back, one stitch in from the edge.

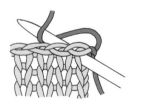 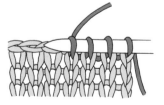

picking up stitches along a bound-off edge

*picking up stitches
along the side*

Remember that a stitch is two strands wide, so you'll always be working two strands in from the edge. Wrap the yarn around the needle and knit the stitch out to the front. If you are picking up along a bound-off edge, be sure to insert the needle into a stitch, not immediately below the bind off. Sock heels are an exception. To prevent an uncomfortable ridge along the edge of the heel flap, pick up just half a stitch from the edge.

....

Q My borders always seem to be too loose or too tight. How can I pick up the right number of stitches on the first try?

A Generally, in Stockinette you should pick up three stitches for every four rows, or five stitches for every seven rows along the side of the knitting. To be sure of this ratio, compare your rows per inch to your stitches per inch. Three stitches are likely to measure about the same as four rows. Across the top of the knitting, you can usually pick up one stitch for each stitch. Bottom bands, wristbands, and

neck bands are normally worked on 10 percent fewer stitches
to keep them from stretching out of shape. In inelastic fibers,
such as cotton, linen, silk, or mohair, the bands may be worked
on 15 percent or 20 percent fewer stitches, as long as this
doesn't make them so tight they are uncomfortable or don't
fit over your head.

If you have trouble picking up the right number of stitches,
or if you see noticeable holes or unevenness along the picked-
up edge, you can do the following. Pick up a stitch in every
row along a side edge and in every stitch along a top edge, then
decrease on the first row (evenly spaced across the length of
the border) to the number of stitches you really need. Here are
a few more tips.

▶ **Too tight?** If your borders are consistently too tight,
add more stitches to them, use a needle that is one size
larger, or simply bind off more loosely.

▶ **Too loose?** If your borders are consistently too loose,
pick up fewer stitches, use smaller needles, or bind off
more tightly.

▶ **Test your borders** on your swatch before putting
them on your garment. Follow the instructions for
making a shaped swatch to get a curved edge to work
with. Pick up along this edge as you would for your
border, then work a border the same width and in the
same pattern stitch, on the same size needles, as you
plan to use on your garment. If it flares, you need fewer

stitches. If it pulls in, you need more stitches. You can also test a straight border along one of the straight sides of the swatch.

SEE ALSO: *Making a Shaped Swatch, p. 277*

 When I pick up stitches around a neckline, sometimes there are gaps. How do I avoid these?

 Working neatly around corners and curves always presents a challenge in knitting. Here are some suggestions that may help.

▶ **Stay clear of edges.** Sometimes these gaps are caused by working decreases or increases too close to the edge of the fabric. Working shaping at the very edge can cause some stitches to be too tight, so always work your shaping one or two stitches in from the edge.

▶ **Avoid stretching.** If you are knitting up your stitches just a half stitch (one thread) in from the edge, this will cause the edge stitches to stretch toward the border and look very loose. Picking up a whole stitch from the edge will reduce stretching.

▶ **Be consistent.** As you work up or down along the side of a neck or armhole, be sure to work consistently between the two stitches closest to the edge.

▶ **Watch the corners.** To avoid a gap at a corner, such as at the base of a neck opening, begin knitting into the stitches one stitch before the bind off starts, and continue knitting into the stitches one stitch beyond where the bind off ends. On the bound-off edge itself, knit up one stitch in each stitch across.

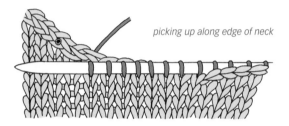

picking up along edge of neck

▶ **Decrease carefully.** If you end up with too many stitches, decrease on the first row of your border, spacing the decreases evenly along the entire length. If you need only a few decreases, place them at the neckline corners where the center bind off begins and ends to prevent these curved areas from flaring.

SEE ALSO: *Page 295 for adjusting neck width*

BUTTON BANDS

Q How do I space buttonholes evenly?

A Work the matching button band first, so you know how many stitches or rows there will be, and then chart it out. You can also mark the spots for buttonholes on the button band using safety pins, and then count the stitches in between. When positioning the buttonholes, you may not be able to get the same number of stitches between every buttonhole, so divide the extra stitches between the ends. Extra stitches are best placed at the bottom, because they are less noticeable than at the top. Even if the buttonholes are not spaced perfectly, you can sew the buttons in exactly

---

An Easy Way to Measure Buttonhole Spacing

Use a piece of elastic ½" or ⅝" (1 or 1.5 cm) wide as a tool. A 15" (38 cm) piece should be long enough for most sweater fronts. Mark the elastic with a pen at regular intervals, perhaps every 2" (5 cm). When it's time to measure the sweater front, pin the top of the elastic where you want the top buttonhole to be. Count down one mark for each button, and then stretch the last mark to where you want the bottom button to be. The marks in between will stretch in perfect proportion. Place safety pins at the points along the front where the marks fall when the elastic is stretched.

the right places. When the garment is buttoned, any slight variations are unnoticeable. It's better to have more buttons, rather than fewer, to prevent gapping.

....

Q **How can I calculate buttonhole placement exactly?**

A You must know the number of stitches in your band, the stitches per buttonhole, and the number of buttons. Follow the instructions below.

INSTRUCTIONS	EXAMPLE
Calculate the number of stitches used for the buttonholes.	3 stitches x 6 buttons = 18 stitches
Deduct this from the total stitches for the button band.	90 stitches – 18 buttonhole stitches = 72 stitches
Deduct some space above the top buttonhole and below the bottom one. Let's say 4 stitches at each end, for a total of 8 stitches.	72 stitches – 8 = 64 stitches
Divide the remaining stitches to fill the spaces between buttonholes. Remember that when there are 6 buttonholes there are only 5 spaces between them.	64 stitches / 5 spaces = 12.8 stitches

The resulting 12.8 stitches is impossible to work, so make adjustments to come up with a workable plan. If you round up to 13 stitches, then the 5 spaces will take up a total of 5 x 13 = 65 stitches, which is only 1 more than you wanted. Steal this extra stitch from either the top or the bottom of the button band. Thus, your calculation is:

SECTION OF BUTTONHOLE	# OF STITCHES
Above top buttonhole	3
Buttonholes: 6 @ 3 stitches each	18
Spaces between: 5 @ 13 stitches each	65
Below bottom buttonhole	4
Total	90

▶ Check for errors in your buttonhole plan this way to avoid unpleasant surprises during knitting.

Q How do I calculate buttonhole placement when I'm working the button band from top to bottom?

A You can follow the same procedure to place the buttonholes, substituting rows for stitches. You'll need to know the number of rows for the length of the band, the number of buttonholes, and how many rows to allow for each buttonhole.

BUTTONHOLES

Q **How do I decide which buttonhole to make?**

A There are many different kinds of buttonholes to choose from. Make your selection based on how they look and whether they fit your button. Test your buttonholes by adding a button band to your swatch. This gives you the opportunity to try several different buttonholes and to make them different sizes. Make sure the hole is barely big enough for the button to pass through. Simple eyelets work anywhere, horizontal buttonholes fit best into horizontal patterns such as Garter Stitch, and vertical buttonholes are least noticeable in ribbing.

· ·

Q **Just how do I make the buttonhole itself?**

A The most basic buttonhole is a simple eyelet. This is the smallest type you can make, and it is especially good for

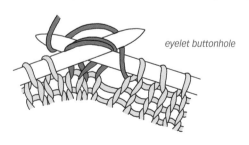

eyelet buttonhole

bulky yarns or for tiny buttons on baby clothes. Make a yarn over where you want the buttonhole, then knit (or purl) the next two stitches together. You may find it looks better in your pattern stitch to reverse the two, decreasing first and then working the yarn over.

SEE ALSO: *The Yarn Over, p. 81; and Decreases, p. 264*

Q Is there a good buttonhole for Garter Stitch?

A Horizontal buttonholes are especially good in Garter Stitch, where they can be hidden in the valley between two ridges. The Tight One-Row Buttonhole explained on the following page is a little more complicated than the Loose Three-Row Buttonhole, because the yarn is woven in and out between the stitches to prevent the buttonhole from stretching. Choose between them based on which fits your button best.

Mark Before You Knit!

Before you begin to work the buttonholes, decide exactly how many stitches you need for each buttonhole and how far apart they will be. Place markers on your needle or in your knitting before you make the buttonholes, to prevent confusion as you work across.

Q How do I make a Tight One-Row Buttonhole?

A These instructions are for a three-stitch buttonhole, but you can use any number of stitches. An odd number works best. Note that "yarn forward" and "yarn back" mean that you move the yarn between the two needle points, either to the front or to the back. These are not yarn overs; they do not add any stitches. The instruction to "bind off 1" means to pass the second stitch on the right needle over the first one. No additional stitches are knit in order to bind off.

TIGHT ONE-ROW BUTTONHOLE

GET READY: Work across to the point where you want the hole.

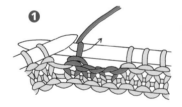

HOW TO DO IT:

1. Yarn forward, slip 1, yarn back, slip 1, bind off 1, yarn forward, slip 1, yarn back, bind off 1, slip 1, bind off 1. Slip the last stitch back to the left needle.

last cast-on stitch

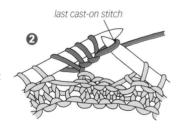

2. Use the cable cast on to cast on 4 stitches. Slip the last cast-on stitch to the right needle.

3. Bind off 1. Yarn forward, slip 1, yarn back, slip 1, yarn forward, slip 1, yarn back. The buttonhole is complete. Continue across the row.

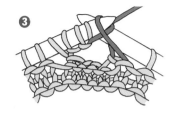

SEE ALSO: *Cable Cast On, p. 15; and The Slipped Stitch, p. 75*

Q How do I make a Loose Three-Row Buttonhole?

A This buttonhole can be done on any number of stitches.

LOOSE THREE-ROW BUTTONHOLE

GET READY: Work to the point where you want the buttonhole.

HOW TO DO IT:

1. Bind off the desired number of stitches. Continue to the end of the row.

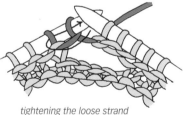

tightening the loose strand

2. When you come to the gap created by the bound-off stitches on the next row, cast on the same number using the Loop Cast On. Continue to end of row.

Elizabeth Zimmermann gives us tips for making this buttonhole neater. On the second and third row, if there is a long strand after the last bound-off or cast-on stitch, pick up the strand, twist it and put it on your left needle. Work it together with the next stitch to tighten it. On the third row, knit into the cast-on stitches so that they twist. (For more information, check Zimmermann's *Knitting Without Tears*; see Resources, p. 363.)

SEE ALSO: *Loop Cast On, p. 12*

Q Is there a good buttonhole to use in ribbing?

A Vertical buttonholes are unobtrusive in ribbing. They disappear nicely into a purl rib.

BUTTONHOLE FOR K1P1 RIBBING

ROW 1. On the wrong side, work across in ribbing, but knit into the front and back of each stitch where you want a buttonhole.

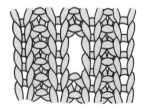

ROW 2. On the right side, work across in pattern until 1 stitch remains before each increased stitch, SSK, yarn over twice, K2tog.

buttonhole for k1p1 ribbing

ROW 3. Work across in pattern on the wrong side. When 1 stitch remains before each double yarn over, P2tog, yarn over, SSP.

ROW 4. Work across in pattern on the right side, purling into each buttonhole under both strands of yarn.

BUTTONHOLE FOR K2P2 RIBBING

ROW 1. On the right side, work in pattern until 1 knit stitch remains before the 2 purl stitches where each buttonhole will be placed, SSK, yarn over twice, K2tog.

ROW 2. On the wrong side, work in pattern until 1 stitch remains before each double yarn over, P2tog, yarn over twice, SSP.

ROW 3. On the right side, work across in pattern. K1, P1 into each double yarn over, working under both strands.

To make a smaller buttonhole, skip Row 2 and work Row 3 on the wrong side instead.

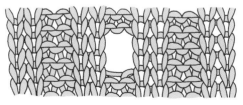

buttonhole for k2p2 ribbing

SEE ALSO: *The Yarn Over, p. 81; and Decreases, p. 264.*

Q My buttonhole is too loose. Can I tighten it?

A Yes. Take matching yarn and sew across one or both ends to make the buttonhole shorter, weaving the yarn in and out along both sides to prevent stretching. You can also work buttonhole stitch around the buttonhole, using yarn or sewing thread.

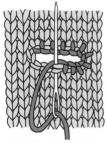

tightening buttonhole

Q I'm missing a buttonhole. Is there any way to add one after the knitting is done?

A Yes. Once again Elizabeth Zimmermann has provided us with a solution. In fact, you can do all your buttonholes this way if you prefer to place them after the bands are completed. Snip one stitch at the center of the buttonhole. Unravel this just a stitch or two to each side (three stitches usually make a reasonable width). Use the Sewn Bind Off to bind off the bottom, going one stitch beyond the opening, then turn and bind off the top the same way, joining to the beginning of your bind off. Weave in all the ends on the back. (For more on "Afterthoughts" check Zimmermann's *Knitting Without Tears*; see Resources, p. 363.)

SEE ALSO: *Sewn Bind Off, p. 99*

BUTTONS

Q How do I sew on the buttons?

A Sew on the buttons using either sewing thread or yarn. With yarn, the holes in the button must be large enough for a tapestry needle and the yarn to pass through easily. Line up the button band with the buttonhole band and sew the buttons opposite the buttonholes. Use one long piece of yarn, weaving it in along the back of the button band between buttons to avoid creating two additional tails for each button. With fragile buttons, or ones that cannot be washed or dry-cleaned, you may want to use safety pins designed for attaching buttons (available at sewing stores) rather than sewing them on. They have a bend at the center to hold the button in position.

Infant Insight

If you don't know whether it's a boy or a girl, make button-holes on both bands and sew the buttons on the correct side when the baby is born. Buttons can be repositioned later for subsequent siblings of the opposite sex.

At Loose Ends

Q How do I deal with all these ends?

A The ends should be woven in on the wrong side of the fabric. If the ends are at a seam line or the edge of a border, weave them through the seam stitches on the inside of the garment. If they are in the middle of a row, cross the two ends and use a yarn needle to zigzag loosely through a row of the purl bumps on the back of the fabric, in the same direction the yarn was originally traveling along the row. Stretch the knitting a bit, so you can be sure that the ends will stay buried as the fabric stretches, then snip each end close to the knitting. Wool, mohair, and other animal fibers present no problems if handled this way. Slippery fibers like silk or cotton, however, need to be locked in place by reversing direction and splitting the original yarn each time you cross it. You may find it easier to do this with a sharp, pointed needle rather than a yarn needle.

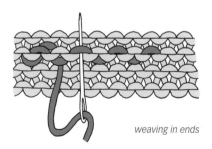

weaving in ends

If you're working with lots of colors, consider letting the ends serve as a decorative embellishment, such as braids on the outside of the garment. You can also add tassels or beads, if you like.

Q **What do I do when I don't want the ends to show on lace or a reversible scarf?**

A Use Duplicate Stitch to weave the ends, following the path of a single strand of yarn. If there will be fringe, incorporate any tails at the edge into the fringe. Avoid creating ends while you knit by splicing them together as you go.

SEE ALSO: *Duplicate Stitch, p. 360; and p. 146 for splicing*

Q **The ends are too short to thread through a needle and sew in. What do I do?**

A It's always a good idea to leave ends 4"–6" (10–15 cm) long because they're much easier to work with. But if you didn't, you can use a crochet hook instead of a needle to draw the tails through the stitches on the back of the knitting. You can also insert the yarn needle through the stitches where you want to weave in, then thread the short yarn end through the eye and pull the needle through.

Solving Problems during Finishing

Q **The two halves of my sweater don't match, and my sleeve and my armhole don't seem to be the same size. What do I do?**

A If you're pretty sure you knit the correct number of rows for both sides of your sweater, then the problems may be caused by variations in tension, making one piece tighter than the other, or because one bound-off edge is tighter than another. Try blocking each piece to the correct dimensions, stretching one and minimizing the other. If this doesn't work, figure out which piece is not the correct size by measuring it and comparing it with the pattern specifications. You may need to unravel and reknit it, or redo the bind off.

· ·

Q **I just finished sewing up my sweater and I found a dropped stitch in it. Do I have to take it all apart?**

A No. Use a crochet hook to reknit the rows that are loose above the stitch, if there are any. Pull the unsecured stitch through to the inside of the garment. Thread a yarn needle with matching yarn and pull it through the stitch, then weave in and trim off both ends. This will keep the stitch from unraveling again.

SEE ALSO: *Fixing Mistakes, p. 65*

Q I just finished sewing up my sweater and I found a hole in it. Do I have to take it all apart?

A First, determine whether it's caused by an inadvertent yarn over or if there's a dropped stitch involved (see previous question). To close a yarn over, use a piece of matching yarn, threaded in a yarn needle, to encircle the hole on the inside of the garment and gently pull it closed. Weave in and trim both the ends.

SEE ALSO: *At Loose Ends, p. 340*

Q When I knit mittens, I always have little holes at the base of the thumb after I pick up the thumb stitches. Any suggestions?

A Pick up a few extra stitches at both ends of the thumb opening and decrease to get rid of them on the first row or two. If any small holes remain, close them up when weaving in the ends on the inside.

Wash and Wear

Q **Now that my garment is done, how do I care for it?**

A Check the yarn label for washing instructions. If you don't have the label, test the yarn to see if the color runs. If it does, wash with cold water; otherwise, use warm water. Fill a basin with water, add soap or mild detergent and stir with your hands. Avoid creating a lot of suds, which can be difficult to rinse out. Press the garment into the water and gently squeeze a few times. If it's made of wool or other animal hair, too much handling or agitation may cause it to felt. If the garment is multicolor and any of the colors run, remove it immediately. Otherwise, let the garment soak for a few minutes.

When you lift the garment out of the water, it will be heavy. Support it from underneath to prevent stretching. Squeeze out the excess water and set the garment aside. Empty out the soapy water and refill the basin with clean water of the same temperature, to avoid felting. Put the garment back in and squeeze a few times. Repeat with clean water until all soap has been removed. Squeeze the water out of the garment gently. Roll it in a towel to remove more moisture. Lay the garment out flat to dry, pulling or patting it gently into the desired shape. Using a sweater drying rack of nylon mesh helps your garment dry more quickly. If you are impatient, place the rack near a fan or a heating or air-conditioning vent.

SEE ALSO: *Page 154 for how to tell if the color will run; and Blocking, p. 306*

Don't Felt It!

Natural animal hair fibers can felt (shrink in size and become densely matted) very easily. When washing wool, mohair, alpaca, angora, or other animal fibers, follow these rules to avoid felting.

▶ Keep water temperature consistent while washing and rinsing.

▶ Do not run water directly onto garments.

▶ Avoid agitation; just squeeze items gently a few times.

▶ Do not scrub or wring.

Q **Can I wash hand knits in the washing machine?**

A Some wool yarns are "superwash" and don't felt. Check the label for washing instructions: Your sweater may be machine washable and dryable. If you have a very bulky sweater or a lot of hand-knit garments to wash at once, you can use your top-loading washing machine to speed the process. Sort the garments by color first, in case any of the colors run. Fill the washer with cold water if you suspect the hand knits may run, or lukewarm if you think they're colorfast. Put in enough water to cover the garments. Add some soap or mild detergent and agitate a little, but avoid creating lots of suds, which are difficult to rinse out. Now press the garments gently down into the water. By hand, squeeze the water through them. Leave them to soak for a few minutes. Use the spin cycle to spin out the water. Be especially careful if your washer sprays rinse water into the tub during the spin cycle, because this may cause felting. Stand by your washer prepared to stop it immediately if this spray function begins. Remove the garments and fill the machine again with the same temperature water for rinsing. Press the garments into the rinse water and squeeze water through them. Spin out the water. Repeat the rinse process until no soap or detergent remains. Lay the garments flat to dry, shaping them properly.

CHAPTER 13

Embellishments

There are numerous flourishes you can add to your knitting: beads, cords, braids and tassels are just a few. Don't assume that these additions are superfluous. Embellishments can be used to secure loose ends of yarn and to cover mistakes. Fringes neaten up uneven edges and can be used to join two layers of a scarf together. The weight of a tassel can effectively hold the flap of a purse closed or keep the point of a shawl stretched.

Beads

Q Can I add beads to my knitting?

A Yes. You can string them, and then position them on the surface of the fabric as you knit; you can string each one onto the stitch as you knit it; or you can sew the beads on later. Here's how to accomplish each method.

PRESTRINGING BEADS

This is a good choice if you know beforehand exactly how many beads you will need, and if it's easy to string the beads on your yarn. Use a smooth, tightly spun yarn. If the yarn is textured, fragile, or loosely spun, the simple act of stringing may damage it. Be sure to choose beads with holes large enough for the yarn to fit through comfortably. You may need to use a small round file to smooth the inside of the beads.

HOW TO DO IT:

1. String all your beads onto one ball of your yarn, but don't use this ball until you get to the point where you actually need the beads.

2. At the beginning of the first beaded row, switch to the yarn with the beads on it. Knit to the point where you want a bead. Bring the yarn forward and slip the bead along the yarn close to your knitting.

3. Slip the next stitch purlwise, bring the yarn to the back of the fabric, and knit the next stitch. This places the bead on a strand of yarn in front of the fabric, with the yarn going through it horizontally.

As you knit, you'll probably need to slide all the unused beads down the yarn to keep them out of your way. When you've finished a beaded area and are ready to knit a section with no beads, change back to one of the balls of yarn without beads. (For more on bead knitting, check Chin's *Knit and Crochet with Beads*; see Resources, p. 363.)

SEE ALSO: *The Slipped Stitch, p. 75*

Beading Your Knits

Regardless of the method you use to attach the beads to your knitting, beware of placing them too densely. Beads can make the fabric very heavy and cause most knitted fabrics to stretch. You may want to place them only in borders or scatter them lightly across the fabric. In most cases, place the beads no closer than every other stitch and every other row. A good effect can be achieved, however, by placing them farther apart.

STRINGING BEADS AS YOU KNIT

This technique works best if you aren't sure where you want the beads or how many you'll need, and if the hole of the bead is large enough to accept a double strand of your yarn.

HOW TO DO IT:

1. Work to the point where you want to add a bead. Using a tiny crochet hook, put the bead on the hook, hook the first stitch on the left needle, pull it through the bead, and return the beaded stitch to the left needle.

2. Knit or purl this stitch. Purling this stitch on the previous row and on the current row frames the bead with the characteristic bump created by the purl stitch and prevents it from slipping around.

SEWING THE BEADS ON LATER

If your beads have holes too small to be strung easily on your yarn, simply sew them on after the knitting is done using a fine matching yarn or beading thread. To make precise placement easier in plain Stockinette Stitch, purl the stitches where you'll later sew on a bead.

Making a Stringing Tool

Beading suppliers carry bead spinners (which greatly speed the process of stringing small beads) and giant needle threaders (also available from fishing tackle suppliers), but here's how you can make your own.

▶ **Fishing line.** Fold an 8"–12" (20–30 cm) piece of monofilament fishing line in half. Push the two ends through as many beads as will fit comfortably. Put the end of the yarn through the loop at the opposite end of the fishing line and slide the beads onto the yarn.

▶ **Dental floss threader.** Use this threader, available from your local drugstore, in the same way as the folded fishing line.

▶ **Sewing needle and thread.** Thread the needle and knot the doubled thread so it won't pull out. Push the needle through as many beads as fit comfortably on it. Put the yarn through the loop formed by the thread where it meets the eye and slip the beads onto the yarn.

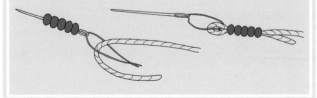

Bobbles

Q My bobbles are flat, lopsided, and ugly. Is there a better way to make a bobble?

A The best one I have found is on a child's hat in Gladys Thompson's *Patterns for Guernseys, Jerseys & Arans* (see Resources, p. 363. It holds its shape and is nicely symmetrical. Note that you need to start working this bobble one stitch earlier than you might think.

GLADYS THOMPSON'S BOBBLE

HOW TO DO IT:

1. Knit into the front, back, front, back, front of the stitch where you want the bobble (making 5 stitches in 1).

2. K1, turn, P5.

3. Turn, K5.

4. Turn, P5, then slip, one at a time, the second, third, fourth and fifth stitches on the right needle over the first stitch and off the needle (decreasing the 5 stitches back down to 1).

5. Turn once more and knit into the back of the bobble stitch. Continue across the row.

Cords

Q How can I make cords for my knitting?

A If you need a drawstring for a bag, ties for a hat, or a cord for a purse, you have lots of choices.

▶ **Twisted cord.** Figure out how long you want your cord to be. Add about one-third to this measurement, then cut a piece of yarn four times this long. Fold the yarn in half and make a knot at each end. Have a friend hold the folded end or hook the end over a doorknob. Twist until the yarn is very tightly twisted, keeping it stretched taut at all times. Pinch the yarn at the center, then fold it in half, keeping it stretched out as you do so. (For long cords, you'll need help doing this.) Slowly release a few inches at a time starting from the folded end, allowing the cord to twist back on itself, resulting in a sturdy four-strand cord.

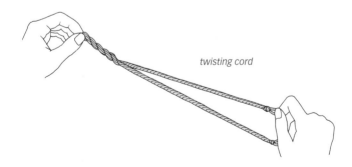

twisting cord

▶ **Braided cord.** Figure out how long you want the cord to be, then add about half to that measurement. You'll need at least three strands this length, but the yarn can be doubled or tripled for a thicker cord. Make an overhand knot at one end and secure the knot on a hook, pin it to a board, or clip it to a clipboard. Work a three-strand braid by alternately bringing the right strand over the middle, then the left strand over the middle, and so on. Knot the other end together when the braid is complete.

▶ **I-Cord.** Using two double-pointed needles, cast on three or four stitches. *Knit across. Slide the stitches back to other end of the needle without turning. Pull the yarn firmly across the back. Repeat from * until the cord measures the desired length. This cord is identical to that produced by knitting nancies or knitting spools. Working it on double-pointed needles is substantially faster. Elizabeth Zimmermann dubbed this knitted cord "Idiot's Delight," which has been shortened by popular use to "I-Cord." You can purchase an I-Cord knitter that rapidly produces knitted cord at the turn of a crank.

▶ **Cast-on/bind-off cord.** Cast on enough stitches for the length of your cord, then bind off immediately on the next row. Be careful of your tension when binding off or your cord will spiral.

▶ **Finger cord.** For this cord, use two balls of yarn in two different colors.

1. Make a slip knot at the end of one yarn and place the loop over one index finger. Hold the second yarn together with the first one in the same hand. Stick your other index finger through the loop and pull through a new loop of the second color.

2. Drop the first color off the index finger, switch the ends of the yarn to the other hand, and pull on the working end of the first color to tighten the loop.

Continue to draw a loop of the contrasting color yarn through the loop on your finger and tighten the old yarn until the cord is long enough. Cut both strands of yarn, then pull one end through the final loop of the other color to fasten off.

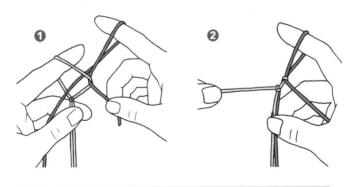

Pompoms, Tassels, and Fringe

Q **How do I make a pompom?**

A You can purchase a pompom-making tool or you can make one out of a piece of cardboard. Of the many ways to make pompoms, I find this method the easiest.

HOW TO DO IT:

1. Cut a square of stiff cardboard a little larger than the diameter of the pompom you want to make.

2. Cut a slit down the center of the cardboard, stopping just past the center point.

3. Cut a 12" (30 cm) length of yarn and insert it into the slit so both ends hang down equally.

4. Wrap additional yarn around the cardboard, changing colors if desired. Make about 100 wraps for a 2½" (6.5 cm) pompom. Use more wraps for a larger one, fewer for a smaller one. Cut the yarn.

5. Tie the piece of yarn hanging in the slit tightly around the wrapped yarn.

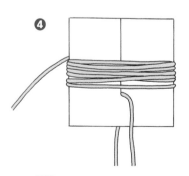

6

6. Cut the wrapped yarn along both edges of the cardboard.

7. Remove the cardboard, shake out the pompom, and trim any uneven ends.

Note: *If you have a fork that is wide enough, you can use it in place of the cardboard. Tie the pompom between the center-two tines.*

Q How do I make a tassel?

A Tassels are even easier to make than pompoms.

HOW TO DO IT:

1. Cut a stiff piece of cardboard into a rectangle a little longer than you want the tassel and about 4" (10 cm) wide. Wrap the yarn lengthwise around the cardboard about 50 times. Cut the end of the yarn even with the edge of the cardboard.

2. Cut a piece of yarn 24" (60 cm) long. Fold this piece of yarn in half, insert it between the cardboard and the wrapped yarn,

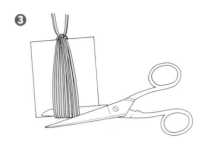

and slide it up to one edge of the cardboard. With half of the yarn extending on either side, tie the two ends tightly around the wrapped yarn.

3. With a pair of sharp scissors, cut through the wrapped yarn at the end opposite the tie.

4. Cut a 12" (30 cm) length of yarn. Wrap it tightly around the tassel two or three times, about 1" (2.5 cm) from the top. Tie it securely. Using a yarn needle, pull the ends of this tie through to the inside of the tassel so that they hang down inside. Shake out the tassel and trim off any uneven ends.

Note: You can use any stiff flat object to make a tassel. A CD case works well for a 5- or 6-inch (13–15 cm) tassel.

Q How do I add fringe?

A Cut lengths of yarn twice the desired length of the fringe. To make cutting the lengths of fringe easier, wrap yarn around a book or piece of cardboard as wide as the desired fringe, then cut along one side. Fold the lengths of yarn in half, draw the folded ends through the edge of the fabric using your fingers or a crochet hook, then pull the cut ends through the loop at the fold. If you wish, add beads or knot the fringes together after they are attached.

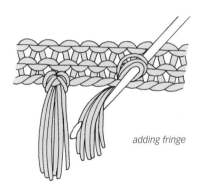

adding fringe

Duplicate Stitch

Q What is Duplicate Stitch and how do I do it?

A Duplicate Stitch, also called Swiss Darning, is embroidery where yarn is sewn into the knitted fabric, exactly duplicating the structure of stitches that are already there. Duplicate Stitch is worked on the right side of the fabric to cover individual stitches, either as an embellishment or to disguise an error. It's also useful for weaving in ends on items like scarves that are reversible, and for neatly hiding color changes on the purl side in circular knitting.

HORIZONTAL ON THE KNIT SIDE

Use this method to work across a row of stitches on the knit side that you want to cover up. It's good for hiding mistakes or adding embellishments, such as as monograms.

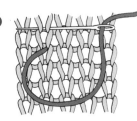

HOW TO DO IT:

1. Bring the point of the yarn needle up through the bottom of the stitch.

2. Sew behind two strands along the top of the stitch.

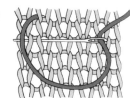

3. Sew back through the bottom of the stitch, and under two strands to the bottom of the next stitch.

Repeat steps 2 and 3 to make a horizontal row of stitches. Right-handed knitters may prefer to work from right to left, left-handed knitters from left to right.

VERTICAL ON THE KNIT SIDE

Use this technique to work up a column of stitches on the knit side. This is used to hide mistakes or to add embellishments.

HOW TO DO IT:

1. Bring the point of the yarn needle up through the bottom of the first stitch.

2. Sew behind two strands along the top of the stitch.

3. Sew back through the bottom of the stitch and pull the yarn through to the back of the fabric. Bring the needle and yarn up through the center of the stitch just completed, ready to begin again with the next stitch above.

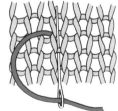

Repeat steps 2 and 3 to work vertically from bottom to top.

HORIZONTAL ON THE PURL SIDE

Duplicate Stitch on the purl side is not supposed to show on the knit side of the fabric. It's used only for working ends in invisibly. This assumes that the purl side is the wrong side of the fabric.

HOW TO DO IT:

1. Sew under two purl bumps from bottom to top.

2. Sew under the next two purl bumps from top to bottom. You may work right to left or left to right, whichever is most comfortable for you.

Repeat steps 1 and 2 to work a horizontal row of stitches.

ᐁᐁᐁᐁᐁᐁᐁᐁᐁᐁᐁᐁᐁᐁᐁᐁᐁᐁᐁᐁ

Resources

ᐁᐁᐁᐁᐁᐁᐁᐁᐁᐁᐁᐁᐁᐁᐁᐁᐁᐁᐁᐁ

Where else can you go for knitting help? Visit your local yarn shop, join a local knitting group and the national guild, look for books and magazines at bookstores, and search the Internet. Sign up for knitting classes at your yarn shop, through your recreation department, or at knitting conferences and retreats.

Information Sources

YOUR LOCAL YARN SHOP

Your local yarn shop is traditionally the first stop for information. If you do go there to ask questions, please keep in mind that this is a business that relies on sales. They need to wait on other customers and may not be able to spend large amounts of time helping you if they are busy. They will be much more likely to be helpful on an ongoing basis if you purchase your yarn, needles, and pattern from them. Ask them about classes or scheduled knitting help sessions.

BOOKS

Those listed in the bibliography below are just some of the ones I've found most helpful. Luckily, knitting books are available through many bookstores, even in areas where there aren't yarn shops.

KNITTING MAGAZINES

The knitting magazines listed below are the most readily available in the United States. Some are sold only by subscription. Others are also available anywhere magazines are sold. Most knitting magazines include a reference section that explains the techniques called for in their instructions. They also include articles on specialized techniques, reviews of new books, and information about yarn and tools. The advertisements can be a lifeline if you're looking for knitting events and supplies. Desktop publishing has made possible the advent of many small, independently-published newsletters. These are promoted knitter-to-knitter, especially via the Internet, and an Internet search for "knitting newsletter" is the best way to find them. Many knitting guilds publish their own newsletter with patterns by members, techniques, articles, and announcements. Guilds are frequently willing to send these to non-members for a small fee to cover their costs.

GUILDS AND KNITTING GROUPS

Guilds and knitting groups can put you in contact with your local knitting community. Some are more formal than others, arranging educational programs and joint projects, while others meet to chat and knit. The Knitting Guild Association (TKGA) is the national knitting guild in the United States. Membership in TKGA includes a subscription to their magazine *Cast On* and access to their educational programs. To find a guild, look for notices in your local paper and check the guild directories at the TKGA web site (www.tkga.com), www.woolworks.org, www.knitting.about.com, or any of the other sites that list guilds. Do a search for your town name and "knitting guild" on the Internet. If there is a local needlework group, quilting group, weaving or embroidery guild, attend a meeting and ask if anyone knows about a local knitting group. Some of the members will be knitters and may be interested in starting a group. Or start your own group. Put up notices, put an announcement in the paper, and announce the meetings on the Internet.

THE INTERNET

These days there's nothing that can't be found on the World Wide Web. There are sites with explanations of knitting terms, translations between languages, step by step instructions, videos, free patterns, lists of shops and guilds by location, calendars of events and, of course, sources for supplies. In addition to the Web sites, there are knitting forums, listservs, and personal blogs. Participating in any of these can put you in touch with other knitters who can answer your questions and commiserate with your problems. The listing of Internet gateways on page 376 will help you get started.

KNITTING CLASSES

Knitting classes are offered by many YMCAs, local recreation departments, large craft shops, knitting shops, and at retreats and knitting conferences. If there are none in your area, tell the organizations that sponsor adult education and recreation classes that you'd like them to offer knitting in the future.

OTHER KNITTERS

Other knitters are the best source of information and inspiration. We all learn by sharing what we know with others and, at the same time, we ensure that the art and craft of knitting will endure. Recognize that there are many ways to accomplish the same thing, and collect as much information as you can from as many knitters as you can. Use common sense and experimentation to find what works best for you. Then, go on to share what you know with other knitters.

Books and Articles

Hand-Knitting Techniques: From Threads Magazine, Taunton
    Press, 1991.

Knitting School: A Complete Course, Sterling Publishing
    Company, 2003.

Standards & Guidelines for Crochet and Knitting, Craft Yarn
    Council of America, 2003. Available for download at
    www.YarnStandards.com.

Abbey, Barbara. *Barbara Abbey's Knitting Lace*, Schoolhouse
    Press, 1993.

Bartlett, Roxana. *Slip-Stitch Knitting: Color Pattern the Easy Way*,
    Interweave Press, 1998.

Bordi, Cat. *Socks Soar on Two Circular Needles: A Manual of Elegant
    Knitting Techniques and Patterns*, Passing Paws Press, 2001.

Brown-Reinsel, Beth. "Beyond the Basics: Different Ways to Knit,"
    Interweave Knits, Spring 2004, pp.72–77.

Brown-Reinsel, Beth. *Kniting Ganseys*, Interweave Press, 1993.

Buchanan, Rita & Deborah Robson. *Socks: A Spin-Off Special
    Publication for Knitters and Spinners*, Interweave Press, 1994.

Budd, Ann. *The Knitter's Handy Guide to Yarn Requirements*,
    Interweave Press, 2004. A pamphlet with yardage guidelines
    for standard projects and all weights of yarn.

Burns, Missy, Stephanie Blaydes Kaisler & Anita Tosten. *Knitting With Hand-Dyed Yarns: 20 Stunning Projects*, Martingale and Company, 2004.

Bush, Nancy. *Folk Socks: The History & Techniques of Handknitted Footwear*, Interweave Press, 1994.

Cartwright-Jones, Catherine & Roy Jones. *The Tap Dancing Lizard: 337 Fanciful Charts for the Adventurous Knitter*, Interweave Press, 1993.

Chin, Lily M. *Knit and Crochet with Beads*, Interweave Press, 2004.

Eckman, Edie. *The Crochet Answer Book*, Storey Publishing, 2005.

Eckman, Edie. *Learn to Knit Socks*, American School of Needlework, 1999.

Epstein, Nicky. *Knitting on the Edge: Ribs * Ruffles * Lace * Fringes * Flora * Points & Picots — The Essential Collection of 350 Decorative Borders,* Sterling Publishing Company, 2004.

Fassett, Kaffe. *Family Album: More Glorious Knits for Children and Adults*, Taunton Press, 1999. Like all Fassett's books, fabulous intarsia and inspirational use of color.

Fassett, Kaffe. *Glorious Knits*, Clarkson N. Potter, 1985.

Fassett, Kaffe. *Kaffe Fassett's Glorious Inspiration for Needlepoint and Knitting*, Sterling Publishing, 2000.

Fassett, Kaffe. *Kaffe's Classics*, Little, Brown and Co., 1993.

Fassett, Kaffe & Sally Harding. *Kaffe Fassett's Pattern Library: Over 190 Creative Knitwear Designs*, Taunton Press, 2003.

Fee, Jacqueline. *The Sweater Workshop: Knit Creative, Seam-Free Sweaters on Your Own with Any Yarn*, Down East Books, 2002. Sweater design.

Feitelson, Ann. *The Art of Fair Isle Knitting: History, Technique, Color & Patterns*, Interweave Press, 1996. Especially useful for thoughtful experiments in the use of color.

Gayle, Lori. "Beyond the Basics: How Much Yarn Do I Need?," *Interweave Knits,* Spring 2003, pp.72-73.

Gibson-Roberts, Priscilla A. *Simple Socks: Plain and Fancy*, Nomad Press, 2004.

Gibson-Roberts, Priscilla A. & Deborah Robson. *Knitting in the Old Way: Designs & Techniques from Ethnic Sweaters*, Nomad Press, 2004. Explanation of traditional sweater structures, including how to estimate yarn needs.

Hansen, Robin. *Fox & Geese & Fences: A Collection of Traditional Maine Mittens*, Down East Books, 1991.

Hansen, Robin. *Knit Mittens! 15 Cool Patterns to Keep You Warm*, Storey Publishing, 2002.

Hansen, Robin. *Sunny's Mittens: Learn-to-Knit Lovikka Mittens*, Down East Books, 2003. Learn to knit felted Lovikka mittens along with Sunny.

Hansen, Robin, with Janetta Dexter. *Flying Geese and Partridge Feet: More Mittens from Up North & Down East,* Down East Books, 1991.

Heathman, Margaret. *Knitting Languages,* Schoolhouse Press, 1996.

Keele, Wendy. *Poems of Color: Knitting in the Bohus Tradition,* Interweave Press, 1995. History of the Swedish knitting cottage industry, with examples and instructions.

Khmeleva, Galina & Carol R. Noble. *Gossamer Webs: The History and Techniques of Orenburg Lace Shawls,* Interweave Press, 1998.

Kinzel, Marianne. *First Book of Modern Lace Knitting,* Dover Publications, 1990. Basics of lace knitting techniques and pattern stitches.

Kooler, Donna. *Donna Kooler's Encyclopedia of Knitting,* Leisure Arts, 2004.

Lewis, Susanna E. *Knitting Lace: A Workshop with Patterns and Projects,* Taunton Press, 1992.

Ligon, Linda, editor. *Homespun Handknit: Caps Socks Mittens & Gloves,* Interweave Press, 1987. Great source of instructions for small projects.

MacDonald, Anne. *No Idle Hands: The Social History of American Knitting,* Ballantine Books, 1988 & 1990.

McCarthy, Betsy. *Knit Socks!,* Storey Publishing, 2004.

McCuin, Judith MacKenzie. "Discovering Novelty Yarns," *Interweave Knits,* Spring 2003, pp.50-52

McGregor, Sheila. *Traditional Fair Isle Knitting*, Dover Publications, 2003.

Melville, Sally. *The Knitting Experience Book 1: The Knit Stitch*, XRX Books, 2002.

Melville, Sally. *The Knitting Experience Book 2: The Purl Stitch*, XRX Books, 2003.

Menz, Deb. *Color Works: The Crafter's Guide to Color*, Interweave Press, 2004.

Modesitt, Annie. *Confessions of a Knitting Heretic*, ModeKnit Press, 2004.

New, Debbie. *Unexpected Knitting*, Schoolhouse Press, 2003. Out-of-the ordinary knitting concepts.

Newton, Deborah. *Designing Knitwear*, Taunton Press, 1998. Practical and complete guide to designing.

Pizzuto, Joseph J., Arthur Price, Allen C. Cohen & Ingrid Johnson. *Fabric Science, 7th Edition*, Fairchild Books & Visuals, 1999.

Potter, Cheryl. *Handpaint Country: A Knitter's Journey,* XRX Books, 2002. Showcase of U.S. yarn dyers and projects using their yarns.

Potter, Cheryl & Carol R. Noble. *Lavish Lace: Knitting with Hand-Painted Yarns*, Martingale and Company, 2004.

Righetti, Maggie. *Knitting in Plain English*, St. Martin's Press, 1986.

Roberts, Luise. *1000 Great Knitting Motifs*, Trafalgar Square Publishing, 2004.

Rosen, Evie. *The All New Teach Yourself to Knit*, Leisure Arts Leaflet #623, 1992.

Rowley, Elaine. *Socks, Socks, Socks: 70 Winning Patterns from Knitter's Magazine Sock Contest*, XRX Books, 1999.

Royce, Beverly. *Notes on Double Knitting*, Schoolhouse Press, 1994.

Rutt, Richard. *A History of Hand Knitting*, Interweave Press, 2003.

Stanley, Montse. *Knitter's Handbook: A Comprehensive Guide to the Principles and Techniques of Handknitting*, Readers Digest, 1999.

Starmore, Alice. *Alice Starmore's Book of Fair Isle Knitting*, Taunton Press, 1993. History of Fair Isle knitting, plus complete explanation of construction and design, collection of charted pattern stitches, and incomparable colorwork.

Stuever, Sherry & Keely Stuever. *Intarsia: A Workshop for Hand & Machine Knitting*, Sealed With a Kiss, 1998. The authoritative reference on intarsia, including finishing techniques.

Szabo, Janet. *Handbook of Aran Sweater Design*, Big Sky Knitting Designs, 2001-2004.

Thomas, Mary. *Mary Thomas's Knitting Book,* Dover Publications, 1972. A small book with a huge amount of information.

Thompson, Gladys. *Patterns for Guernseys, Jerseys & Arans: Fishermen's Sweaters from the British Isles*, Dover Publications, 1995. Sweaters and pattern stitches collected in the British Isles.

Timmons, Christine, ed. *Hand-Knitting Techniques: from Threads Magazine,* Taunton Press, 1991.

Vogel, Lynne. *The Twisted Sisters Sock Workbook: Dyeing, Painting, Spinning, Designing, Knitting*, Interweave Press, 2002.

Vogue Knitting Magazine Editors. *Vogue Knitting: The Ultimate Knitting Book*, Sixth & Spring Books, 2002.

Walker, Barbara G. *A Treasury of Knitting Patterns*, Schoolhouse Press, 1998. Barbara Walker's capacious books are the most complete source of knitting pattern stitches.

Walker, Barbara G. *A Second Treasury of Knitting Patterns*, Schoolhouse Press, 1998.

Walker, Barbara G. *Charted Knitting Designs: A Third Treasury of Knitting Patterns*, Schoolhouse Press, 1998.

Walker, Barbara G. *A Fourth Treasury of Knitting Patterns*, Schoolhouse Press, 2000.

Walker, Barbara G. *Knitting from the Top*, Schoolhouse Press, 1996. Practical instructions for creating top-down sweaters.

Walker, Barbara G. *Mosaic Knitting*, Schoolhouse Press, 1997.

Wilkes, Angela & Carol Garbera. *An Usborne Guide: Knitting from Start to Finish*, E.D.C. Publishing, 1986. A small but surprisingly complete and informative learn-to-knit book.

Williams, Joyce. *Latvian Dreams: Knitting From Weaving Charts,* Schoolhouse Press, 2000. Source for wonderful color patterns.

Wiseman, Nancie M. *The Knitter's Book of Finishing Techniques*, Martingale & Company, 2002. Compact and complete reference for finishing techniques. Clear explanations and clear photographs—you'll never need another book on this topic.

Zilboorg, Anna. *Fancy Feet: Traditional Knitting Patterns of Turkey*, Lark Books, 1994. Socks, yes, but also an excellent source of color patterns for other uses.

Zilboorg, Anna. *Knitting for Anarchists*, Unicorn Books, 2002. Philosophical support for the free-thinking knitter plus a superlative investigation of knitted and purled stitch formation and orientation.

Zimmermann, Elizabeth. *Knitting Around*, Schoolhouse Press, 1989. The seminal work on circular knitting.

Zimmermann, Elizabeth. *Knitting Without Tears*, Encore Editions, 2000. Reference for those who "want to knit better" as well as a good read. This book launched a huge number of designers in their careers, including the author.

Knitting Magazines

PRINT KNITTING PUBLICATIONS

Cast On, published by The Knitting Guild Association,
www.tkga.com

Creative Knitting, published by House of White Birches,
www.creativeknittingmagazine.com

INKnitters, published by Fiber Circle Publishing, www.inknitters.com

Family Circle Easy Knitting, published by SoHo Publishing
Company, www.fceasyknitting.com

Interweave Knits, published by Interweave Press,
www.interweave.com

Knit 'N Style, published by All American Crafts Inc.,
www.knitnstyle.com

Knitter's Magazine, published by XRX Inc.,
www.knittinguniverse.com

Rebecca, published by Rebecca, www.rebecca-online.com

Rowan Knitting Magazine, published by Rowan Yarns,
www.knitrowan.com

Sandra, Anna, and *Verena Stricken*, GLPnews offers subscriptions to
these European knitting magazines through www.GLPnews.com.

Vogue Knitting, published by SoHo Publishing Company,
www.vogueknitting.com

Other excellent magazines that frequently include knitting content are Spin-Off, PieceWork, and Fiberarts, all published by Interweave Press, www.interweave.com

ONLINE KNITTING MAGAZINES

KnitNet, at www.knitnet.com

Knitter's Review, at www.knittersreview.com

Knitty, at www.knitty.com

Web Sites

The World Wide Web is constantly evolving, with new sites appearing, old ones falling into disuse, and domains appropriated for other uses on a daily basis. It's hazardous to recommend any Web site, since it may disappear immediately; therefore, the sites listed below are those that I have found most consistently useful over the years and that I expect to be maintained in the future.

KNITTING

Each of these sites contain tips, explanations of techniques, free patterns, links to supply sources, lists of retail stores and local guilds, book and magazine reviews, plus many links to other Web sites.

Craft Yarn Council of America, www.craftyarncouncil.com, has information on yarn and sizing standards, national and local events, and national knitting and crochet initiatives.

Knitting at About.com, www.knitting.about.com, is very well established, with more information than you'll ever get all the way through, and constantly updated.

wiseNeedle, www.wiseNeedle.com, provides reviews of yarns and patterns, submitted on-line by knitters.

Woolworks, www.woolworks.org, was the first major knitting site and is a huge compendium of information.

Searches for "knitting" on the major search engines will result in hundreds of thousands of results, so it is best to be more specific by adding "tips", "patterns", "hand techniques", "classes", and the like to your keywords.

LAUNDRY SYMBOLS

Ginetex, www.ginetex.org, offers complete information about European textile care symbols.

The Soap and Detergent Association, www.cleaning101.com, has complete information about U.S. textile care symbols.

Textile Industry Affairs, www.textileaffairs.com, also has information about U.S. textile care symbols.

Common Abbreviations Found in Knitting Patterns

ABBREVIATION	DESCRIPTION
[]	work instructions within brackets as many times as directed
()	work instructions within parentheses in the place directed
* *	repeat instructions between the asterisks as directed
*	repeat instructions following the single asterisk as directed
"	inch(es)
alt	alternate
approx	approximately
beg	begin/beginning
bet or btw	between
BO	bind off
CA	Color A
CB	Color B
CC	contrasting color
cm	centimeter(s)
cn	cable needle
CO	cast on
cont	continue
dec	decrease/decreases/decreasing
dpn	double-pointed needle(s)
fl	front loop(s)
foll	follow/follows/following
g	gram

ABBREVIATION	DESCRIPTION
inc	increase/increases/increasing
k or K	knit
k2tog	knit 2 stitches together
kwise or kw	knitwise
LH	left hand
lp(s)	loop(s)
m	meter(s)
M1	make one — an increase — several increases can be described as "M1"
M1 p-st	make one purl stitch
MC	main color
mm	millimeter(s)
oz	ounce(s)
p or P	purl
p2tog	purl 2 stitches together
pat(s) or patt	pattern(s)
pm	place marker
pop	popcorn
prev	previous
psso	pass slipped stitch over
pwise or pw	purlwise
rem	remain/remaining
rep	repeat(s)
rev St st	reverse Stockinette Stitch
RH	right hand
rnd(s)	round(s)

ABBREVIATION	DESCRIPTION
RS	right side
sk	skip
skp	slip, knit, pass stitch over - one stitch decreased
sk2p	slip 1, knit 2 together, pass slip stitch over the knit 2 together; 2 stitches have been decreased
sl	slip
sl1k	slip 1 knitwise
sl1p	slip 1 purlwise
sl st	slip stitch(es)
ss	slip stitch (Canadian)
ssk	slip, slip, knit these 2 stitches together - a decrease
sssk	slip, slip, slip, knit 3 stitches together
st(s)	stitch(es)
St st	Stockinette Stitch/stocking stitch
tbl	through back loop
tog	together
WS	wrong side
wyib	with yarn in back
wyif	with yarn in front
yd(s)	yard(s)
yfwd	yarn forward
yo	yarn over
yon	yarn over needle
yrn	yarn around needle

Chart Symbols for Knitting

☐	I	Knit on right side, purl on wrong side
−	☐	Purl on right side, knit on wrong side
	O	Yarn over
	℔	Knit into the back (creates a twisted stitch)
	℔	Purl into the back (creates a twisted stitch)
	V	Slip stitch with yarn on wrong side of fabric
	¥	Slip stitch with yarn on right side of fabric
/	⋀	Knit 2 together on right side, purl 2 together on wrong side
\	λ	SSK or SKP on right side, SSP on wrong side
	≥	Purl 2 together through the back loop on the right side
	⋜	Purl 2 together on the right side
	⋏	Knit 3 together
	⋏	Purl 3 together
	⋏	Raised double decrease: Slip 2, Knit 1, Pass slipped stitch over
	Λ	Decrease number of stitches specified
	୪	Make one increase
	⋎	Increase (left-slanting)
	⋁	Increase (right-slanting)
	V̄	Increase number of stitches specified
	⋒	Knit into the stitch one row below
	A	Purl into stitch one row below
	●	Make bobble

Garment Sizing Guidelines

Reprinted from *Standards & Guidelines for Crochet and Knitting*, (April 2003), with permission of the Craft Yarn Council of America.

FIT

VERY-CLOSE FITTING: Actual chest/bust measurement or less
CLOSE-FITTING: 1–2" (2.5–5 cm)
STANDARD-FITTING: 2–4" (5–10 cm)
LOOSE-FITTING: 4–6" (10–15 cm)
OVERSIZED: 6" (15 cm) or more

LENGTH FOR CHILDREN

WAIST LENGTH: Actual body measurement
HIP LENGTH: 2" (5 cm) down from waist
TUNIC LENGTH: 6" (15 cm) down from waist

LENGTH FOR WOMEN

WAIST LENGTH: Actual body measurement
HIP LENGTH: 6" (15 cm) down from waist
TUNIC LENGTH: 11" (28 cm) down from waist

LENGTH FOR MEN

Men's length usually varies only 1–2" (2.5–5 cm) from the actual "back hip length" measurement *(see chart)*

Baby's size		3 mo.	6 mo.	12 mo.	18 mo.	24 mo.
Chest	in.	16	17	18	19	20
	cm	40.5	43	45.5	48	50.5
Center Back	in.	10½	11½	12½	14	18
Neck-to-Cuff	cm	26.5	29	31.5	35.5	45.5
Back Waist	in.	6	7	7½	8	8½
Length	cm	15.5	17.5	19	20.5	21.5
Cross Back	in.	7¼	7¾	8¼	8½	8¾
(Shoulder to	cm	18. 5	19.5	21	21. 5	22
shoulder)						
Sleeve Length	in.	6	6½	7½	8	8½
to Underarm	cm	15.5	16.5	19	20.5	21.5

Child's size		2	4	6	8	10
Chest	in.	21	23	25	26½	28
	cm	53	58.5	63.5	67	71
Center Back	in.	18	19½	20½	22	24
Neck-to-Cuff	cm	45.5	49.5	52	56	61
Back Waist	in.	8½	9½	10½	12½	14
Length	cm	21.5	24	26.5	31.5	35.5
Cross Back	in.	9¼	9¾	10¼	10¾	11¼
(Shoulder to	cm	23.5	25	26	27	28.5
shoulder)						
Sleeve Length	in.	8½	10½	11½	12½	13½
to Underarm	cm	21.5	26.5	29	31.5	34.5

Child's (cont.)		12	14	16
Chest (in.)	in.	30	31½	32½
	cm	76	80	82.5
Center Back	in.	26	27	28
Neck-to-Cuff	cm	66	68.5	71
Back Waist	in.	15	15½	16
Length	cm	38	39.5	40.5
Cross Back	in.	12	12¼	13
(Shoulder to	cm	30.5	31	33
Shoulder)				
Sleeve Length	in.	15	16	16½
to Underarm	cm	38	40.5	42

Woman's size		X-Small	Small	Medium	Large
Bust	in.	28–30	32–34	36–38	40–42
	cm	71–76	81–86	91.5–96.5	101.5–106.5
Center Back	in.	27–27½	28–28½	29–29½	30–30½
Neck-to-Cuff	cm	68.5–70	71–72.5	73.5–75	76–77.5
Back Waist	in.	16½	17	17¼	17½
Length	cm	42	43	43.5	44.5
Cross Back	in.	14–14½	14½–15	16–16½	17–17½
(Shoulder to	cm	35.5–37	37–38	40.5–42	43–44.5
Shoulder)					
Sleeve Length	in.	16½	17	17	17½
to Underarm	cm	42	43	43	44.5

Woman's *(cont.)*		1X	2X	3X	4X	5X
Bust	in.	44–46	48–50	52–54	56–58	60–62
	cm	111.5–117	122–127	132–137	142–147	152–158
Center Back	in.	31–31½	31½–32	32½–33	32½–33	33–33½
Neck-to-Cuff	cm	78.5–80	80–81.5	82.5–84	82.5–84	84–85
Back Waist	in.	17¾	18	18	18½	18½
Length	cm	45	45.5	45.5	47	47
Cross Back	in.	17½	18	18	18½	18½
(Shoulder to	cm	44.5	45.5	45.5	47	47
Shoulder)						
Sleeve Length	in.	17½	18	18	18½	18½
to Underarm	cm	44.5	45.5	45.5	47	47

Man's size		Small	Medium	Large	X-Large	XX-Large
Chest	in.	34–36	38–40	42–44	46–48	50–52
	cm	86–91.5	96.5–101.5	106.5–111.5	116.5–122	127–132
Center Back	in.	32–32½	33–33½	34–34½	35–35½	36–36½
Neck-to-Cuff	cm	81–82.5	83.5–85	86.5–87.5	89–90	91.5–92.5
Back Hip	in.	25–25½	26½–26½	27–27½	27½–27¾	28–28½
Length	cm	63.5–64.5	67.5–68	68.5–69	69.5–70.5	71–72.5
Cross Back	in.	15½–16	16½–17	17½–18	18–18½	18½–19
(Shoulder to	cm	39.5–40.5	42–43	44.5–45.5	45.5–47	47–48
Shoulder)						
Sleeve Length	in.	18	18½	19½	20	20½
to Underarm	cm	45.5	47	49.5	50.5	52

Head Circumference Chart

Circumference

	INFANT/CHILD				ADULT	
	Premie	Baby	Toddler	Child	Woman	Man
in.	12	14	16	18	20	22
cm	30.5	35.5	40.5	45.5	50.5	56

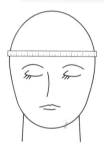

▶ For an accurate head measure, place a tape measure across the forehead and measure around the full circumference of the head. Keep the tape snug for accurate results.

Acknowledgements

First and foremost, because knitters learn most from each other, I thank all of the anonymous knitters who have generously shared their knowledge and personal discoveries with other knitters. It is impossible to credit everyone who made a discovery and told a friend, posted the idea on the Internet, or mentioned it to another friend while shopping, and passed the discovery on into our body of general knowledge.

Secondly, I would like to thank all of the knitters who have learned from me over the years, whether in class or in less formal settings. You forced me to investigate, analyze, and develop answers to questions that I never would have dreamed of on my own.

And then there are the knitters, teachers, writers, and designers, from whom I've personally learned so much over the years. Your knowledge and generosity continues to astonish me.

More personally, I must thank my mother Norma Tucker Katz, who taught me to knit sometime before my eighth birthday; Martha Armstrong, who taught me a better cast on and took me on my first steps beyond the basics; my colleagues, Susan Coughlin, Edie Eckman, and Merike Saarniit, who have encouraged and supported me since the beginning of my professional knitting career and became friends along the way; my long-suffering daughters Anna and Allegra, who patiently accept my many hours of writing and knitting, cheerfully test techniques for me, and listen good-naturedly to my excited chatter whenever I am inspired by a new idea; my husband David, who understands the demands of large projects, in both space and time; and finally, the staff of Storey Publishing, who made this book a reality: Gwen Steege, my editor, who came up with the original concept for the Knitting Answer Book and then gave me the freedom to make it my own and Sarah Guare, who kept track of the thousands of details.

Index

Page numbers in *italics* indicate illustrations. Page numbers in **bold** indicate tables.

A

abbreviations, 170–71, 378–80
alpaca, 128, 345
American method, 46–47
angora, 128, 145, 345
animal fibers, 141, 152, 310, 340, 345
armholes, 104, 271, 276–78, 297, 324–25, 342
asterisks, 182, 185
Australia, 162

B

baby clothes, 141, 332, 339, 383, 386
Backward Loop Cast On, 13–14, 25, 41, 215
bag, 106, 119–23
ball winders, 124
Basic Bind Off (BO), 38, 88–89, 91

beads, 341, 348–51
biasing, 137, 158
binding off (BO), 38, 87–104, 232–33. *See also* edge.
blocking, 65, 163, 198, 208, 251, 306–310, 342
bobbin, 249
bobbles, 198, 352
body measurements, 183, 280, 382–86
books and articles, 364, 367–74
border, 184, 199, 204, 270–71, 314–15, 324–39
bottom bands, 325–26
boucle, *135,* 319
brackets, 182, 185
bulkiness, 39, 284, 313
bump in knitting, 43, 48, 51, 79, 218, 237, 238
burn test, 152–53

button bands, 329–31
buttonholes, 329–38
buttons, 339

C

Cable Cast On, 15–16,
    23–25, 40, 43, 215
cabled yarns, 135
cable needle (cn), 118–99,
    201–04
cables, 44, 102, 111, 115,
    201–06, 231
Canada, 130, 162
casting off. *See* binding off
cast ons (CO), 11–44
    basic, 12–21
    circular knitting, 215–17
    increase, 219–20, 263
    problem solving, 39–44
    special situations,
        26–31, 219–21
    twisted, 222
    See also specific
        technique
chart symbols, 173, 174–75,
    381
chenille, *135,* 137–38, 319
chevron pattern, 103

children's clothes, 25, 352,
    382, 383–84, 386
chokes, 151
circular knitting, 59, 209–34
    basics, 210–21
    binding off, 232–33
    changing from flat,
        233–34
    chart instructions for,
        180
    colors, changing,
        156–57, 228–30
    gauge, 221–22
    pattern stitches, 230–31
    stranded knitting,
        240–41
    stripes, 236
    for tubes, 107
    with variegated yarn,
        254
    working on project,
        222–28
circular needles, 70, 111,
    115, 212–13, 224–25,
    228
circular yoke, 284
cleaning instructions,
    129–30, 144, 377

color, 139, 235–54, 157
 change, 184, 228–30
 charts for, 173–74, 179
 between packages,
  155–56
 running, 154, 345
 "salt and pepper," 230
 two colors, 52, 240–42,
  278
Continental Cast On, 18
Continental method
 knit stitch (K), 47, 50,
  51–52, 56, 57, 58
 purl stitch (P), 49, 51
cords, 353–55
cotton, 128, 282, 310,
  326, 340
counting rows and stitches,
  53–55, 167
Craft Yarn Council of
  America, 127, 281, 290
crimp, 128
crochet, 99, 319–20
Crocheted Cast On,
  32–34, 38
crochet hook, 66, 67, 89,
  122

D

decorative effect, 26, 60, 99
decreases (dec), 26–61,
  263–69
 distance from edge, 275
 double (DD), 268–69
 K2tog, 264
 K3tog, 268
 Knit 2 Together Through
  the Back Loop, 266
 nonstandard, 63, 267
 pattern stitches, 276–77
 P2tog, 264
 P3tog, 268
 Purl 2 Together Through
  the Back Loop, 267
 raised double, 269
 safety pins for, 181
 Slip, Slip, Knit (SSK), 265
 Slip, Slip, Purl (SSP), 266
 Slip 1, Knit 1, Pass
  Slipped Stitch Over, 265
 Slip 1, Knit 2 Together,
  Pass Slipped Stitch Over,
  269
diagonal edge, 50–51, 74,
  104, 197, 274

diamond-shaped insert, 297–98

double decreases (DD), 278

Doubled Long-Tail Cast On, 25–26

double increases, 260–61, 278

double-pointed needles (dpn), 107, 167, 205–06, 211, 213–15, 218–19, 226–27

double yarn over, 83

dropped cast on, 41–43

dropped stitch, 66–68, 342

Duplicate Stitch, 60–62, 157, 341

E

ease, 281

edge, 78–80, 91, 93, 183
    curling, 199–200, 287, 306, 324
    diagonal, 74, 104, 197, 274
    increase or decrease at, 275
    ripples, 44, 102

e-mail, 185, 188

embellishments, 157, 341, 347–62

embroidery. See Duplicate Stitch

English method
    knit stitch (K), 46–47, 50, 51–52, 56, 57, 58
    purl stitch (P), 48–49, 51

European symbols, 129

exiting incorrectly, 73

eyelash yarn, *135,* 319

eyelets, 74, 199, 259, 332

F

fabric, 86, 282–83

Fair Isle knitting, 184, 210, 229, 239–40

felting, 92–93, 344, 345, 346

fiber content, 139, 152–53, 326
    blocking and, 310
    natural, 128, 141, 152, 310, 340, 345
    seams, 320
    synthetic, 128, 152–53, 309, 310

finishing, 305–46, 342–43

fitting, 279–304, 382–86

flat knitting, 59, 180, 210–11, 233–34, 254
foreign knitting terms, 181
fringe, 31, 200, 208, 341, 359
frogging, 71

G

garment construction, 200, 210, 283–84, 382–86
Garter Stitch, 50, 54, 68, 136
    buttonholes for, 332, 333
    circular knitting, 230–31
    edge stitches, 79, 80, 200
    Kitchener Stitch in, 321–22
    side seams for, 313–14
    stripes, *237*
gauge, 131, 162, 163
    needle, *108,* 114, 120
    pattern and, 282–83
    stitch and row, 86, 121, 163–67
    swatch for, 164–66, 221–22
German method, 47
gusset, 297–99

H

hats, 86, 163, 211, 220, 232–33, 352, 386
health considerations, 84
Helix Knitting, 230–31
hems, 38–39, 102–03
holes, 71, 74–75, 200, 205, 242, 250, 303, 326, 343

I

I-Cord, *220,* 221, 354
I-Cord Bind Off, 95–96
incomplete stitch, 71–72
increases (inc), 256–63, 275
    vs. cast on, 263
    double, 260–61
    eyelet, 259
    knit into front and back, 256
    lifted Make 1, 257–58, 261
    Make 1 (M1), 256–57, 261–62
    paired, 259
    pattern stitches, 276–77
    row below, 257–58
    safety pins for, 181
    selecting side for, 263

selecting type of, 262

yarn over (YO), 258

information sources,
364–66

inserts, 297–300

intarsia, 184, 211, 248–51

Internet, 115, 171, 178, 181,
188, 365, 366, 374–77

Invisible Cast On, 34–36

J

joining, 215–17

K

K1P1 ribbing, 231, *238*

best cast on for, 25

buttonhole for, 337

Cable Cast On for, 15

English knitters, 52

Ribbed Cable Cast On
for, 16, 24

seams, 314–15

Tubular Bind Off for, 96

Tubular Cast On for, 26,
27

K2P2 ribbing, 226, 231,
314–15, 337

k2tog (knit 2 together), 28,

63, 102, 206

Kitchener Stitch, 299–300,
311, 321–23

Knit 2 Together Bind Off, 89

knit into back of stitch, 60,
61, 194, 213

knit into front of stitch, 61,
213

knit into stitch below, 191

knit into the back loop, 60

knit side, 92, 360–61

knit stitch (K), 46–47, 48,
50, 51, 60, 64, 65, 66.
See also stitches

Knitted Cast On, 14–15, 23,
31, 40, 42–43

knitting, 58, 175–84, 224,
317

charting text
instructions, 179–80

direction, 63, 224

marking your place,
195–96, 226

nonstandard, 58, 63, 76

knitting charts, 172–73,
179, 180

Knitting Guild Association,
The (TKGA), 365

knitting guilds, 185, 188, 365

knitting jargon, 186–87

knitting needle, 205–06, 170
    circular, 70, 115, 212–13
    gauge, 108, 120
    markers on, 176, 196, 207, 225
    material, 64, 108, 112–13, 116, 207, 218
    problem solving, 69, 15–16
    shapes, 110–11
    size, 39, 40, 70, 78, 86, 93, 106, 109, 130, 211, 224
    stitch orientation, 58–59
    switching, 114, 117–18, 182
    types, 106, 107, 118–19

knitting tools, 105–24, 169–70, 181, 351

ktog (knit 2 together), 38

L

lace, 29–31, 74, 99, 106, 206–08, 253, 341

Lace Cast On, 24, 29–31

laundry symbols, 129–30, 377

left-handed knitters, 47, 55–56

legs of stitch, 73

length, 183, 292–94

linen, 128, 310, 326

Long-Tail Cast On, 18–21, 22, 23, 24, 25, 26, 42

Loop Cast On, 12–14, 22, 23, 25, 29, 32, 41, 215, 220

looseness, 80, 226–27, 245, 286, 338

Loose Three-Row Buttonhole, 333, 335–36

M

magazines, 364–65, 374–75

magnetic document holder, 24, 176, 195

markers on needle, 196, 225

marled yarns, 134

Mattress Stitch, 239, 299, 312–13, 313–14, 315, 317

measurements, 168, 287–89, 382–86

men's clothes, 382, 385, 386

mistakes, 55, 85, 200
    fixing, 65–75, 77
    in lace, 206, 208
    in pattern, 185, 188
    See also tinking
mitered corners, 197
mittens, 210, 211, 233, 343
mohair, 128, 310, 340, 345
mosaic knitting, 247–48
multipart projects, 169
"multiple yarn
    management," 249
multi-ply yarns, 37, 136

N

natural fibers, 128, 141
neck opening, 295–96,
    302
    boatneck, 283
    gaps, 327–28
    picking up stitches,
    324–25
    shaping, 104, 271–74,
    276–78, 284, 301, 326
    two balls of yarn, 272–74
needle, 122, 339, 343
New Zealand, 162
niddy noddy, 151

nonstandard orientation,
    58, 63, 76
nostepinnes, 124, 133
"no stitch," 174–75, 180
novelty yarns, 135, 142, 143

O

"one size fits all," 162
Open Cast Ons, 32

P

paired increases, 259
parentheses, 182, 185
pattern (patt), 159–88
    abbreviations, 378–80
    adding cables to, 204
    adjustments, 86,
    183–84, 233–34
    chart symbols, 381
    circular, 229–30, 231
    creation, 285
    instructions, 169, 173,
    174, 177, 182, 226
    seamless, 158
    size choice, 160–62, 282
pattern stitches, 189–208,
    194
    binding off, 102, 103

charting, 196

for circular knitting,
230–31

combining, 197–98

common, 190, **192–93**

increases and decreases,
276–78

modifying, 197, 198–99

needles for, 111, 198

pattern instructions, 172

problem solving, 68,
199–200

stripes in, 238–39

personal knitting style,
56–57

picot hem, *38,* 102

plies, 134

point protectors, 122

pompoms, 356–57

problem solving, 63–65

provisional cast ons, 32–39

purl into back of stitch, 194

purl side, 92, 362

purl stitch (P), 48–49, 51, 60,
61, 66–67, *82,* 190, 242.
See also stitches

R

raglan sleeves, 197, 284

ravel cord, 37

resources, 363–87

reverse shaping, 271

Reverse Stockinette
(rev St st), 102, 201

Ribbed Cable Cast On,
17, 24, 25

ribbing, 60, 234

bind off in, 91

blocking, 310

at border, 200, 270–71

buttonhole for, 336–37

circular knitting, 231,
234

corrugated, 246

fixing mistakes, 68

needle change after, 182

pattern adjustments, 183

ribbon yarn, 149

right-handed method (knit
stitch), 46–47

right leg of stitch, 58

"right side," 23

row gauge, 166–67, 197

rows, 23, 53

rulers, 120, *165, 166*

S

safety pins, 181, 207, 208, 226

scarves, 25, 199–200, 210, 238, 310, 341

schematics, 168

seams, 14, 286, 311–19

Seed Stitch, 52, 184, 190, 200

selvages, 78, 183

sewing pieces together, 311–17

Sewn Bind Off, 91, 99–100, 338

shaping, 195, 255–78, 302

shawls, 24, 74, 86, 162, 210

shoulders
    drop-, 286, 315
    hanging from, 291
    seams, 304, 311–12
    shaping, 104, 284, 302
    too wide, 296–97
    two balls of yarn, 272

silhouette, 281, 283

silk, 37, 128, 310, 326, 340

sizing, 85, 160–62, 382–86

skeining yarn, 151

sleeve
    fitting, 183, 288–90,
    292–94, 298, 299–301
    increases for slope, 270, 274
    joining to body, 315–17, 342
    styles, 256, 284
    wrist bands, 325–26

Sling Shot Cast On, 18

Slip, Slip, Knit (SSK), 206

slip knot, 17, 22, 26, 43–44

slipped stitch (Sl), 75–78, 79–80, 195

socks, 26, 79–80, 106, 163, 199, 210, 211, 219, 302

special stitch
    manipulations, 191, 194

splicing, 146–47, 208, 341

split markers, 207, 225, 226

'stair step' bind off, 104

standard orientation, 58

starting off wrong, 74

"steeks," 246–47

sticky notes, 123, 176, 195

stitches, 26, 53, 78, 90
    cast on, problems, 41–42
    dropped, 66–68, 81, 342
    legs of, 58, 73
    measuring, 165–67

picking up, 324–28

problems, 60–62, 65, 71–72, 246–47, 250

steeks, 246–47

textured, 252–53

two-stitch repeat, 278

See also knit stitch; purl stitch

stitch gauge. *See* gauge

stitch holders, 121

stitch markers, 120

Stockinette Stitch (St st)

at edges, 79, 199–200

fixing mistakes, 67

hem, 38, 102, 325

Kitchener Stitch in, 321–22

knit and purl sides, 51

side seams for, 312–13

yarn type for, 136, 143

straight needles, 106, 107

stranded knitting, 184, 210, 229, 239–47, 278

stretchiness, 24, 86, 94, 99, 291

stringing tool, 351

stripes, 157, 184, 229, 236–39

swatch, 163–66, 170, 221–22, 223, 277, 326

sweater, 86, 158, 163, 285

best cast on, 24

cabled, yarn for, 136

drop-shoulder, 315

finishing, 342–43

fitting, 160–62, 183, 279–304

knitting instructions, 176, 290–91

shaping, 271–74

Stockinette Stitch for, 199

swatch test for, 163–64, 277

swifts, 124, 133–34, 151

Swiss Darning, 360–62

synthetic fibers, 128, 152–53, 309, 310

T

tail of yarn, 17, 21, 22, 92, 144, 225

tapestry needle, 339

tassels, 341, 357–58

tension, 57, 64, 162, 221, 251, 342

textile care symbols, 377

thickness, 142

Three-Needle Bind Off, 100–101, 300, 304, 312, 317, 319

Tight One-Row Buttonhole, 333, 334–35

tight rows, 78

tight stitches, 39–40, 64, 78, 93, 217

tinking, 69, *72*, 77

Tubular Bind Off, 91, 96, 97–98

Tubular Cast On, 25, 26, 27–29, 32

Twisted Loop Cast On, 31

twisted stitches, 60–62, 191, 213, 222, 262

twisted yarn, 242–43

twisting cardigan, 158

2-ply yarn, 136

two-stitch repeat, 278

Two Strand Cast On, 18

U

unevenness, 80, 245, 326

uneven pieces, 318–19, 342

United Kingdom, 162

United States, 106, 126, 130, 162, 168, 171

unraveling work, 26, 70, 71–72, 74, 205–06, 342

untwisted stitches, *60*

V

vests, 195, 199, 272, 301

W

washing instructions, 154–55, 344–46

waste yarn, 27–29, *34,* 36, 144

weaving edges, 311, 317

weaving yarn ends, 92, 147, 225, 241, 251, 340–41

Web sites, 130, 181, 185, 365, 366, 374–77

wet blocking, 309, 310

width, 73–74, 168, 295–301

women's clothes, 384–85, 386

wool, 128, 141, 282, 286, 310

working yarn, 27, *34,* 63, 144, 148–49, 182, 200

worming, 137–38

"worsted" yarn, 136, 282
woven tape, *135*
wrap and turn, 303
wrist bands, 325–26
"wrong side," 23, 90, 213

Y

yarn, 125–58, 136
  ball, 108, 126, 131,
    145–47
  choice, 135, 138–39, 141
  color, 139, 154, 155, 157,
    252–54
  combining types of,
    143–44
  double strand, 253
  dye lot, 129, 156–57
  fiber content, 128–29,
    138–39, 152–53, 169
  holding techniques, 50,
    62
  labels, 126–31
  packaging, 131, 152–53
  quantity, 126, 140–41,
    169
  reused, 37, 150
  for sewing, 319–20
  shrinkage, 154, 163–64
  skein, 126, 131, 132
  slipped stitch placement,
    76–77
  slippery, 37, 145, 149, 340
  spinning, 150
  structure, 127, 134–36,
    139, 142, 143
  substitutions, 142
  suitability, 139–40
  tests, 152–53, 157, 158,
    163–64
  thickness, 138–39, 169
  variegated, 252–54
  winding, 132–34
  See also working yarn
yarn bras, 124, 149
yarn guide, *243*
yarn needles, 122, 341, 343
Yarn Over Bind Off, 94
yarn over (YO), 74, 81–83,
    199, 200, 208, 258
yarn shop, 364
Y Cast On, 18

Z

Zimmermann, Elizabeth,
    336, 338